W9-AFR-773

THE CYCLE OF MODERN POETRY

E 369

21

LONDON: HUMPHREY MILFORD
OXFORD UNIVERSITY PRESS

THE CYCLE
OF MODERN POETRY

A SERIES OF ESSAYS
TOWARD CLEARING OUR PRESENT
POETIC DILEMMA

BY G. R. ELLIOTT

ST. JOSEPH'S UNIVERSITY — STX
PR502.E46
The cycle of modern poetry;

3 9353 00031 4136

PRINCETON
PRINCETON UNIVERSITY PRESS
1929

COPYRIGHT, 1929, PRINCETON UNIVERSITY PRESS

PR502
E46
co.2

PRINTED AT THE PRINCETON UNIVERSITY PRESS
PRINCETON, NEW JERSEY, U. S. A.

TO
MY WIFE

PREFACE

THE final chapter of this book, on "Milton and the Present State of Poetry," was read in part for the Cole lecture in Bowdoin College, January, 1928. That paper, or series of paperettes, forms a sort of frame for the preceding essays. These were written at intervals during the past dozen years and appeared in various periodicals. But they have been revised, extended, and in some parts entirely recast for the present publication. If a reader lights upon a passage that he perused before, let him not assume that the ensuing passage is also unchanged. Byron would say, "I won't be changeless and I will be re-read"—though I dare not echo the original form of the famous saying that I have just parodied.

The paper on Keats as first published was attacked by a number of Keatsians—including myself. Setting it aside for seven years (a Biblical period of service) I restudied this poet completely. The result, some of my former critics may say, is that the new essay, in its main contention, sins more grievously than the old. But I hope they will say that at least it sins more convincingly.

My thanks are due to the editors of the following American journals for permission to reprint material on the poets named in parentheses: *The Dial* (Frost), *The Forum* (Frost), *The Nation* (Frost, Shelley), *The Publications of the Modern Language Association* (Shelley, Byron, Keats, Arnold, Hardy), *The Sewanee Review* (Browning), *The South Atlantic Quarterly* (Hardy), *The Southwest Review* (Longfellow), *The Virginia Quarterly Review* (Frost). Also I am obliged to Henry Holt and Company for permission to quote from Frost's poetry; and to The Macmillan Company for permission to quote from Hardy's *Collected Poems*, copyright 1925, and from Hardy's *The Dynasts*, as well as for permission to reprint some sentences from my Introduction to *Keats* in "The Modern Readers' Series." Certain points of view indicated in the notes of *English Poetry of the Nineteenth Century*, edited by Norman Foerster and me for The Macmillan Company, 1924, are fully developed in the present book, which may indeed be regarded as a critical companion to that collection.

AMHERST COLLEGE,   G.R.E.
March, 1929.

CONTENTS

INTRODUCTION

MANY critics agree that poetry today has come into a kind of dilemma, but their opinions differ as to the kind. Most of the views I have read seem to me either too exclusive, considering the comprehensive nature of poetry; or too contemporaneous, considering that the main impulsions of our present poetic movement are at least a century old. The outstanding fact is that the great poetic impulse that rose in the later eighteenth century and culminated in the nineteenth, the Romantic or Naturistic impulse or whatever one wishes to call it, is now pretty well exhausted. The wheel has come full circle; a cycle is ending. Poetry today, in England and America, is groping for a fresh direction. Many sharp tangents have been tried during the past twenty years; but they have proved to have a sharp *recurvous* tendency. Meteors hailed as heralding a new system, a twentieth-century poetry, have proved to be rockets. In short, poetry has not yet hitched her wagon to a new star. She is still caught in the dying orbit of the nineteenth-century mind and art.

In the ensuing chapters I have examined at close range some significant phases of poetry from Wordsworth to the present, at the same time trying to see in what general direction poetry should presently move if she is again to find a real highway. I did not set out to establish any single thesis, least of all an abstract or exclusive thesis. The book is largely devoted to particular poets and particular poems. Yet the reader will find emerging in each chapter, under one aspect or another, the age-old idea of the vital and mysterious doubleness, so to call it, of human nature—the idea that Arnold rendered with didactic bluntness in the lines:

> Man must begin, know this, where Nature ends;
> Nature and man can never be fast friends;

the idea that young Keats wrapped in the loveliness of his brooding when he yearned above "the moving waters" toward that which is "still steadfast, still unchangeable"; the idea that looked out upon Rossetti through the eyes of his loved one:

> Sometimes thou seem'st not as thyself alone
> But as the meaning of all things that are,
> A breathless wonder shadowing forth afar
> Some heavenly solstice hushed and halcyon;

the idea that mightily engaged Shakespeare at the height of his dramatic power and, indeed, did much to bring him to that height, for man is most highly dramatic when seen as a "quintessence of dust" which is "in apprehension how like a god!"

In "apprehension," not *comprehension!* Recurrently in the history of human thought the conceited comprehensions of rationalism, ignoring the "mighty opposites" of real experience, have striven to explain our life in terms of a single power, either spirit or Nature.[1] In this respect rationalism is the foe at once of poetry and of common sense. When the eyes of common sense are not befogged by current theorizing, they see in life not a single power but two powers, the interaction of which can be guided, but never *comprehended*, by reason: the power of appetite and the power of control, the power that is shaped and the power that shapes—the dust and the deity. Common sense knows that a man cannot be "at one with himself," in any worthwhile way, unless he recognizes in himself two natures and succeeds in keeping "his better nature" more or less on top: a vital and admirable *oneness* of personality implies a *twoness* of nature. This everyday mystery is near the very source of the greatest poetry. Keats averred that there is nothing less poetic than a true poet. The converse epigram would be, there is nothing more poetic than a man of true common sense. Poetry has no mystery deeper than that underlying the phrases I have quoted from the vocabulary of common sense: "at one with himself," "his better nature.". . . Reflecting on such phrases, one's thought may pass, without becoming esoteric, into the inner shrine of Rossetti's *House of Life*:

> Lo! what am I to Love, the lord of all?
> One murmuring shell he gathers from the sand,
> One little heart-flame sheltered in his hand.
> Yet through thine eyes he grants me clearest call
> And veriest touch of powers primordial
> That any hour-girt life may understand.

No doubt this passage is remote enough in tone from the practical citizen, especially if he does not happen to be in the extreme stage of love. Yet its immanent idea is the same as that of the passage in *Hamlet*, cited above, which has passed into common currency and

---

[1]An extraordinary chronicle and criticism of this rationalistic tendency are provided by Paul Elmer More in his noble series of volumes on *The Greek Tradition* (Princeton University Press).

expresses the common conviction. Rossetti's "murmuring shell" gathered from the sand is Shakespeare's "quintessence of dust." And throughout *The House of Life*, as throughout Shakespeare's chief tragedies, goes the sense, at once a poetic sense and a common sense, of two different natures that meet unaccountably in human personality. Rossetti experiences so poignantly the gulf between love and Love, between the "heart-flame" and that which is not a flame at all, that he is *awed* by their intimate union in a single "hour-girt life." He knows he is in the presence of "powers primordial."

If the reader wishes to try a curious and revealing experiment, let him pass directly from Rossetti's great sonnet-sequence to Shelley's *Epipsychidion*. Here he will find an ethereal brightness, a fresh brilliance of poetic energy, quite lacking in Rossetti, and applied, ostensibly, to the very same theme. Shelley's loved one is "an image of some bright eternity." He experiences a union of spiritual and sensuous love that fills him with rapturous adoration and opens for him, he thinks, "the fountains of our deepest life." But the reader, the unbiased reader, will not feel here, or indeed in the whole series of Shelley's love-poems, the real awe that often touches him in *The House of Life*. He will recognize that Shelley, unlike Rossetti, has *not* the "clearest call and veriest touch of powers primordial."

And the reason, as I have tried to demonstrate below in connection with other important poems of Shelley, is that he had no profound sense of the *opposition* between the two powers he was dealing with. Therefore he could have no profound sense of their potential harmony. He experienced them in ecstatic confusion, not in deep-toned harmony. He never really *apprehended* the mysterious duality of human nature because he was so sure that he *comprehended* it. He was mastered by the conceited comprehension emanating from the enormous modern study of nature:

> Anon out of the earth a fabric huge
> Rose like an exhalation, with the sound
> Of dulcet symphonies and voices sweet,
> Built *like* a temple. . . .[2]

The emotional, often religionistic, monism of Shelley, of his master Wordsworth in his creative period, of Browning, of Emerson even, of Whitman, and of the poetry of the present day—I mean, the *feeling* that life is a single immense stream of tend-

[2] Italics mine.

ency—is in "dulcet symphony" with the rationalistic monism of Huxley and the metaphysicians, with the endeavour, still going on, to explain human life and "behaviour" in terms of a single Nature.

To be sure, some of Wordsworth's successors made fine attempts to break through the charmed circle. I trust I have done some justice to those attempts in the course of this book; I have already instanced the case of Rossetti. But generally speaking those attempts were comparatively weak from the *imaginative* standpoint. They did not have behind them the main drive of the modern imagination. That is why Shelleyan or Whitmanian monism has still such a hold on our poets and other imaginative writers today. Consider, for instance, their attitude toward sexual love. If questioned, would not most of them assert that Rossetti's view of passion is quite naïve and out of date, and that they themselves, though inferior to him in poetic art, are much more closely in touch with the "powers primordial"? Until this conceit is deflated, poetry cannot solve her present dilemma, cannot make a great move forward, and, incidentally, cannot take a real hold of the common sense.

Our poetry from Blake and Wordsworth on has continually believed itself to have the "clearest call and veriest touch of powers primordial" when, really, the "call" was a distant echo and the "touch" was a passing breeze of naturistic or spiritistic doctrine—for these two varieties of absolutism foment each other, and now that electrons are beginning to look like angels, God knows what variety of the Unseen All may come next! That is why modern poetry, with its remarkable array of poetically gifted persons, from Wordsworth to Hardy, could not come near the highest level of the Renaissance on the one hand, nor make a sustained appeal to common sense on the other. Whitman intended, more than any poet had ever done, to represent common humanity—and he became the prophet of an esoteric, aesthetic cult. The real poet of common humanity must imaginatively realize, as Shakespeare and Milton realized, and as common humanity feels, that the "powers primordial" are two *opposed* natures, a lower and a higher, meeting terribly or beautifully in human personality. This realization would lift up poetry again to awe, and broaden it out again to common sense.

No doubt the idea that I have sketched above wears something of the air of a thesis when isolated and presented in such a summary fashion. If the reader disagrees with it he may at least be stimulated to draw up his own answer to the following question: how may poetry win a larger and freer spirit than she has just now—or has had, indeed, for two centuries past? However, if the reader is one who dislikes inclusive questions, or thinks that they ought to be confined to the field of science, he may note that the bulk of this book is a study of particular aspects of modern poetry that interested me, in the first instance, for their own sake. My recurrent "thesis," if such it must be termed, grew from particular studies. In other words, the book has two gears, and at certain points in the journey it shifts from one to the other. I wish the reader might enjoy the whole drive as much as I have: then he wouldn't mind a little jolting when the shifting is rather sudden. Ideal readers, I think, belong to the order of Kipling's *Sons of Martha*:

It is their care in all the ages to take the buffet and cushion the shock.
It is their care that *the gear engages*, it is their care that the switches lock.

THE SOLITUDE OF SHELLEY

MAN AND POET

POOR Shelley's after-fame is now almost as fluctuant as that scene of his ending, a hundred years ago, when the waves bore him "darkly, fearfully, afar" (July 8, 1822). His status as a poet is involved in peculiar uncertainty. Writers who have agreed fairly well on other matters have differed widely in their evaluation of Shelley's style, particularly as compared with the styles of Wordsworth, Byron, and Keats. And almost any company of *immediate* poetry-lovers—I mean, those who maintain a healthy distrust of professional critics and a warm faith in their own predilections—can wax uncommonly disputatious if one of their number affirms that Shelley was a very real poet, or a very unreal one. Apparently his art is quite singular in its capacity to captivate and to repel. As a whole, it so repelled Matthew Arnold that it appeared to him a maze which wise men should rather walk around than penetrate. Though he surveyed it tellingly, he never passed right through it with his hand on an unbroken clue; nor have his followers done so. Critics of another type have yielded themselves so fully to the poet's fascinating meanders that eventually they could not emerge, with undimmed vision, into the open country beyond. In short, it has proved very difficult to bring the captivating and the repellent qualities of Shelley's work under a single impartial scrutiny.

The same is true of his life. His biographers have either taken sides, or, presenting both sides, have failed to make them cohere. The official *Life* by Professor Edward Dowden, in its elaborate attempt at impartiality, flattens Shelley out but does not make him believable. He appears as an English gentleman of genius whose conduct, from the standpoint of domestic morality, must sometimes be regarded as exceedingly ill-advised. But if this is a Victorian compromise, Arnold's essay, reviewing Dowden's book, is an Arnoldian compromise. Arnold's head and heart, as not infrequently, were divided. The Jovian head nodded Shelley out of heaven, but the Romantic heart tossed him a pair of wings. Their "luminous beating" arrested

Jove's sight; he got the angelic vision on the brain: "The Shelley of actual life is a vision of beauty and radiance . . . a beautiful and ineffectual angel." Professor Peck, in the latest biography, terms him a "will-o'-the-wisp" and, with industrious frankness, displays him as such in the whole course of his life.[1] Yet in his poetry, Mr. Peck evidently believes with Arnold that "still our ideal Shelley, the angelic Shelley, subsists."

It is hard to surrender the angel altogether, the messenger with *some* "airs from heaven." Where there is such loveliness, we feel that there ought to be an *atmosphere*, at least, of great human Truth. Yet if we regard the lovely, and sometimes mephitic, mists of dawn as radiations from the sun, our notion of the nature of sunlight gets sadly confused. That has happened considerably during the past hundred years, with baleful results for poetic truth today. The nature of physical light has been cleared amazingly by science. At the same time the sun-god himself, the god of poetry, has been hidden by growing superstition:

> And from the mirrored level where he stood
> A mist arose, as from a scummy marsh.
> At this, through all his bulk an agony
> Crept gradual, from the feet unto the crown. . . .[2]

Keats, at the very sunrise of our modern poetry, felt (deeper than his words) that the god was being distorted, that our vision of Him needed a full rebirth. Today, at the sunset of the nineteenth-century movement, the vapour has risen far higher, "as from a scummy marsh." Many persons today assume that the god himself is the source of the mists. Our need is to believe, with Keats and the Greeks, that He is the eternal foe of mists, though they rise toward Him.

He *plays* with them, passingly. That is the special loveliness of mists—and of Shelley. He has a misty luminosity. He has the "luminous wings" of the mist, not of the angel. For an angel is illumined, very considerably, from within. That was the case, for example, of Mrs. William Wordsworth, who had "something of angelic light" in her life as well as in her husband's poem. But Shelley's light is literary and derivative. Emerson was right (before Arnold and more decisively than Arnold) in denying to him an original

---

[1] W. E. Peck, *Shelley, His Life and Work*, Houghton Mifflin, 1927.
[2] Keats's *Hyperion*, I, 257ff.

vision of any importance.[3] Saturated with the outlook of Wordsworth in particular, Shelley was a devotee of poetry in general, from Homer to Keats. He basked and trembled in the long light of poetry like a cloud floating in sunshine. He transfused rather than transformed it, in his own writings, pouring it upon the things in Nature that he loved. But when we inquire for his love, when we pierce the misty glamour of the landscape in search of the ray peculiar to Shelley himself, the whole scene darkens considerably. Then we descry the flicker of the will-o'-the-wisp.

Just here some readers might exclaim that I myself, after noting the bias of other commentators, have proceeded to take sides against Shelley. But my point is that the very effort to be impartial, to find a fair clue for the whole maze of his life and work, leads us to the conviction that Shelley the man and Shelley the poet must undergo a single plain judgement: extraordinarily fascinating, extraordinarily shallow. His shallowness of personality was the complement of his magical nature-poetry—like the forest pool that always delighted him with its reflection of the traceries of the upper air:

> Sweet views which in our world above
> Can never well be seen,
> Were imaged by the water's love
> Of that fair forest green:
> And all was interfused beneath
> With an Elysian glow,—
> An atmosphere without a breath,
> A softer day below.

That "water's love" is wonderfully free from depth. And we spoil that "interfused Elysian glow" of Shelley when we persist in retaining for him "something of angelic light." We miss the very quality of the Shelleyan *reflection* if we read into it, knowingly or furtively, any human depth or height whatever. We can be just to Shelley only by seeing how shallow he is.

His thinking was shallow, eager, recent, and imitative, conventionally unconventional. In fact it was the kind of mental originality that has spread to so many writers and young people today. Shelley never got his head above the doctrines of eighteenth-century thinkers,

---

[3] Emerson is a good authority on this point. He was very sensitive to poetic originality. On the other hand, he was not prejudiced against Shelley as a man: he over-praised him.

from Locke to Godwin.[4] In his poetry the materialistic metaphysic persisting from the previous century, was raised and beautified by lyric art without changing its essential quality; as the dust of the earth, lifted and diffused by the wind, provides the colours of our most superb sunsets. His mind was not philosophic, as he fancied, but oratorical. One may agree with Trelawney that "however great Shelley was as a Poet, he was greater as an Orator." All his life he orated, drawing materials from his incessant reading. He would read and talk himself tired, and then suddenly fall asleep, and presently awake to talk and read again. He disobeyed every one of the Baconian commandments: "Read not to contradict and confute, nor to believe and take for granted, nor to find talk and discourse, but to weigh and consider." Shelley did not weigh and consider. He was abnormally devoid of meditation. And as Mr. Peck points out, he could never have endured the life of seclusion which he often yearned for but which, in moments of experience, he shrank from: "the dismaying solitude of myself . . . the horror, the evil, which comes to self in solitude."

He needed people, a variety of people. I think it was this need, even more than his devotion to the principles of Benevolence and of "Reason" (as he called it), that made him the centre of such a curious network of dependencies. Mr. Peck recounts in convincing detail the tragi-comic story of his expenditures of time and money and sympathy upon his needy acquaintances. If these flies, and particularly that fat fly William Godwin, loved to be caught in the shimmering web of his benevolence, we must remember that the kindly spider himself drew from the game a certain vital sustenance. His nature craved continual, but not profound, relationships with persons. He was not Cor Cordium. He was a friendly will-o'-the-wisp, dependent on human companionship but devoid of any deep passion for human Personality.

His love for women was an electric desire that would never have seemed very passionate if it had not been abnormally uncontrolled. It was not "an entirely human inflammability" as Arnold said. It was a sort of erotic congeniality, diluted with priggish theorizing. At the end of his married felicity with Harriet Westbrook, he endited to the "sister of his soul," Eliza Hitchener, the following gem of

[4] As shown in Professor S. F. Gingerich's recent book on the Romantic poets.

oratorical priggishness: "I ought to count myself a favoured mortal with such a wife and friend (these human names and distinctions perhaps are necessary in the present state of society)."[5] Miss Hitchener, so decorously drawn by Dowden, is shown by Mr. Peck to have had in her nature that which would naturally lead Shelley to pronounce her a "Brown Demon." Her letters to him are a tremendous farrago of flattery, idealism, and ill-concealed earthly passion. Apparently she had a passionate temperament with which she made the mistake of trying to capture Shelley. The will-o'-the-wisp never cared for that kind. He wanted somebody who could out-Harriet Harriet.

The whole subject of his transition from Harriet to Mary is dealt with vividly by Mr. Peck. After dismantling the flimsy charges against the former, he remarks: "If Harriet *was* at any time unfaithful to her marriage bond, is anything else established than that a simple honest girl, who by all accounts was as good as she was fair, eloped with, married, and bore children to a man who corrupted her morals with Godwinian poison and, afterwards deserting her, set her adrift in an evil world to follow his own teachings and his own example? Certainly there can be no exoneration for *him* in any act of *hers*." Considering this situation, Mr. Peck confesses himself nonplussed by the coldness of Shelley's references to Harriet after her suicide. But that coldness is not out of keeping with the whole genius of his life and poetry. His beneficiary, Leigh Hunt, naturally called him an "angel of charity." Arnold added: "In many respects Shelley really resembled . . . an angel of charity." But though he spoke with the tongues of angels and bestowed his goods to feed the poor, he had not Charity. He never sacrificed to others what he much desired for himself. He would not give up a jot of his self-righteousness for the sake of the woman whom he led into ghastly misery. Yet it is uncharitable to assume that Shelley had heart enough to be greatly bad, or greatly good. Let us attribute all we can to the mysteries of nature:

> Maiden still the morn is; and strange she is, and secret:
> Strange her eyes; her cheeks are cold as cold sea-shells.[6]

The definitive exposal of his shallow-heartedness is his attitude toward Mary during the last years of his life. He was now mature;

[5] Dowden's *Life of Shelley*, I, 247.
[6] From George Meredith's *Love in the Valley*.

she was his avowed mate in mind and spirit; and she had suffered very much for him and with him. But his heart became more and more unfaithful to her, as Mr. Peck's book demonstrates. He yearned away from her, and expressed to others his sense of her cold limitations—just as he had done in the case of Harriet. The emotions as well as the thoughts of this man revolved and repeated themselves, without finding any human goal; like the circulations of wind, stream, and cloud in his poetry. His life imitated nature, and in his best writings nature imitated him. "Rivers are not like roads, the work of the hands of man," so writes our naiad; "they *imitate mind*, which wanders at will over pathless deserts, and flows through nature's loveliest recesses, which are inaccessible to anything besides."

But he had a vague yearning to break through the shallow round of his nature—like a naiad who doesn't understand what a human person is, but moans because she isn't one. This yearning is the most humanly poignant thing in Shelley's life and poetry. A blind self-despair loomed up more and more behind his priggishness, his humble conceit, his dissatisfaction with others. Browning's opinion that if Shelley had lived he would have become a Christian may not be plausible, and yet it expresses a keen intuition into a kindred poet. Half of Shelley, at the least, was a born institutionalist—like his father Timothy or, if you will, like Nature herself. He was convinced of the vast importance, for good or ill, of wholesale systems. Even in the midst of composing *Prometheus Unbound* he could say: "I consider poetry very subordinate to moral and political science, and if I were well, certainly I would aspire to the latter; for I can conceive a great work, embodying the discoveries of all ages, and harmonizing the contending creeds by which mankind have been ruled." The systematic creed that he needed as a poet, however, was one that would give him,—what he could not get from his own experiences as a man among men,—some real grip and image of the inmost meaning of Personality, its mingled dust and deity. In the thirteenth century, Catholic theology would have fascinated and formed him; Oxford could have made him a fairly human monk. As it was, he was tragically unfortunate. He was dismissed from Oxford in his second year. Thereupon he was lured into a stultifying confusion of his sensuous and his ideal impulses. In his early wanderings he missed contact with men who could have guided him.

"I *might* have been of use to him," said Coleridge, many years later, "and Southey could not; for I should have sympathized with his metaphysical reveries, and the very word metaphysics is an abomination to Southey, and Shelley would have felt that I understood him." He needed a gifted and religious friend—and he got Byron. He needed a god—and he got Godwin. And so, in certain despairing verses written a few months before his death, he cried:

> I loved I know not what—but this low sphere,
> And all that it contains, contains not thee,
> Thou whom, seen nowhere, I feel everywhere.
> From heaven and earth, and all that in them are,
> Veiled art thou, like a star.[7]

POET OF JOY

But that veil, in Shelley's mood of delight, can appear as the misty atmosphere of springtime in which "the lamps of Heaven flash with a softer light."[8] Such, it happens, is the time and weather outside my window now; and Shelley is there. He blends with a roving thought of early-summer vacation. One feels like taking afresh from his poetry the sheer pleasure there is in it—forgetting all battles of the books and struggles of the world, in some quiet country-place, or at least in the lonely places of fancy. Shelley's joy is at once the very spirit, and the quick relief, of solitude. It transports us (unless we are anti-Shelleyan) out of our everyday lives; but it does not impel us (unless we are pro-Shelleyan) toward the difficult heights of thought. It moves in an airy, neutral region,

> where do inhabit
> The shadows of all forms that think and live . . .
> Dreams and the light imaginings of men,
> And all that fate creates and love desires,
> Terrible, strange, sublime and beauteous shapes.
> There thou art, and dost hang, a writhing shade,
> 'Mid whirlwind-peopled mountains; all the gods
> Are there, and all the powers of nameless worlds,
> Vast, sceptered phantoms; heroes, men, and beasts;
> And Demogorgon, a tremendous gloom;
> And he, the supreme Tyrant, on his throne
> Of burning gold. . . .[9]

[7] From *The Zucca.*
[8] *Adonais*, stanza 19.
[9] *Prometheus Unbound*, Act I, lines 197ff.

This gilded Tyrant, this Jupiter of things as they are; and that vague tremendous being (Demogorgon) which is certain to change things presently, for better or for worse; and even one's own Promethean self, ideally writhing under the idealized oppression of things as they are: all these are there, in shadowy form, stripped both of power and of pain.

> And see! more come,
> Like fountain-vapours when the winds are dumb,
> That climb up the ravine in scattered lines.
> And hark! is it the music of the pines?
> Is it the lake? Is it the waterfall? [10]

Their movements have the loveliness of cloud-volutions, and their voices commingle in rarest music. Ultimately, the peculiar ambiguous charm of these visions derives from the fact that their creator was at once a devotee and an obscurer of sublime reality. Shelley was not content to take his place in the numerous and delightful company of poets who shrug their shoulders at the mysteries of the universe, and sing for us merely "the light imaginings of men"; though it seems that Nature, in a very considerable measure, had shaped his poetic powers with that end in view. He longed to envisage the highest truths of life, and "all that fate creates or love desires." He is a daemon of mid-air, invoking the gods of the upper and the under worlds. They must all make some fine response, so wistfully piercing is his incantation; but into his region they can send only phantoms of themselves. These come streaming about us, when we enter that region, and curtain us in the loneliness of mountain mists. They relieve us from reality; yet, being wraiths of reality, they can yield us for a time recreative companionship.

Love is the chief of "sceptered phantoms" here. It is a strangely composite figure. But the holidaying reader shall escape the sway of its special joy whenever he examines it analytically, for praise or for blame: whenever it appears to him Christian, Platonic, humanitarian, erotic, or anything other than Shelleyan. When Arnold pronounced Shelley "extremely inflammable," and yet also "angelic," he did not go on to show how these two contradictory images are solved in the spirit of Shelley's poetry. Angels are comparatively cool creatures, from the carnal standpoint. We may accept Milton's opinion that they:

[10] *Prometheus Unbound*, Act I, line 666.

Can either sex assume, or both; so soft
And uncompounded is their essence pure.

And perhaps these lines, so airily hermaphroditic, suggest the quality
of Shelley's love; and help to illuminate the procedure of his Witch
of Atlas when "by strange art she kneaded fire and snow together."
Deficient in deep intensity, Shelley was animated by a quick, vague
affection. He never followed his emotions *through*, into the ways of
full lust or of firm devotion, either in his life or in his poetry.
Properly, his love is neither a flame nor an angel, but a daemon of
the cloud-region. It is not a harmony of diverse realities, but a
distillation from them: a mingling of emotions so vapour-like that
they seem to blend into one. It is poetically incapable, as "Epipsychidion" demonstrates, of the harmony that rises in great verse from
the combination of rich, distinct emotional tones. Its finest voice is
the melodious wraith, so to speak, of love's full harmony:

> The Fountains mingle with the River
> And the Rivers with the Ocean,
> The winds of Heaven mix for ever
> With a sweet emotion;
> Nothing in the world is single;
> All things by a law divine
> In one spirit meet and mingle:
> Why not I with thine?

Beneath this subtle music, and running through Shelley's whole
poetry of joy, is the yearning solitude of a spirit removed from love's
realities, and "peopling the lone universe" with love's shadows.
Unlike Romeo's dreams—

> Ah me! how sweet is love itself possessed,
> When but love's shadows are so rich in joy!—

Shelley's visions do not converge upon actuality. When he does
attempt the joy of "love itself possessed," in Canto Sixth of *The
Revolt of Islam*, the hero of his story becomes a sort of discoloured
Romeo,—at once more sensual, more ethereal, and less passionate than
Shakespeare's. And among the tangled meshes of this episode, the
reader can see the poet's genius struggling, in curious fashion, to
escape into the region of the "sceptered phantom," the shadowy
cloud-power:

> Which leads the heart that dizzy steep to climb
> Where far over the world those vapours roll
> Which blend two restless frames in one reposing soul . . .
> It is the shadow which doth float unseen,
> But not unfelt, o'er blind mortality. . . .

That "reposing soul" is like the pause which clouds seem to make at the moment of mingling, accenting their restlessness. Shelley's love-joy is a shadow floating incessantly between man's earth and man's heaven; and blending in magical beauty with all the motions of the clouds.

In this regard, Shelley, more than any other English poet, "is made one with Nature." His verse is instinct with the fact that Nature, whatever else she may be, is made of movement, movement ranging through innumerable degrees: corrosion of rocks, push of plant-fibres, creep of worms, swaying of branches, rush of rivers, flight of birds, sweep of clouds, darting of sunbeams. When we are in the mood to strip these things of their colour, and of the colour lent them by the human spirit, they can all merge into a vast, dim fabric, hanging screen-like about us, every thread of which is incessantly moving, swiftly or slowly, among the others. Shelley, like everyone else, projected his own colours upon that huge shifting screen. But his fancies, his very inmost tendencies of thought, were of such a quality as to blend, extraordinarily, with its intervolving strands. Nature herself is Shelleyan. She is not extensively Wordsworthian, or Keatsian. Nor should our pleasure in Shelley's representation of her be sapped by the more "realistic" view which developed in the later nineteenth century and remains prominent in the poetry of the present time. For the "vital onrush," the blind cruelty, the red-veined geniality of Nature—these are temporal reflections from human life, like the religionistic and moralistic colours of the external world in other ages; or like the millennial vision of Shelley when in his youth he cherished the belief that the very poles of the Earth would in time become warm and habitable:

> And fragrant zephyrs there from spicy isles
> Ruffle the placid ocean-deep, that rolls
> Its broad, bright surges to the sloping sand,
> Whose roar is wakened into echoings sweet
> To murmur through the heaven-breathing groves
> And melodize with man's blest nature there.[11]

[11] *Queen Mab.*

But the real charm of this passage—prophetic of Shelley's best mature style—is in the subtle shiftings of its music, as one movement of air or water glides into another. His rhythms are Nature still, but Nature *melodized*.

Motion subtly passing into other motion, or twining its way through it—this is very Nature, persistent behind all the colours of the human ages. Her chief circulation—the chief series of her vast, threading movements, as they impress our human senses—is that of water-vapour; and Shelley is the poet laureate of water-vapour. His joy takes it as it rises from streams and seas, speeds with it on the winds, comes down with it in dew and rain, and floats away again with it through all mists and clouds. The age-old fancy in which clouds are the *breath* of Nature, instinct with all her complex motions, reaches its culmination in Shelley. Whenever he touches a cloud, he touches it, or it touches him, into poetry: a sort of electric cloud-life runs throughout his verse. In long mediocre stretches of his more ambitious works, the cloud-spirit seems hovering in darkness close behind the scene, awaiting its cue:

> Doth the cloud perish when the beams are fled
> Which steeped its skirts in gold? or, dark and lone,
> Doth it not through the paths of night unknown,
> On outspread wings of its own wind upborne,
> Pour rain upon the earth? . . .[12]

The ways of other things are continually assimilated by this poet to the ways of clouds. The streams on which his imagination is continually journeying are never compulsive tides of passion, in the full human sense of this word, any more than the remote shores and glades, to which they bear him, are firm lands of thought. His streams have the speed, drift, and swirl of vapours; and the stillness of his landscapes is the hovering of clouds.

The exquisite hovering movement which distinguishes Shelley's style comes mainly from an incessant fluctuation in his feeling for stillness. He swiftly longs for rest, and swiftly shrinks from it, like a sea-bird circling a reef. His joy "wantons in endless being"; he continually associates quietness with dull conventionality, with desolation and lifelessness; yet he craves a point of repose, ever on beyond:

[12] *Revolt of Islam.*

> Silence! Oh, well are Death and Sleep and Thou
> Three brethren named, the guardians gloomy-winged
> Of one abyss, where life, and truth, and joy
> Are swallowed up—yet spare me, Spirit, pity me,
> Until the sounds I hear become my soul,
> And it has left these faint and weary limbs,
> To track along the lapses of the air
> This wandering melody until it rests
> Among lone mountains in some . . .

This fragment, written some years before his death, was perhaps left unfinished because it is well-nigh unfinishable. The repose for which the last lines yearn, returns toward the quiet that the opening lines shrink from. Here the poet is Ariel caught in a human circle. He can escape, however, from the sad orbit of mortality, into the circulations of Nature, through a kind of magic trance. It involves a species of self-hypnosis which present-day psychology, not I, should investigate accurately. Generally speaking, the trance-state so frequent in Shelley's work, from *Queen Mab* on to the end, is an effort, as Lady Macbeth's shrewd doctor would say, "to receive at once the benefit of sleep and do the effects of watching." Its most reposeful phase is imaged in the state of an enchanted personage in *The Witch of Atlas*:

> And there the body lay, age after age,
>   Mute, breathing, beating, warm, and undecaying,
> Like one asleep in a green hermitage,
>   With gentle smiles about its eyelids playing,
> And living in its dreams beyond the rage
>   Of death or life, while they were still arraying
> In liveries ever new the rapid, blind
> And fleeting generations of mankind.

Here is complete escape from the cycle of human laws. Here (if we may run the vision to earth thus) is such a lull as a tired worker might enjoy at the beginning of his summer vacation, in the gently swinging hammock of some "green hermitage," delightfully daydreaming of the pell-mell responsibilities he had just left behind. And when presently he bestirs himself, and, still considerably entranced, hurries out to enjoy the free region, he shall find Shelley there too, ever on ahead, circling among the winds, trees, and clouds. For the slumbrous stage of the Shelleyan trance is merely transitional. Through this porch the poet passes out into the joy of "the rapid, blind, and fleeting" movements of Nature. Absolved from all that wearies mankind, he is also absolved from the normal need of rest.

But of course, for a human being, no such absolution is without its penance. The delighted trance, like the fresh delight of one's summer vacation, threatens ever to end. As he revolves in his beautiful Nature-orbit, where unimpeded motion alternates swiftly with light repose, our poet is constantly pulled, by sheer force of human gravity, toward the human orbit, where heavy desire alternates with high need of peace. Recurrently—as in the fragment *To Silence* quoted above, the *Stanzas Written in Dejection near Naples*, and elsewhere—Shelley wakens to find himself caught motionless between the two orbits, in a region of lonely desolation, which I shall deal with later. But there is an antecedent moment in which he not only makes desolation beautiful, but finds there a quiet joy; for instance, among the disinterred walls of Pompeii:

> Around me gleamed many a bright sepulchre
> Of whose pure beauty, Time, as if his pleasure
> Were to spare Death, had never made erasure;
> But every living lineament was clear
> As in the sculptor's thought; and there
> The wreaths of stony myrtle, ivy and pine,
> Like winter's leaves o'ergrown by moulded snow,
> Seemed only not to move and grow
> Because the crystal silence of the air
> Weighed on their life; even as the Power divine,
> Which then lulled all things, brooded upon mine.[13]

That lovely transcription of the winter-pause of leaves (where else in modern verse is the worn word "crystal" so reanimated?) has the maximum of stillness, so to speak, that Shelleyan joy can absorb. Its delicate implication of potential movement is developed in the immediate context of the passage quoted. And from here one's fancy easily passes to "the sapless foliage of the ocean" suddenly trembling, in the *Ode to the West Wind*; and to many another passage presenting a fragile, momentary stillness, often bordering on desolation, always instinct with coming change. From such region, when the wings of his joy are strong enough, Shelley soon speeds away. And one may follow him through all degrees of motion, up to the magical swiftness of *The Cloud*. This wonderful lyric is a sort of quick gathering and distillation of all the cloud-joy in his poetry. Its absolute freedom from the sad tones heard in Shelley's other late

[13] *Ode to Naples.*

pieces, seems due to a sort of desperate vacation-mood: a determined throwing away of the cares that come "when winter comes," and a concentring of all his fancy upon the congenial fluidity of Nature. In pursuing here the full circulation of the world's water-vapour,

> Over the rills, and the crags, and the hills,
> Over the lakes and the plains,
> Wherever he dream, under mountain or stream,
> The Spirit he loves remains. . . .

he makes the full circuit of his own joy. He sustains his mood on a sort of tranced acceleration of movement, with now and then a quick, delighted hovering. He reaches the acme of entrancement at the close when he hovers for a moment toward a quiet death in the sky—and then with daemon-laughter resumes his circling "like an unbodied joy whose race has just begun":

> I am the daughter of earth and water,
> And the nursling of the sky;
> I pass through the pores of the ocean and shores;
> I change, but I cannot die.
> For after the rain, when with never a stain
> The pavilion of heaven is bare,
> And the winds and sunbeams with their convex gleams
> Build up the blue dome of air,
> I silently laugh at my own cenotaph,
> And out of the caverns of rain,
> Like a child from the womb, like a ghost from the tomb,
> I arise and unbuild it again.

The shiver in the second last line is of a cometary spirit pulled, for an instant, by the human orbit, but ever mocking at human birth and death; finding not a human tear in all the rain, nor a touch of human Peace in the "blue dome" which it loves to unbuild. When we let ourselves "float and run" with Shelley, the kind of joy that animates Shakespeare and Milton seems "distant in humanity." When the Shelleyan joy is purest, it is least human; at the same time it is poetically accomplished. What is it when it mingles with sorrow?

POET OF JOY AND SORROW

That question may be faced most squarely, perhaps, in connection with *Adonais*, which, while thoroughly representative of Shelley, has proved itself more generally satisfying to his readers than any other of his major poems. Certainly, in its own way, *Adonais* may be

regarded as the most fascinating treatment in English poetry of an
old human subject: regret for the transitory, and high yearning for
the changeless—these two feelings companioning and enhancing each
other, like variants of a single theme, until the "immortal longing"
can burn intensely, in a final moment, through the very air of death.
The rhythm, almost unexampled in its combination of prevailing
dignity with fluent shifting of tone, carries the duple theme magically and culminates with it in the closing passage:

> That Light whose smile kindles the Universe,
> That Beauty in which all things work and move,
> That Benediction which the eclipsing Curse
> Of birth can quench not, that sustaining Love
> Which through the web of being blindly wove
> By man and beast and earth and air and sea,
> Burns bright or dim, as each are mirrors of
> The fire for which all thirst, now beams on me,
> Consuming the last clouds of cold mortality.
>
> The breath whose might I have invoked in song
> Descends on me; my spirit's bark is driven
> Far from the shore, far from the trembling throng
> Whose sails were never to the tempest given;
> The massy earth and spherèd skies are riven!
> I am borne darkly, fearfully afar;
> Whilst, burning through the inmost veil of heaven,
> The soul of Adonais, like a star,
> Beacons from the abode where the Eternal are.

At once a rhythmic and a thematic triumph is that "Light" which
kindles wistfully in the opening verse, and passes changefully
through the ensuing lines like a leaping and subsiding torch-flame
borne by a swift messenger, and beacons steadily for a moment at
the close, as though from the goal. The passage can be fascinating,
if we are in the mood for it. But at another time, when we regard it
with a certain degree of poetic intentness, it may easily become
repellent, driving us back on our memory of lines that render an
"immortal longing" in a more satisfying manner, such as Cleopatra's

> Give me my robe, put on my crown; I have
> Immortal longings in me; now no more
> The juice of Egypt's grape shall moist this lip. . . .

To be sure, the whole speech of nineteen lines, if lifted from its
context in Shakespeare's play and placed alongside the Shelley

passage, takes on some air of cheapness. Its half dozen superb verses are surrounded and tinged with the common soil of Elizabethan rhetoric. Shelley's rhetoric and rhythm are more evenly distinguished, and his subject is more aspiring. Nevertheless, when our aim is sheer *poetic* pleasure, the Shakespeare passage is the more satisfying of the two. For its author, unlike Shelley, is intent in a very high degree upon the specific kind of emotion he is rendering: namely the "immortal longing" of a passionate and egotistic nature now weary of the world, and eager to project its love and earthly splendour, painlessly, into eternity. The passage is remarkable for its variety of emotional tones, swiftly succeeding each other, yet dominated by a single homogeneous quality. Shelley, on the other hand, twines together two quite different qualities of emotion, in such a way as to frustrate both. His stanzas yearn upward toward a Light that is absolutely beneficent, "beyond the clouds of cold mortality," and "like a star" in its eternal and awful peace. But this thread of high "immortal longing" is woven confusedly into a warp of restless mortal sympathies. The poet feels for the earthy "web of being" in which we are all enmeshed, the blind, warm life that pulses through "man and beast and earth and air and sea"; and thereupon, somewhat diverging from that gregarious emotion, comes a rush of sympathy for his own unconventional spirit, far from the routine existence of "the trembling throng." In short, the mixed emotion of the passage is so restless that it fails of elevation, and so anxious for elevation that it is thin and warped in its human implications.

Just previously (stanza 52) Shelley had been able to touch the same two spheres of feeling in swift alternation and yet without confusion:

> The One remains, the many change and pass;
> Heaven's light forever shines, Earth's shadows fly;
> Life, like a dome of many-coloured glass,
> Stains the white radiance of Eternity. . . .

Here it seems that the poet has contemplated his "immortal longing" so intently that it can become, for a sufficient moment, a white and quiet light of emotion inundating all else. The "white radiance of eternity" is felt distinctively; so is this "many-coloured" life of ours which dims and entirely stains that radiance, and yet transfuses it, in transitory domed splendour. Why then, in the sequel, does the poet collapse that dome and reduce that radiance to a kaleidoscopic figuration which mingles the white and coloured lights factitiously? His palpable aim in the two final stanzas is to draw together, in one pattern, several topics which he has treated scatteringly in the course of the poem. But beneath that design is a deeper one. Consciously or not, he wishes to close the poem on his favorite note of high aspiration interwoven, indistinguishably, with wide sympathy.

Here, indeed, is the central purport of Shelley's work as a whole, from *Queen Mab* to *Hellas*. He wished to express an unhampered sympathy with the wide "web of being" in men and Nature; and, at the same time, a pure devotion to "the Good," or whatever one may choose to term the highest life of the spirit. He had an exceptionally keen sense for the old human longing to combine such sympathy with such devotion, "harmonizing this earth with what we feel above." But he had an abnormally slight sense for the real divergency, and the continual opposition, of these two emotions in the general human heart. It is a matter of common experience, in individual lives and in history, that a heightening of our sentiment for "the Good" will narrow our sympathy with those features of life that seem most remote from it; and that a broadening of our sympathies, in an effort at readjustment, will pull down considerably our love of "the Good." But this competition scarcely appears in Shelley's work. So that, instead of striving as the human heart strives when it is most vital, toward a real harmony in which each of those two emotions should retain its own distinctive quality, Shelley quickly merged and denatured them.

Hence the extraordinary sense of frustration which we experience when we try to read, with poetic intentness, his most ambitious work, *Prometheus Unbound*. The poem appeals at once to our yearning for universal sympathy and to our yearning for human perfection. These two sentiments, when stimulated, tend to diverge and to develop themselves in competition with each other. But Shelley will not have them do so. From the first, he keeps winding and fusing them together in a single stream of undifferentiated emotion. For example, he merges more and more the qualities of the two principal personages, Prometheus and Asia. If these two characters had been made the vehicles, respectively, of ethical elevation and wide sympathy, their eventual reunion could have won a fine human and poetic significance, suggesting that fullness of life which the human spirit recognizes as its greatest potentiality. But in the course of the story, the initial nobility of Prometheus is soon softened down by his rising pity for all things, including the powers of evil (Act I, scene i, lines 53, 305, 480); and finally this active striver for mankind becomes a retired well-wisher, throbbing only with millennial reverie and sympathy (Act III, scene iii). On the other hand, the Aphroditic quality of Asia, her imaging of the universal pulsing desire that weaves the "web of being," remains inchoate; for the poet wishes her to adumbrate also the higher kind of love that urges human perfection. Thus the outlines of Prometheus and his Asia fade into each other: the two are not married, but merged. The poem as a whole frustrates and repels our poetic sense by attempting the music of the spheres on a single string.

Since Shelley's longing for human harmony means a denaturalization of the emotions which must take part in such harmony, it is essentially unpoetic. It has rhetorical zest and rhythmic sweep, but it lacks *poetic* spontaneity. Whatever spontaneity may mean in personal life, surely in verse it means that, for the moment, all the artist's powers are intensely preoccupied in bringing out the full specific quality of his emotion, and in thus making it poetically real. But Shelley, as in the two final stanzas of *Adonais*, is intent on shaping up his theme, not on shaping out his emotion. The pattern achieved in that passage, as previously suggested, is rhetorical and rhythmic, rather than poetic. It does not consist in a poetic realization of the writer's emotions. Such unreality pervades Shelley's more ambitious works, becoming acute in climactic passages. Its source, in the last analysis, is his peculiar longing for harmony— in other words, the kind of love, aspiration, and hope that run centrally through his poetry. These emotions failed to grow more specific and shapely, as Shelley's powers in verse became more mature, for the simple reason that his interest in them was not mainly a poetic interest. He did not experience them with any depth of poetic originality and spontaneity. Accordingly, those who have found in Shelley's work an extraordinary and dominant spontaneity have had their eye (and often unwittingly) upon his temperament rather than upon his art. Those who have condemned his poetry for *mere* spontaneity have left the gate open to those who have praised it for *sheer* spontaneity.[14] Neither phrase is properly applicable.

However, through the false harmonies of Shelley runs a captivating melody: the cry of "the spirit of solitude,"—the most exquisite note of utter loneliness in English poetry. His solitude is that of a spirit hovering between rich human sympathy and high self-satisfaction, not realizing either. Loneliness of this sort has been notably common during the past hundred and fifty years; but it hovers perpetually in the outskirts of human life. It is a mood that awaits any one whenever his dissatisfaction with human institutions and conventions begins to veil from him their deepest meaning. Through convention, in the finest sense of that nowadays degraded word, human sympathy and aspiration are at once restricted and, in some degree, made real. But Shelley would see only the deadening tendency of convention, and could therefore have no real fellowship with the deep convention-making power in our nature which imperfectly builds, and rebuilds, the house of life. That living structure, even while his nature craved its shelter and could find nothing

---

[14] Paul Elmer More's essay on Shelley deals most penetratingly with the confused nature of Shelleyan criticism, and the actual nature of the Shelleyan temperament. But his treatment of the subject of spontaneity in Shelley's poetry seems inadequate. In reference to Francis Thompson's remark upon the closing scenes of *Prometheus Unbound*—"the spell on which depends such necromantic castles is some spirit of pain charm-poisoned at their base"—Mr. More says: "That charm-poisoned spirit was nothing less than the peculiar romantic illusion of the Revolution which ignored the native impulse of evil, ever lurking in the heart of man, ready to leap forth when its chains are shaken, and which valued the emotions in accordance with their mere spontaneity and intensity" (*Shelburne Essays*, Seventh Series, p. 18). But surely "the native impulse of evil" is itself among the emotions which are spontaneous and intense. Therefore Shelley's failure to give a proper value to that impulse means that his criterion was not "mere spontaneity and intensity," and suggests that this phrase is not an exact key to his poetic art. The whole question would seem to turn on a proper distinction of the poetic mode from the moral mode of controlling emotion. Though these two modes are complementary, a too close approximation of them will produce confusion in the criticism of poetry. Certainly, the man Shelley was deficient enough in self-control, and often followed the impulse of the moment: this may be called "mere spontaneity." But it is equally true that he was deficient in the artistic instinct of following an emotion *through*, into its full specific nature: this means that his poetic spontaneity was very shallow.

beyond it but shadowy hopes and fears, could appear to him an idle painted veil:

> Lift not the painted veil which those who live
> Call Life; though unreal shapes be pictured there,
> And it but mimic all we would believe
> With colours idly spread,—behind, lurk Fear
> And Hope, twin Destinies, who ever weave
> Their shadows o'er the chasm sightless and drear.
> I knew one who had lifted it—he sought,
> For his lost heart was tender, things to love. . . .

Most poets, when their love is thus inadequate to the constructive life of mankind, can float their homeless imagination for a while on the beating tides of common desire—from which Shelley shrank. A few can build up, through meditation, a higher companionship —for which Shelley was too wilful. At once exceptionally refined and extraordinarily restless, he found neither the relief of full desire nor the steadiness of calm thought:

> Alas! I have nor hope nor health,
> Nor peace within nor calm around,
> Nor that content surpassing wealth
> The sage in meditation found,
> And walked with inward glory crowned—
> Nor fame, nor power, nor love, nor leisure . . .

But he found the very cadence of utter solitude.

Shelley's verse is at its best when he best realizes, poetically, his loneliness. His dominant mood is then trance-like, for it is made of emotion which is withdrawing itself from the sources of emotion. It is a thin love of life, circling above an abyss of nothingness: thrilling upward, again and again, in an ecstasy poignant with a sense of its own coming dissolution; but sinking down, with increasing frequency, in a state of despairing apathy. He achieved a fine art in the representation of apathy. Often it comes out in dramatic touches, imaging either his own state of lonely suspension, as in the fragment *To the Moon*, which breaks off so suggestively:

> Art thou pale for weariness
> Of climbing heaven and gazing on the earth,
> Wandering companionless
> Among the stars that have a different birth,—
> And ever changing, like a joyless eye
> That finds no object worth its constancy?
> Thou chosen sister of the spirit,
> That gazes on thee till it pities . . .

or the kind of apathy, opposite in origin and complementary to his own, which descends upon mechanically conventional persons, such as the dead Ginevra's husband:

> Some few yet stood around Gherardi there,
> Friends and relations of the dead,—and he,
> A loveless man, accepted torpidly
> The consolation that he wanted not;
> Awe in the place of grief within him wrought.

But this vein is richest, of course, in Shelley's lyric and sensuous stanzas. They range in tone all the way from the deathly languor of this passage in *The Invocation to Misery*:

> There our tent shall be the willow,
> And mine arm shall be thy pillow;
> Sounds and odours, sorrowful
> Because they once were sweet, shall lull
> Us to slumber, deep and dull . . .

to the piercing desolation of *When the Lamp is Shattered*. The whole movement of this wonderful little piece is that of a love swaying down, so to speak, toward insensibility. In other poems, such as *To a Skylark*, the same love spirals upward, in swift, ecstatic joyance: creating for a moment, in its longing to escape languor, a region where "languor cannot be." Shelley's delight and apathy must be felt, by a reader who would touch the finest pulse of his verse, as diastole and systole, as the lift and fall of a single wave of emotion. His joy is unique in English poetry because it is uniquely near to apathy:

> The passing wind which heals the brow at noon,
> And may strike cold into the breast at night,
> Yet cannot linger where it soothes the most,
> Or long soothe could it linger. . . .[15]

Other poets have deeper sorrow and richer joy than his. No other has his exquisite hovering movement of delight: his lonely joy, swaying cloudlike between heaven and earth, always about to dissolve and pass.

From its very nature, Shelley's lonely emotion could rarely assume real poetic shape: I mean, that inner form, synonymous with poetic reality, which is created by the union of sincere impulse and focal theme. Such union is not consummated in the bulk of Shelley's work.

[15] From a fragment of an unfinished drama.

Sometimes, as in *The Witch of Atlas*, he follows his shifting moods, veraciously, through a thin and diffusive theme. At other times, as in *Epipsychidion*, he pursues a focal idea—a deliberately thought-up topic, more or less derived from his reading—which his own actual emotion cannot properly fulfil. For when vitally ingenuous his poetic spirit is so liable to formless volutions that, when deliberately architectured, it is always likely to become factitious and inane, like the human shapes which a fanciful, determined eye finds in the clouds. But a real shape of poetry, now and then suddenly emerging in these cloudy regions, has a magic beauty, an inevitability, quite singular in English verse. We feel that an "unbodied joy" has found for a moment, as if by chance and after long vain journeyings, the only theme in which it could really be clothed. Such a theme was the autumnal west wind which Shelley listened to in a forest near Florence. The *Ode* which ensued is an harmonious texture of fancies which had been drifting scatteredly through his previous works, and which were now drawn into a single rhythm under the sweep of a movement in Nature wonderfully correspondent to the tenor of his own lonely mood. "Make me thy lyre even as the forest is," he prays: and never was poetic invocation more magically answered. Wraith-like fancy, tumultuous yearning, and delighted brooding— spectral leaf, surging cloud, and quivering wave—all flow into one "deep autumnal tone, sweet though in sadness." The poem is a sudden apparition, in lovely form, of the spirit of utter solitude.

The continual though obscured presence of this spirit can lure us on, by hints and gleams of itself, through the inanities of Shelley's more ambitious works. We feel that at any moment the true daemon may take shape, and sing; as in the rich sylvan solitude of Act II, scene ii, of *Prometheus Unbound*,

> When there is heard through the dim air
> The rush of wings; and rising there,
> Like many a lake-surrounded flute,
> Sounds overflow the listener's brain
> So sweet, that joy is almost pain.

In *Adonais*, more than elsewhere, this music of isolation is sustained through a highly architectured theme. An instinct finely true to himself, though untrue to Keats, led Shelley to place in the forefront of the poem an image of Adonais in a "twilight chamber," gone from life, but not yet covered with the darkness of decay: lying

there in "deep and liquid rest, forgetful of all ill"; closely attended
still by his own fading aspirations, surrounded in the near distance
by the shifting vital powers of Nature, visited by the eternal spirit
of poetry herself—but insensible, now, to them all (stanzas 7, 8).
This is the noblest form of that picture of entranced loneliness
which, first appearing in the opening stanzas of *Queen Mab*, is
painted and repainted throughout Shelley's work,—in hues more
deathful toward the close. Something of nobility is sacrificed, but
the suggestiveness of the picture is heightened, by the "one frail
Form" who is featured so vividly among the poetic mourners of
Adonais (stanzas 31-34). Properly considered, this figure is a pathetic
variant of the central Adonais-image. It represents the Shelleyan
temperament not yet absolved from life, but on the verge of dissolution: "a pard-like Spirit beautiful and swift," hunted to the end by
its own lonely aspirations:

> A phantom among men; companionless
> As the last cloud of an expiring storm
> Whose thunder is its knell. . . .

The episode prepares the way for an increased emphasis upon the
poet's yearning to be free from life, and to become "what Adonais
is." It is a yearning which shrinks away from earthly personality,
from "the world's bitter wind," and from the processes of natural
decay; but falls short of a real devotion to that immortality which
is at once the most organic and the most peaceful life of the human
spirit. Essentially, it is a yearning for a sort of perpetual trance, as
of a being suspended between time and eternity, oblivious of its
utter solitude.

   This longing is the most vitally felt emotion in the last third of
Adonais. But the poet's inner shaping of it is confused and imperfect: so that this part of the work, though the most popular, is sub-
stantially the least adequate, from the standpoint of art. Shelley
endeavours, as previously suggested, to focus his theme upon the
idea of a Light, or Power, which solves all discords,

> Which wields the world with never-wearied love,
> Sustains it from beneath, and kindles it above.

These verses are inept and mediocre, not because entirely void of
human truth, but because Shelley has not intently experienced the
two-sided truth they hint at. Their neat rhetorical harmony is in
strong contrast with the real melody that flows whenever the poet

contemplates, with intent longing, the Adonais-image; which, at the beginning of this part of the poem (stanzas 38-40), is rapt away from its initial "twilight chamber," and established in an ideal state beyond decay:

> He has outsoared the shadow of our night:
> Envy and calumny and hate and pain,
> And that unrest which men miscall delight,
> Can touch him not and torture not again . . .

Such music belongs to the spirit of solitude, in its yearning for Lethe. Its echoes can carry us through all ensuing inanities, even through the rhetoric of the two closing stanzas, quoted previously. Behind their elaborate and tangled imagery; behind the poet's desire to have his "spirit's bark" driven by the breath of eternity, far over a tempestuous sea, beyond the riven "massy earth" and "sphered skies," toward the "inmost veil of heaven"—behind all this rhetorical pomp of ocean and air, we can hear, if we will, that clear small voice of poetry which speaks most perfectly, perhaps, in the lonely, mysterious murmuring of the following verses from another poem, where sea and sky are quieter:

> Yet now despair itself is mild,
> Even as the winds and waters are;
> I could lie down like a tired child,
> And weep away the life of care
> Which I have borne and yet must bear,—
> Till death like sleep might steal on me,
> And I might feel in the warm air
> My cheek grow cold, and hear the sea
> Breathe o'er my dying brain its last monotony.

II

BYRON AND THE COMIC SPIRIT

TODAY we need to remember Byron's poetry, and forget Byron. But who could turn from such a magniloquent figure without a look behind? Of the vast fame that once was his, let us save this glimpse: Goethe's Eckermann in the 1820's noted that "all young travelling Englishmen carry volumes of Byron." (What volumes carry they in the 1920's?) Of the man himself as he lived, let Leigh Hunt speak a final word—from the days when, as Byron's house-mate in the Casa Lanfranchi at Pisa, he sat writing before a window that opened upon the interior courtyard: "Lord Byron, who used to sit up at night writing *Don Juan* (which he did under the influence of gin and water), rose late in the morning. He breakfasted; read; lounged about, singing an air, generally out of Rossini; then took a bath, and was dressed; and coming down stairs, was heard, still singing, in the courtyard. . . . His dress was a nankin jacket, with white waistcoat and trowsers, and a cap, either velvet or linen, with a shade to it. In his hand was a tobacco-box, from which he helped himself occasionally to what he thought a preservative from getting too fat. Perhaps also he supposed it good for the teeth. We then lounged about, or sat and talked; Madame Guiccioli, with her sleek tresses, descending after her toilet to join us. . . . None of her graces appeared entirely free from art; nor, on the other hand, did they betray enough of it to give you an ill opinion of her sincerity and good-humour."[1]

This scene is pure food for the Comic Spirit; which in recent decades has been struggling, with imperfect success, to sit up and take nourishment. During its century of sleeping-sickness, it has been hectored by the vision of Byron as a Titan. And this phantom still lingers. For the nineteenth-century spirit, in which we still move and have our being, loved Titanism. During the past four or five decades, writers who have professed a balanced and disillusioned view of Byron, have continued the illusion, in one guise or another, that he

[1] Leigh Hunt's *Autobiography*, 1850, Vol. II, page 134.

was Titanic. Minute and solemn investigation of his sins has continued; but this seems practically closed, now, for want of fresh material. When the last of the Lovelace books was published in England several years ago, the *London Times* reviewer, who seemed richly informed, gave a lengthily conscientious verdict: to wit, that in the case of Lady Byron versus Lord Byron the available evidence on both sides seemed now complete; that unfortunately the very nature of the affair prevented the evidence from being perfectly conclusive; but that it seemed clear, on Lord Byron's behalf, that he was never plainly informed of his lady's chief charge against him; whereas, on Lady Byron's behalf, there emerged a strong probability that this charge was justified and that Byron was actually guilty of. . . . But alas! the whole great triangular tragedy—Byron, Lady Byron, and Astarte—is three straws on the rising stream of twentieth-century laughter.

Byron's other sins are not much more Titanic; nor are his notable virtues. In 1881, Matthew Arnold still felt so strongly the pull of his boyhood's hero that, adopting for once a Swinburnian hyperbole, he insisted on Byron's "splendid and imperishable excellence which covers all his offences and outweighs all his defects: the excellence of sincerity and strength." But how ironic that word "imperishable" appears when Arnold goes on, in maturer vein, to state that Byron "has no light, cannot lead us from the past to the future"; and that he "shattered himself to pieces" in attacking the bourgeois cant of the earlier nineteenth century! Sincerity and strength are "imperishable" in proportion as they cut through the passing forms, to the perennial forces, of human cant. Olympus itself is antagonist of the true Titan. He makes no compromise with its minions (all this ought to be couched in blank verse) and when he falls, falls deep. Byron made the compromise called "Byronism"; and fell—into the arms of *fairly congenial* Guiccioli, "with her sleek tresses" and "none of her graces entirely free from art." Well, shall we not let him saunter— this Titan in "nankin jacket, with white waistcoat and trowsers," "singing an air out of Rossini," and adored in the background by crowds of "young travelling Englishmen"—let him saunter pleasantly over the rear horizon?

His poetry, the best of it, may then rise unclouded on the horizon ahead. It has not yet had its clear and full day. It was cloudily wor-

shipped by Byron's contemporaries. The Victorians partly mispraised
it and partly reacted from it. The poetic spirit of our own time,
rejecting the Victorians and casting back for inspiration to the early
writers of the century, has loved the Shelleyan dream and the "colour-
ful" imagery of Keats. But Byron could offer neither. Moreover,
though recent writers have re-created a cult and a cant of free
individualism that is often reminiscent of Byron, no recent writer
has *consciously* desired to be Byronic—so strongly has this poet
inoculated his posterity against Byronism! In the academic sphere,
apparently, Byron's work has of late made some headway. But here
as everywhere, his poetry and his individuality have remained too
closely intertwined. In his worst passages the worst features of the
man Byron are industriously made plain. In his best passages the
higher Byron is shown forthstepping,—"that true and puissant personality, with its direct strokes, its ever-welling force, its satire, its
energy, and its agony" (Arnold). His spiritual career—"that Titanic
strife"—is closely followed in the succession of his poems up to *Don
Juan*. The remarkable essay on Byron by Paul Elmer More concludes:
"he wrung from the tragedy of his own life the irony and pathos of
Don Juan, a poem which in its own sphere is so easily supreme that this
achievement alone would rank him great among the strongest, if not
among the wisest."[2] In short, Byron is viewed as an extraordinary
personal force, coming out now in irony or satire, now in agony or
pathos or romantic sentiment, and therefore reaching its fullest expression in the medley of *Don Juan*.

But how much of that *personal* force was really *poetic* force? This
question now presses to the foreground; and no doubt it will be
gradually answered during the next hundred years or so. Doubtless
many passages of Byron that are still favourites will sink. For example, if this "direct stroke" should arrest the future lover of verse,

> No more—no more—Oh! never more on me
> The freshness of the heart can fall like dew . . .

all the more would he hurry over the remainder of that well-known
passage.[3] It has Byronic pathos and irony; but, for poetry, it is far
too sprawlingly showy. This is obviously the main defect of Byron's

[2] Introduction to *Byron's Poetry* in the Cambridge Edition.
[3] *Don Juan*, I, stanzas 214-15.

work; but the nature of it needs to be made plainer. Its main source is not insincerity, nor slipshod technique, nor predilection for rhetorical effect. Many faults of this nature, as in the Elizabethan poets, can be floated on a current of real *poetic mood*. But just here is Byron's deficiency. Poetic mood, in general, is of course the artist's poise of spirit when, with his peculiar abilities at full tide, he is intent, not on expressing himself or impressing his public, but simply on the making of true verse. The mood comes as a brooding and creative presence that demands complete obedience. It demands that all *personal* interests and powers that the artist may have as a man among men, shall be submitted to it, and rejected in so far as they cannot serve its purpose. It burns quietly above the apex of all excitements, like a star over Vesuvius. Its mark is a certain mysterious serenity, quite distinct from all other serenities—moral, philosophic, and so on—though it may hold much of these in solution. This kind of serenity is comparatively rare in Byron's work. Perhaps no other English writer has had so many poetic capabilities and, at the same time, been so deficient in sure poetic mood. Just for this reason, however, his verse affords the most remarkable examples of that mysterious process which underlies all good verse: the transition from the personal to the poetic mood. In the following stanza, a certain familiar interest of Byron the man is completely lifted and changed into poetry, excepting the first line:

> Her eye (I'm very fond of handsome eyes)
> Was large and dark, suppressing half its fire
> Until she spoke; then through its soft disguise
> Flashed an expression more of pride than ire,
> And love than either; and there would arise
> A something in them which was not desire,
> But would have been, perhaps, but for the soul
> Which struggled through and chastened down the whole.[4]

Here is the broad wholeness of effect that Byron was master of—in easy force of phrasing, and linked, mounting rhythms. But in this case there is also a true poetic mood that rises through "and chastens down the whole," curbing the rhetoric and enriching the mettle of poetic suggestion. The mood is *deeply comic*, developing through a sort of stoic compression and composure. A little further on it flows out ripplingly into this:

[4] *Don Juan*, I, stanza 60.

Yet Julia's very coldness still was kind;
And tremulously gentle her small hand
Withdrew itself from his, but left behind
A little pressure, thrilling, and so bland
And slight, so very slight, that to the mind
'Twas but a doubt; but ne'er magician's wand
Wrought change with all Armida's fairy art
Like what this light touch left on Juan's heart.

Taken together, these serenely comic stanzas point the way of Byron's destiny. It was not the way of romance or satire. For highest distinction in satire, he was too emotional, and he lacked the subtlety of wit that shines in the eighteenth-century masters whom he revered. His feelings sought romantic expression. For romance, however, he lacked the subtlety of imagination that gleams in Wordsworth, Shelley, Keats, and Coleridge. They were penetrated by the romantic mood, and he was merely cloaked in it. It made him swagger because it fitted him imperfectly. His romantic poetry is diffuse and showy not just because the man was an egotist, but because the artist was not at home there. His gift of poetic mood was not apt and certain in transmuting personal feelings into romantic verse. His proper genius was the comic spirit, which loves large symmetry, and neither slashes nor weeps and yearns; though of course it may employ satire and sentiment intermittently when they are soluble in its purpose. Not the satirico-romantic mode was Byron's *goal*, but a sort of stoical and comic art, akin, in spirit, to that which George Meredith was later to essay. Byron's destiny demanded that, through an increasingly stoic outlook on life, he should learn to hold his crowded experiences at a certain cool distance, where he could view them, not with contempt or sighs, but in the light of the comic vision. For an obvious example of the rise in the quality of his style when he views life at stoic distance, consider stanza 182 of *Childe Harold*, Canto Fourth—"Thy shores are empires," etc.—in contrast with the preceding passages, where his personal feelings are too close to the scene. The stanza, though serious, is on the road leading to the comic vision of life because it views an old paradox of human society with poetic serenity. When Byron travels the road *toward* the comic vision he sings his best song: his mood is firmest and his touch most sure. In this point of view, *Heaven and Earth* and *Sardanapalus*, written in 1821, are his two most significant poems, and throw *Don Juan* into the shade. They have been neglected because, as it seems to me, they have not been shown in their proper relationship with his preceding work.

The works of 1816-17 have been regarded too exclusively as the volcanic result of Byron's English career, with all its passions and troubles and its abrupt decline. In reality, just how mountainous were those troubles (so the critical reader has queried) and how sincere the throbs and groans of the downcast Titan beneath? This question has confused the critical evaluation of the poems of the time. Properly, these may be viewed as a series of shifting efforts, on the part of a slow-maturing poet, to find his way ahead in his art. *Childe Harold*, Canto Third, is far superior to the earlier works—the dulcet lyrics, the half-baked satires, the flaring *Oriental Tales*—mainly because Byron was trying with maturer earnestness to surmount Byron, to win a new lift and veracity of poetic mood. So intense and continual is this effort that it warms all the atmosphere and creates a mirage-like reflection in which the scattered objects seem to form a single landscape. From a rapid and sympathetic reading of this extraordinary piece, one may always win an illusion of poetic completeness. Actually, however, such completeness is achieved only in particular passages, as in that describing the Rhine castles:

> And there they stand, as stands a lofty mind,
> Worn, but unstooping to the baser crowd,
> All tenantless, save to the crannying wind,
> Or holding dark communion with the cloud.

Here Byron's personal trouble has been stoically accepted and submerged, and rises again as pure poetry.[5] Identical in tone with this passage is the companion poem to *Childe Harold*, *The Prisoner of Chillon*, where Byron won superb success in mood and organism by confining himself to his hatred of tyranny, and throwing it into a cool Alpine distance. But he could not well continue on such narrow tracks. In *Manfred*, he cast back upon the rich and various experiences of *Childe Harold*—the loss of love, the despair, the appeal to surrounding nature, the proud independence, the craving for Lethe —and tried to reweave them into a single dramatic design. But the design is factitious and superficial: it is the result of a rhetorical, not a poetic, concentration. The fresh lift and glow of the earlier poem are gone; and this reassembly of its feelings serves only to

[5] In contrast, for instance, with stanza 114: "I have not loved the world nor the world me," etc.

show how little they had been subdued, in the meanwhile, to the service of real poetic purpose. Manfred himself is obviously designed to be of far larger calibre than he actually is: his actions presuppose a resolution that one who so unpacks his heart with words could not have; he contradicts that strength of his own despair on which the whole theme turns. Therefore those who have praised the piece for its extraordinary unity of theme, while deprecating its romanticism, have turned it wrong side out, under the sway of a false criterion. The romantic emotions of *Manfred* are potential poetry: its whole mood and mode are nonsensical.

Byron deliberately tasted blood in *Manfred*, and the taste lingered. In the ensuing poem, *Childe Harold*, Canto Fourth, he demands his soul to stand "a ruin amidst ruins." The naïveté of Canto Three is gone. He is groping toward the satiric vein of *Don Juan*. In this famed work, begun in 1818, the lust of rhetorical self-expression culminates, and well-nigh swamps Byron the poet. Continually he gets his head above the tide, like "some strong swimmer in his agony," only to be submerged again by a wave of stale regret or commonplace wit. The alternating of sentiment and satire was, in itself, a sound comic idea, and marked an advance toward Byron's goal. But this mode demands a firm comic mood, which Byron did not yet have. His incertainty of mood and purpose, ingenuously confessed by himself at the beginning of Canto Fourth, made the poem as a whole a failure. The author is still a drawing-room lion,— monologuing with clever variegation to "a large and attentive audience," but spoiling his whole effect by an extraordinary lack of self-possession. He is undecided as to what kind of lion he is—or whether he *is* one after all. The poem degenerates in its whole spirit, more or less steadily, after Canto First. The story of Juan and Julia in that canto is superb sex-comedy, quite unique of its kind in English verse. But in the ensuing episode of Juan and Haidée, comedy is lost in a queer mixture of romance and burlesque. The poet is tangled in his own feelings, and uncertain as to their quality. By cheap joking he tries for comic footholds in the marshy sentiment that lures him on. The romantic theme in itself is a failure: Haidée, the centre of it, is a mechanic composition, part Arcadian and part Oriental.[6] A natural sequel is the episode of Juan and Dudu, Canto

---

[6] What a glaring inconsistency in regard to her "pure ignorance" appears in stanzas 190 and 193 of Canto Second! It is noteworthy that her situation

Sixth, which reads like a burlesque of the Juan and Julia affair. Here Byron moves easily, in obvious laughter. Indeed, the recurrent strain of burlesque or "low comedy" in *Don Juan* stays happily with the reader. If isolated, it could have made a complete poem on a frankly lower level, like *The Vision of Judgement* (1821). As it is, *Don Juan* is a rich but monotonous display of the little Byronic world; with a very special interest for us, which should not be confused with lasting poetic interest; and with the true comic spirit touching it here and there, and yearning to work it over into organic poetry.

The call of his finer genius led Byron in 1821 to set aside *Don Juan*, for nearly two years, in favour of poetic drama. The two Italian plays, *Marino Faliero* and *The Two Foscari*, with their stiff attention to form, mean a revulsion from the expressional dissipation of *Don Juan* and a striving for shapeliness. This self-imposed discipline was beneficent for Byron's remaining pieces; but he could not move far in the bonds of historical tragedy, and his imagination sought the mythological fields of *Sardanapalus*, *Cain*, and *Heaven and Earth*. The last two are closely related. *Cain*, despite its absurd "air-service" provided by Lucifer, is in its main mood a far firmer and truer work than *Manfred*. The rhetorician of the Alps yields here to a real human sinner, Cain, who has a spirit worthy of a destiny not conceivable for Manfred:

> Think and endure, and form an inner world
> In your own bosom—where the outer fails;
> So shall you nearer be the spiritual
> Nature, and war triumphant with your own.

Still firmer in its stoicism, and far deeper in imaginative power, is *Heaven and Earth*. This poem is the apex of Byron's serious verse. It has the superb tone-architecture of *The Prisoner of Chillon* on a wider basis of thought. It has the moody, scenic power of *Childe Harold*, but with poetic concentration. It is *Manfred* purged and re-created after five years. Just here an objector might exclaim: "But *Heaven and Earth* is like a stiff wall-painting; it lacks the glowing detail of Byron's earlier works." My reply is: "Are you not confusing *personal* and *poetic* glow? The value of style, beyond detail,

is used again and more successfully in a later poem, *The Island*, as though Byron were correcting himself. There, the mood is purely Arcadian; and the story of Neuha and Torquil is satisfying as a poetic idyl.

depends on poetic mood. A wall-painting, if gloriously done, is better
than a cheap and highly coloured 'portrait of the artist.'" Here Byron
is freest from Byron: his mood is almost sheer poetry. The feverish
thought of his own little fight with society is sunk in the contempla-
tion of mankind's whole struggle with necessity—as imaged in the
conduct of a group of typical figures during the night before Noah's
Flood. So free and intense was the vision that it lifted Byron from
the bonds of conventional drama, and shaped out a fresh mode of
poetry for which his genius had been groping at the time of *Manfred*.
It is a sort of cantata: a series of lyric passages, sometimes dropping
into recitative, sometimes sweeping into choral strains. But the whole
moves steadily forward to the catastrophe, like a gathering storm;
for in the moments of pause the reader is made to feel a fresh
intensity gathering.

The piece opens upon the God-defying love of Aholibamah—a superb, statuesque Amazon—for her descending seraph:

> I can share all things, even immortal sorrow;
> For thou hast ventured to share life with me,
> And shall I shrink from thine eternity?

Then comes the mild tone of Japhet, servant of Jehovah. But his
love of his errant Anah warms his feeling for the doomed world:

> Ye wilds, that look eternal; and thou cave,
> Which seem'st unfathomable; and ye mountains,
> So varied and so terrible in beauty;
> Here, in your rugged majesty of rocks
> And toppling trees that twine their roots with stone
> In perpendicular places, where the foot
> Of man would tremble, could he reach them—yes,
> Ye look eternal! Yet, in a few days,
> Perhaps even hours, ye will be changed, rent, hurled
> Before the mass of waters; and yon cave,
> Which seems to lead into a lower world,
> Shall have its depths searched by the sweeping wave. . . .

His rising sympathy for mankind, straining the leash of his pious
obedience, leads into the song of the mocking nature-spirits:

> Not slow, not single, not by sword, nor sorrow,
> Nor years, nor heart-break, nor time's sapping motion,
> Shall they drop off. Behold their last tomorrow!
> Earth shall be ocean!
> And no breath,
> Save of the winds, be on the unbounded wave!

And the chorus of spirits mounts through this:

> The wave shall break upon your cliffs; and shells,
> The little shells of ocean's least things, be
> Deposed where now the eagle's offspring dwells—
> How shall he shriek o'er the remorseless sea!

to this:

> And to the universal human cry
> The universal silence shall succeed.

A meditative pause ensues, marking the end of the first half of the cantata. Then begins the final ensemble of voices. The current of Aholibamah's passion, meeting more and more the urgency of the servants of Jehovah, rises to a stoic acceptance of fate, and represents grandly the spirit of ultimate independence in humanity:

> Let us resign even what we have adored,
> And meet the wave, as we would meet the sword,
> If not unmoved, yet undismayed,
> And wailing less for us than those who shall
> Survive in mortal or immortal thrall. . . .

She stands aloof, now, while the milder personages plead and question together. And just here, with a sure sense for tonal architecture, the poet brings on the immediate signs of the Flood, answering to the premonitions at the close of the first half of the poem, like nearer thunders. Just before sunrise:

> Hark, Hark! the sea-birds cry!
> In clouds they overspread the lurid sky,
> And hover round the mountain, where before
> Never a white wing, wetted by the wave,
> Yet dared to soar,
> Even when the waters waxed too fierce to brave.

At sunrise:

> The clouds return into the hues of night,
> Save where their brazen-coloured edges streak
> The verge where brighter morns were wont to break.

Never was Byron's command of wide landscapes, rocky grandeurs, and wild waters used with such large *human* effect. The roar of the waters blends with the pathetic Chorus of Mortals flying in vain for refuge. And yet, a tone not of wild despair or revolt but of stoic acceptance dominates this closing scene, and is felt in the regular pulse of the verse. It is the dominant tone of the whole piece and, indeed, of Byron's total work in 1820-21.

Stoical acceptance of life, with concentration of poetic mood and form—this was the avenue through which the author of *Don Juan* had to pass if he were to reach the realm of poetic comedy that was his by right. His nearest approach to that realm is *Sardanapalus*. It is *Don Juan* reborn. The sprawling incertainty of mood is mainly gone. The poet has finally sloughed off, not only the pseudo-Titan, but his uneasiness concerning the status of his own special nature in relation to human nature in general:

> I feel a thousand mortal things about me,
> But nothing godlike—unless it may be
> The thing which you condemn: a disposition
> To love and to be merciful, to pardon
> The follies of my species, and (that's human)
> To be indulgent to my own.

These are words of the central character, Sardanapalus, but they convey the mood of the whole play. The inflated regrets and mockeries of *Don Juan*, jostling together uneasily like a circus handful of toy-balloons, have been cast off. In their place the true comic spirit hovers, rather steadily,—now blessing an honest sentiment, now throwing a sharp-smiling glance upon the religious and political pretensions of mankind. Above all, the comic illumination is turned upon Byronism itself. Consciously or not, Byron was learning to distil the comedy of his own career, which is paralleled in the plot of this play. Sardanapalus, by his truest nature a poetic and humorous onlooker, is set by fate in a high position, acts a showy part for a time, and then breaks with society. He is able to view his own case with a critical smile. For he senses the inevitability of individual temperament and, opposed to it, the inevitability of social convention. Byron had more innate respect than the other chief poets of the time for what might be called the convention-making power in human nature. He loved the spectacle of history, and the reach of poetic tradition. The very bitterness of his clash with British society was due in no small measure to the fact that he had himself a more or less conventional conscience, and, beneath it, a recognition that social customs, cheap or fine, are offspring of an essential human power. A deepened sense of the mystery of that power appears in the works of 1820-21,—especially in his attitude toward the gods of conventional humanity, Jehovah and Baal, who rise somberly in the background of *Heaven and Earth* and *Sardanapalus*, and let fall their shadows upon the moving scene. What are the divine stars beyond those human divinities? the poet seems to ask, and finds no answer:

> There's something sweet in my uncertainty
> I would not change for your Chaldean lore;
> Besides, I know of these all clay can know
> Of aught above it or below it—nothing.
> I see their brilliancy and feel their beauty:
> When they shine on my grave I shall know neither.

Meanwhile, Baal is an "oracular deity":

> . . . his marble face majestical
> Frowns as the shadows of the evening dim
> His brows to changed expression, till at times
> I think the statue looks in act to speak.

He is too human to be feared or hated. But his persecution of human hearts makes him often unlovely. His minions are pathetic; comical, also, in that they turn against their well-wishers. But these well-wishers, these liberators, with their blind impulsiveness or fetterless love of pleasure—with their incapacity for coming to human terms with society's ways—are they not comical, too? In *Sardanapalus*, Byron smiles at himself more wholesomely than ever before. To be sure, the smile is overcast in the later scenes; here the play contradicts its initial tone and works up to a romantic-tragical ending. The cast-off Queen must enter and be apologized to. The lovely and sensible concubine, Myrrha, must in the end mount the funeral pyre with the hero. Before this end, the genial hedonist of the Nineveh palace has to make a sober discovery:

> These slaves, whom I have nurtured, pampered, fed,
> And swoln with peace, and gorged with plenty, till
> They reign themselves—all monarchs in their mansions—
> Now swarm forth in rebellion, and demand
> His death who made their lives a jubilee;
> While the few upon whom I have no claim
> Are faithful! This is true, yet monstrous.

But even here his tone is half jocular. And if he had lived on and looked back, he would soon have seen the full comedy of that situation, with himself at the centre.

If Byron himself had lived on—if he had been more devoted to poetry than to the freedom of Greece—he would have done much, I think, toward the freedom of the comic spirit in himself and in his century. His voluminous power as a writer was far from spent.

A Shelley (or even a Keats) aged fifty and producing a kind of poetry comparable in value with the glamorous verse of his youth, is unthinkable: his race was run. But quite possible was a disillusioned Byron, living on into middle age, and composing his matured comic vision into narratives or dramatic sketches, in verse and lively prose. This author was not *so* beloved by the gods that he needed to die young! In *Don Juan* his powers were cascading, not toward brilliant extinction, but toward a serener level and a comelier flow. Picture him re-collecting himself, as a middle-aged Sardanapalus, with some Myrrha to friend—in a Casa Lanfranchi, or visiting England, if you will—recalling with tolerant amusement young Childe Harold's yearning:

> Oh that the desert were my dwelling-place,
> With one fair spirit for my minister,
> That I might all forget the human race,
> And, hating no one, love but only her!

Such a Byron would have caught both sides of the comic vision: the absurdity of those who fight, as well as of those who worship, the god Baal. The second side has been overdone by recent revivers of comedy. They see the absurdity of Baal-worship; but they themselves are worshippers of cheap and sometimes nasty theories. They flout Baal without really comprehending him, because they have missed the experience of grappling with him Byronically, and of thus modifying profoundly their own self-conceit. One may trace a certain progressive incertainty and conceited narrowness of comic vision from George Meredith, through Samuel Butler, to Bernard Shaw, and on to . . . others. Byron, from premature Elysium, points toward the balance and poetic comeliness of the true comic spirit that we are groping for now.

III

THE REAL TRAGEDY OF KEATS

But the crown
Of all my life was utmost quietude.
(*Endymion*, III, 352.)

THE REAL CONDITIONS

THE verse quoted above has kept recurring to my mind, off and on, during a number of years, when I have reflected upon Keats. His central instinct was for high poetic repose, —for the quietude that comes, not from avoiding life, but from surmounting it. He yearned incessantly toward the kind of serenity that appears in the world's greatest poetry. And only in studying his poems and letters from this standpoint, does one come to realize how lofty was his essential aim—how far beyond his reach was the goal that he was more and more setting for himself in poetry. Herein lies his real tragedy. His early death is bound to lose much of its tragic colour as the centuries revolve upon that day, February 23, 1821. That day belongs to the era of poetry that is now fading and holds for us a kind of personal bitterness, the bitterness of a great loss to our poetry that has not at all been compensated. But that day must become "distant in humanity"—if humanity goes on. The very condition of a new great era of poetry and culture is that the central instinct of Keats shall be, at the least, *better* fulfilled than it could be in the era to which he belonged. In that case the tragedy of his untimely death, of his loss to humanity, will necessarily retire, even while the tragedy of his spirit, of the discrepancy between his capability and his great instinctive aim, will stand out more clearly. This inward tragedy has been obscured for us by the unique and exaggerative atmosphere with which Keats has been invested by the rising admiration of the past hundred years.

The tendency has been to set him more and more apart from his contemporaries. The cumulative nature of this tendency will appear vividly to anyone who will take the time to glance through the criticism of Keats from its beginning until now, pausing reflectively upon the cluster of articles that appeared at the commemoration of the centenary of his death. During the seven years that have elapsed since that devoted occasion, a few critics have capped the climax: they have wanted to set the work of Keats far above, and apart from, the whole nineteenth-century mode of literature. Their desire is natural and significant: their wish is the father of their critical thought, and the parent in this case is immensely superior to the child. Their wistfulness is representative. For us of the early twentieth century, the poetry of Keats is "hung aloft the night," and shines on the highway ahead. It has the *aura* of a universal mode of art that the modern age has longed for, and still longs for, in the midst of its complex preoccupation with singular interests. "I think poetry should surprise by a fine excess and not by singularity," wrote Keats on February 27, 1818; "it should strike the reader as a wording of his own highest thoughts, and appear almost a remembrance."[1] Two months later he turned that maxim into a prayer, in the *Ode to Maia*. He implored this goddess of "old vigour," of fresh life and beauty, to enable him to write verse that would be "rich in the simple worship of a day." He knew that the very genius of poetry is devoted to our "highest thoughts" and that these are simple, universal, and rich in daily worship. He had this conviction in his heart during the ensuing eighteen months while he conceived and accomplished his best work. Therefore his poetry gives us constantly the sense of a greater poetry behind. It is like a scene, that, however lovely in itself, charms us ultimately with its hint of a grander vista beyond its furthest line of trees—in some "untrodden region" of the poet's mind,

> Where branched thoughts, new grown with pleasant pain,
> Instead of pines shall murmur in the wind:
> Far, far around shall those dark-cluster'd trees
> Fledge the wild-ridged mountains, steep by steep. . . .

Other poets of the past century have maturer poems than he; but none have his vista beyond, his magnanimity of poetic intention.

This, however, is not to be identified with poetic *capability*. In the letter quoted above, Keats concludes his maxims with the following: "But it is easier to think what poetry should be than to write it . . . and if poetry come not as naturally as the leaves to a tree, it had better not come at all." Well, the poetry that came thus naturally to Keats, from first to last, was *not* the poetry of our "highest thoughts." He yearned for these. His moral and critical

[1] *Letters of Keats to his Friends* (The Macmillan Company, 1921), page 77.

intellect developed toward them. But it developed away from his poetry, away from his "shaping spirit of Imagination." Indeed Coleridge's *Ode to Dejection*, from which I have just quoted, may fairly be read as a prelude to the tragedy of Keats, unless we insist on disguising the younger poet's situation. He himself saw this situation though of course not fully. If we see it less clearly than he did, we blunt the tragedy of a great young spirit; we misinterpret the course of his development, which now lies plainly enough before us in the succession of his writings; [2] and we blur his relation to his own time and to ours. For a century and more, poetry has been devoted to the "naturalistic interpretation" of life, as Arnold termed it. But during the past fifty years that view of life, while extending itself in quantity, has been disintegrating in quality with ever increasing acceleration. Today it is a shallow maelstrom in which the dregs of a great creative era, mixed with the various muds of new pseudo-science or semi-science, go round and round. In the work of Keats, it was a fresh clear lake, reflecting the landscape, all about, with unexampled loveliness of intimacy. But we spoil it effectually if, insisting that this lake is a sea, we proceed to hide its further shore under a cloudy confusion of ideas. To know Keats, we must know his boundaries. [3]

[2] Amy Lowell's devoted work in dating and collating Keats's poems and letters can outweigh her blind mistreatment of his *Hyperion*, in her remarkable *Life of Keats*.

[3] At the close of his essay on Keats (1880), Arnold says with quaint ambiguity: "For that faculty of moral interpretation which is in Shakespeare, and is informed by him with the same power of beauty as his naturalistic interpretation, Keats was not ripe." A reader with "bounded apprehension and dim faculties," as Arnold might say, would expect that the word "faculty" would be used as the subject of the clause, and that the word "yet" would appear before "ripe." The critic ought to have stated plainly that he did not wish to give an opinion as to whether "that faculty of moral interpretation" was really in Keats, and whether it could have been "informed by him with the same power of beauty as his naturalistic interpretation"; in other words, whether Keats had moral power not only as a man but as a poet. Previously, when speaking of Keats's "intellectual and spiritual passion" for Beauty, Arnold entirely clouds the question of his poetic capability. He was "laden," says the critic, "with a mighty formative thought requiring health and many days and favouring circumstances for its adequate manifestation." Alas, it was scarcely a "thought," and it was not at all "formative," and the "favouring circumstance" it required was a different century. That is just why Keats felt so tragically "laden" with

The other chief poets of the past century are now seen more or less clearly in their proper boundaries. Those of Keats have been kept uniquely vague. His poetic potentiality and his ruining fate have been so continually balanced against each other, with insensible additions now on one side of the scale and now on the other, that both have come to appear much more conclusive than they really were. It has been assumed that his physical disintegration, beginning some eighteen months before his death, stopped his progress just as he was approaching a higher level of poetic achievement. But a dispassionate restudy of his later works and letters convinces one that he was approaching, rather, a radical change in poetic method; a change that was fraught, in his own clear eyes, with dubious results. His verse had been less and less adequately answering his growing inner life, he was feeling insistently for a different mode of self-expression, and the path of poetry ahead of him seemed blind. This crisis, far more deeply interfused than physical weakness, morbid love, and disappointed ambition, was the source of that accumulating misery of spirit which pierces us so keenly, after a century, as we review the succession of his last months. Our sympathy must deepen when we realize that his own fears for his art were justified; that if he lived he could not, in all human probability, have reorganized his poetry without shattering, beyond compensation, its quick-built magic charm. One hears his spirit's fear of this in many a premonitory passage:

> There was a noise of wings, till in short space
> The glowing banquet-room shone with wide-arched grace.
> A haunting music, sole perhaps and lone
> Supportress of the faery-roof, made moan
> Throughout, as fearful the whole charm might fade.[4]

His quick maturity remains wonderful enough when we cease to regard it as more mysterious than it actually was. Inexplicable is

it. In the course of his misfortunate essay on Wordsworth, Arnold says that Keats "utters a moral idea" in the following verse of the *Grecian Urn*: "Forever wilt thou love and she be fair"! In the context, the meaning of this statement becomes clear; but so, I think, does its absurdity. If Arnold had been less ambiguous, perhaps Professor C. D. Thorpe in his book on the *Mind of John Keats* (Oxford University Press, 1926) would have been more circumspect. This book is well thought out, interesting, and suggestive. But the author, in reading a philosopher into Keats, reads out the poet; or, at any rate, misses the real shape of his imagination.

[4] *Lamia*, II, 120ff.

the fact that John Keats, particularly, should have been endowed with the richest poetic nature of the past century. But it should be clear by now that the historical conditions in which he found himself, conditions very abnormal, so acted upon his nature as to bring about an abnormally swift development. In his career we must recognize something of the forced growth of the hot-house plant. His nature, early seeking, like all full poetic natures, for immediate beauty, could flower out swiftly and lusciously in the superheated atmosphere of imagination which encompassed it. Keats took up into himself the whole imaginative intensity accumulated in the so-called rise of the Romantic Movement, of which his work was the acme. If nothing is more wonderful than his ready transmutation of all external influences, nothing is more clarifying than a careful study of the shaping effects exerted upon him by his Romantic predecessors, from Chatterton and the others down to Hunt and Wordsworth. The full import of these effects has been blurred by the emphasis which criticism has thrown upon Keats's affinity with the Elizabethans. From them, to be sure, he quarried many elements of style; but he scarcely reached the essential mode of their imagination. One must wonder how he could be so much penetrated with the beauties of Spenser and Milton, and so slightly swayed by their total envisagement of life, unless one realizes that his imagination was moulded from the very first into the shape of his own time.

Therein is the solution for a certain paradox which has beset the interpreters of Keats: he was sounder than his chief contemporaries as a man among men, and yet more liable than they to mawkishness of poetic mood. Biography, so far, has not succeeded in rendering him entirely lifelike and believable because it has failed to recognize the full depth of the division between the man and the poet. Arnold, by slurring this division even while heavily stressing the opposed sides of Keats's nature, his "lusciousness" and his "flint and iron," intensified the paradox. The plain truth is that the "lusciousness" was very much in the poet, very little in the man; the "flint and iron" were very much in the man, very little in the poet. The poet was shaped by an era that favoured, extraordinarily, the development of the sensuous and romantic imagination, while it discouraged, extraordinarily, the development of the ethical imagination. Keats the man, however, was shaped by the great ethic tradition of his nation; like Wordsworth, he fed upon the character of Milton. His own

character though immature was firm and distinguished. It kept him
clear, or brought him clear, of the ethic and mental bypaths that
entranced his contemporaries—

> Of all the unhealthy and o'erdarkened ways
> Made for our searching. . . .

Coleridgean theorizing and Byronic conduct seemed in his clear eyes
to lead off from the highway of poetry. Accordingly that intense
pressure of imagination which pushed the others into strained acts
or ideas, could move Keats only in the direction of a strained poetic
style. His lusciousness was stylistic. He strove to load, as he advised
Shelley to do, "every rift with ore." The readiest ores were vivid
sensations, and he heaped them with "glowing hand," as Porphyro
his feast of fruits. He packed his verse with quick metal of the
senses, and he did so extremely, because his imagination was not at
all engaged in the more difficult task of quarrying, for poetry, the
"flint and iron" of his own character. His cloying lusciousnesses had
no deep root in his humanity; they were things gathered in eager
haste for the sake of poetry.

This impression attaches most strongly to the mawkish and unreal
love-passages which recur in his verse and which pass over, so to
speak, into his love-letters. Keats did not yet know the very mettle
of love; but he knew that it was golden ore for poetry, and he tried
to catch its hues. The most significant feature of his own love-
story is precisely this, that not till the fall of 1819, when his best
work was over, and his love-letters were nearly over, did love move
toward the centre of his life. Before then, he strove quite successfully (if unconsciously) to keep it in the sentimental outskirts. He
adopted this course ostensibly on practical grounds; but more deeply
because his love threatened to throw his imagination upon a reality
foreign to the kind of verse he was writing. In his verse, as he says,
there is "a tendency to class women with roses and sweetmeats." [5]

[5] Letter of August 1820. The words quoted above are preceded by the
remark: "I am certain that I have said nothing in a spirit to displease any
woman I would care to please." Without doubt he was here thinking of
Miss Brawne, who was at this time nursing him after a desperate turn in his
illness. That she did not accompany him a month later to Italy "was a good
deal through his kindness to me" (she recorded after his death), "for he
foresaw what would happen." This quotation is from Amy Lowell's *Life of
Keats*, which has done so much to correct the prevailing Romantic distortion
of his fiancée's character and of the nature of his love for her.

In his life, there was a tendency to associate them with the great realities of character and passion. His deeper sense, as well as his sentiment, drew him to Frances Brawne. He had previously had some disillusioning and enlightening experiences of young women. Nor did he finally commit himself to this one, apparently, until after he had observed her with a depth and seriousness of penetration which he did not care to display in his letters to his friends and relatives. We should credit to his character the reserve that he showed in this matter, as in other matters that touched him deeply. He chose Miss Brawne deliberately, and thereafter he never swerved from her. That should be testimony to the fact that she was quite worthy of him, in spite of the disparaging comments made upon her by his Romantic and hero-worshipping friends. Those comments, by reflection, have been very damaging to the character of Keats himself, depreciating the quality of his heart and judgement. The truth is that his love was at core normal, firm, and growing. But he had to segregate and protect his Romantic poetry from it.

He tried to submerge below the focus of his imagination all realities which he could not yet transmute into beauty. The *Letters to his Friends*, so frequent in shrewd observations of actual life and sharp passages of realistic thinking, might often seem to have been written by another than the creator of *Isabella* and *Lamia*. We see him continually noting, but segregating so to speak from his verse, a range of realities which poetry since his time has wished to grapple with immediately: the actual cravings of sex, the drab conventionalities of social life, the bloodshed and bitterness of nature, the altered features of religion and philosophy. The quick tide of romantic imagination on which he and his contemporaries were lifted could carry him over obtrusive realities to shores where his lust of beauty could suddenly strike root and come to flower. Hence the most swift and beautiful fruition which the history of poetry has so far seen. But it was necessarily brief.

A rift in the poet's aims appeared even in his early days, and toward the close it widened to a chasm. The best testimony to the essential greatness of Keats's nature is the fact that he could not long be satisfied with Keatsian beauty. He more and more craved for his poetry fullness of life. At the same time he more and more craved for his spirit rich sources of quietude. For he felt that to draw into his verse more of life, external and mental, would be to shatter his mastery of beauty, unless he could learn to shape his fresh materials in that spirit of high repose which he recognized in the greatest poets. Two ways of advance seemed possible. One was the way of "philosophy"; the other, the way of dramatic objectivity. There is no doubt that Keats had more of the real dramatic *attitude* than his chief contemporaries. His sympathy flowed more genially than theirs into standpoints diverse from the poet's own: the freedom from "self-passion or identity" which he noted in himself is often quite Shakespearean. His *Endymion*, even, is more dramatic, and his *Tragedy of Otho the Great* more promising, than critics steeped in lyric atmosphere have perceived. But Keats was too much a man of his age to have found final success in poetic drama. The scale of human values had become too unsettled to permit of that large certainty of judgement,—at its worst, that placid mental conventionalism,—which enabled Shakespeare to watch the struggling spectacle of life with artistic serenity. Keats's dramatic tendency did not permeate his constructive imagination. It seems clear from his most matured pieces, such as *Hyperion* and the *Ode on a Grecian Urn*, that he was moving toward a kind of lyric and narrative poetry more objective in mood than that of his contemporaries, and often quite dramatic in touch, but embodying a more or less deliberated interpretation of life.[6]

"Philosophy," therefore, in the most human sense of that now so frayed term, became increasingly Keats's hope,—not primarily from a desire for truth, but from a growing need of spiritual quiet. His continual feverishness, which appealed to the nerves of a feverish century, should no longer blur our recognition of his notable affinity for quietude. His most memorable attitudes, as a personality, were reposeful. We see him in the presence of the things of nature that he most loved checking himself into intense silence; or sitting motionless with book in hand, "like a picture of somebody reading"; or moving in society with an attitude, predominantly, of quiet geniality. Probably his fits of animation were often his impressible nature's surface-reactions to the voluble artistical company into which he had been drawn. To the loud Haydon, that re-edited Bottam, he seemed socially inept; and one remembers that in 1818 he began to seclude

[6] If read in its *full context*, his letter of November 17, 1819, concerning his outlook in dramatic and narrative poetry, is in agreement with the view expressed above.

himself from the noisy London crew. In his poetry, full images of stillness haunt us, from the closing lines of the sonnet on "Chapman's Homer," and the extraordinary "Cave of Quietude" in *Endymion*, down to the opening passage of *Hyperion*, and the *Ode on a Grecian Urn*. From this side of his nature emanated his remarkable moon-worship. His most persistent devotion was to the "gentlier-mightiest" Diana, with her intensely quiet radiance. It is noteworthy that his young Apollo in *Hyperion* seems more captivated by "the most patient brilliance of the moon" than by the glory of the sun which he is destined to rule. Not the sun-god but his serener sister, the moon-goddess, was the presiding spirit of Keats's poetry; and the philosophic hue which that spirit assumed toward the close of *Endymion* was prophetic of his later mental ambition.

Nothing is more significant in his *Letters* than the definitive alteration, within three years, of his attitude to philosophy. Critics have liked to quote his immaturer doctrines as though characteristic of his final thought. Sir Sidney Colvin in closing his extensive biography of Keats dwells upon his "inspiring conviction of the sovereign, the transcendental, truth of whatsoever ideas the imagination seizes as beauty." But this "inspiring conviction" was uttered by the poet a month after his twenty-second birthday, and in words quite devoid of his biographer's grandiosely definitive metaphysicality: "What the Imagination seizes as Beauty must be truth, whether it existed before or not." It was uttered in the same context with his boyish cry, "O for a life of Sensations rather than of Thoughts!" [7] Some two years later he thinks that poetry may be "not so fine a thing as philosophy—for the same reason that an eagle is not so fine a thing as a truth." [8] For in the meantime he has come to the following opinion of himself, from which misleading excerpts have so often been taken that it should be quoted in full: "I know nothing, I have read nothing, and I mean to follow Solomon's directions, 'Get learning, get understanding.' I find earlier days are gone by; I find that I can have no enjoyment in the world but continual drinking of knowledge. I find there is no worthy pursuit but the idea of doing some good for the world. Some do it with their society, some with their wit, some with their benevolence, some with a sort of power of conferring pleasure and good humour on all they meet

[7] *Letters*, pages 41-2, November 28, 1817.
[8] *ibid.*, page 237, March 19, 1819.

—and in a thousand ways, all dutiful to the command of great Nature. There is but one way for me. The road lies through application, study, and thought. I will pursue it; and for that end, purpose retiring for some years. I have been hovering for some time between an exquisite sense of the luxurious, and a love for philosophy; were I calculated for the former, I should be glad. But as I am not, I shall turn all my soul to the latter." [9]

The fact is that the younger Keats, intent on immediate beauty, had taken over into the "chameleon" surface of his nature the one-sided doctrine of the imagination which was current among his contemporaries.[10] But his deeper nature, demanding a poetic completeness which they lacked, impelled him toward a mental adjustment. That his "love for philosophy," as he termed it, tended at times to be as inconsiderate as the doctrine from which he was unconsciously reacting, appears in the passage quoted above and in later letters, as when we find him preparing to ask Hazlitt for "the best metaphysical road I can take." But his central desire was for more life, and for the larger serenity of spirit which would enable him fully to compose that more of life into beauty. The early round of his beauty was being threatened by inruptions of life, as in the following:

> The rocks were silent, the wide sea did weave
> An untumultuous fringe of silver foam
> Along the flat brown sand; I was at home
> And should have been most happy,—but I saw
> Too far into the sea, where every maw
> The greater on the less feeds evermore,—

[9] *Letters*, page 100, April 24, 1818.

[10] Today, this doctrine—namely that the imagination determines its own validity quite independently of ethical thought—has reached its final stage (one may hope) of absurdity. It has become a shrill and iterative literary convention,—"a raving distracted cuckoo," as Milton termed Salmasius. Arnold, with his Romantic fear of analysis, kept the question in the vague, as in that brief paragraph of his essay on Keats beginning: "For to see things in their beauty is to see things in their truth." He thus left the way open for his successors to write or condone such nonsense as that quoted above from Sir Sidney Colvin upon the "sovereign truth of *whatsoever* ideas the imagination seizes as beauty." Well, today the imagination has seized upon the "sovereign truth" of the idea, for instance, of miscellaneous copulation. This idea is seized "as beauty," with the result that certain writers who pride themselves on calling a spade a spade refuse (unlike the Elizabethans) to call a whore a whore. They call her an idealist.

> But I saw too distinct into the core
> Of an eternal fierce destruction,
> And so from happiness I far was gone.

His glance passes lucidly from the outer to the inner source of his unhappiness:

> Things cannot to the will
> Be settled, but they tease us out of thought;
> Or is it that imagination brought
> Beyond its proper bound, yet still confined,
> Lost in a sort of Purgatory blind,
> Cannot refer to any standard law
> Of either earth or heaven? It is a flaw
> In happiness, to see beyond our bourn,—
> It forces us in summer skies to mourn,
> It spoils the singing of the nightingale.[11]

Reaching beyond the present "bourn" of his verse, he wanted for his imagination a guidance which itself could not supply. A few weeks later he remarks that "extensive knowledge" with "widening speculation" can take away "the heat and fever." High poetic repose was his goal. His prayer to Apollo, uttered on the threshold of the brief period of his best work, sounds a motif that was iterated with deepening poignancy, on to the end:

> God of Song,
> Thou bearest me along
> Through sights I scarce can bear:
> O let me, let me share
> With the hot lyre and thee,
> The staid Philosophy.
> Temper my lonely hours,
> And let me see thy bowers
> More unalarmed.[12]

THE TRAGEDY

His mental reachings for this far goal began to weaken his hold on the kind of poetic beauty which he had so swiftly mastered. His thought was diverging from his imagination. This condition became acute in his last working months, the closing months of 1819. The facts do not warrant the assumption that his physical weakness had thus early become so great as to render him the helpless prey of his

[11] March 25, 1818.
[12] January 31, 1818.

passion for Miss Brawne; and that, under more fortunate circumstances, his poetic power would not have declined. The truth of the matter seems to be just the other way around. If his poetic power had remained at full tide, it would have continued to keep him above his troubles. He would still have tried to insulate his morbid tendency from his active being, as he had done very signally during the preceding months, when he was writing his last great poems. He would have continued to guard his frail health for the sake of poetry, instead of so neglecting it as to open the way for the decisive illness of February 3, 1820. His closest observer, Charles Brown, put the matter in its true sequence when he recorded: "He was too thoughtful, or too unquiet; and he began to be reckless of health." But the deep source of his disquietude, the division in his nature, was of the kind that cannot be fathomed by friends, nor be fully clear to the sufferer himself. It is natural that Keats, as well as his friends, should have been apt to seize upon tangible and superficial factors in attempting to account for his inner disintegration. Therefore the biographic material for this dark period, even if it were not so scanty, could not possibly be so illuminating as the two long fragments, the revised *Hyperion* and *The Cap and Bells*, in which the poet's state is given less consciously and more faithfully. These two pieces, so opposite in nature and yet composed concurrently day by day, shadow out the sharp duality of his spiritual condition.

The *Fall of Hyperion: A Dream* shows Keats reaching anxiously for philosophic truth, and stultifying his poetic perception. *The Cap and Bells* shows him pulled in the other direction by his instinct for immediate poetic effect; and indeed the continued strength of this instinct appears in several ways, during the last eighteen months of his life. It made him project further romantic tales which he hoped would surpass his earlier ones. It made him look back longingly to the days

> When, howe'er poor or particolour'd things,
> My muse had wings,
> And ever ready was to take her course
> Whither I bent her force,
> Unintellectual, yet divine to me—
> Divine, I say!—What sea-bird o'er the sea
> Is a philosopher the while he goes
> Winging along where the great water throes? [13]

[13] From *Lines to Fanny*, October 10, 1819.

But that he could never have recaptured his fine romantic gusto is suggested by his very deliberation of the matter: "As the marvellous is the most enticing, and the surest guarantee of harmonious numbers, I have been endeavouring to persuade myself to untether Fancy, and to let her manage for herself. I and myself cannot agree about this at all. Wonders are no wonders to me." [14] His mental aloofness from romantic story had become definitive. Therefore the romantico-satiric method of *The Cap and Bells*, so far from being merely an amazing lapse occasioned by external factors and a passing mood, is a natural development of the state of mind which was forming behind the scenes of *Lamia*. Though Keats had lived on, *Lamia* must have remained, I think, his last great romance. Its marked deliberation, in contrast to the mood of the earlier *Isabella* and *Eve of St. Agnes*, passes sometimes into factitiousness. And its deepest emotional tone, as suggested by the passage I quoted from it earlier, is elegiac of Keatsian beauty, and premonitory of the coming change. It is the rising tragedy in the poet's own spirit that comes out into the question preluding the dissolution of the lovely serpent-woman under the sage's scrutiny:

> Do not all charms fly
> At the mere touch of cold philosophy?

But even while shrinking from thought's chill cast, he was longing for its elevation. And he was approaching that opinion of his loveliest poems which appears in the well-known sentence: "I have done nothing—except for the amusement of a few people who refine upon their feelings till anything in the understandable way will go down with them, people predisposed for sentiment." [15] This pessimism is fully intelligible only as an exhalation from the real incompetency which had now come over his creative power on account of the division in his spirit; as is suggested, indeed, by another sentence in context with the one just quoted: "Though at this present I have great dispositions to write, I feel every day more and more content to read." To go into retirement for the sake of reading and thought, though at the expense of composition, was his iterated purpose: he knew that his muse was still far from ripe for high philosophy. But at the same time he had "great dispositions to write," as he puts

[14] November 17, 1819.
[15] October 3, 1819.

it, with a depth of pathos beneath the light phrase. A natural outcome of this double mood was the reconstruction of *Hyperion*. It was
a violent and hapless attempt, but for Keats a vitally necessary attempt, to bridge the widening rift between his thought and his verse.
In this view the symbolism of the poem becomes clearer. In the
visionary temple, the marble pavement with its creeping cold is
plainly an adumbration of the numbness,—the loss of "poetic ardour
and fire" mentioned in a letter of this period,[16]—which had come
upon Keats's creative genius in its present ambiguous groping. He
had been sated with the sensuous mode of verse symbolized by the
"feast of summer fruits" at the opening of the poem. He was now
facing the difficult ascent to a poetry of higher outlook,—the arduous
steps to Moneta's shrine in the temple,—as the great way of escape
from the state of cold unproductiveness in which he found himself:

> I strove hard to escape
> The numbness, strove to gain the lowest step.
> Slow, heavy, deadly was my pace: the cold
> Grew stifling, suffocating at the heart;
> And when I clasped my hands I felt them not.
> One minute before death my iced foot touched
> The lowest stair. . . .

Surely these words came, though unconsciously, from the innermost
heart of his bitter experience.

The kind of philosophy that his deepest nature called for was far
beyond his reach. He could not be satisfied with the specialistic
theories which contemporary egotism was hatching on, or out of,
the débris of the past. He refuses to be one who will "brood and
peacock" over his own speculations "till he makes a false coinage
and deceives himself"; he shrinks from "poetry that has a palpable
design upon us," and desires the kind that is "great and unobtru-
sive."[17] His critiques of Wordsworth, Coleridge, Shelley and the
rest are less significant for their mental and moral lucidities, which
delighted Arnold, than for their underlying vague instinct for the
full quality of poetic thought. He was vaguely groping away from
his contemporaries, toward the rich poetic thought of the Renaissance. He wanted to look steadily into all the blackness of human
nature, and to lift his eyes to the something of light and peace he

[16] September 21, 1819.
[17] February 3, 1818.

felt above that. He craved, without knowing it, a "philosophy" of
Miltonic quality. In the spring of 1818, when approaching his great
creative period, he tells us that he had lately begun to "feast upon
Milton" (April 27) : he was yearning afar off toward "the prize,
high reason, and the love of good and ill" (March 25). But he had
lately been studying Wordsworth's *Excursion* admiringly, and in his
well-known letter on the "Chamber of Maiden-Thought'" (May 3),
it is clear that the humanitarianism of Wordsworth was interposing
itself effectually between Keats and the essential vision of Milton.
Keats had been debating "whether Milton's apparently less anxiety
for Humanity proceeds from his seeing further or not than Wordsworth." He now decides that there had been "a grand march of
intellect" since Milton's time, that Milton had been content in his
great poems with the "dogmas and superstitions of Protestantism,"
and finally that "he did not think into the human heart as Wordsworth has done."

This was a fatal opinion for Keats to adopt. He never grew free
of it, in spite of his increasing objections to Wordsworth's mode and
temper. It was Wordsworth who set open the door of his Chamber
of Maiden-Thought, and whose genius seemed to him "explorative
of those dark passages" ahead of him. He never laid hold of the key
held out to him by Milton, the key to the great mansion of the
Elizabethan imagination. He passed it by in the dark. He followed
the nineteenth-century view of Milton, admiring his style and character while convinced that his "philosophy" was obvious and outworn.
In his maturing years, he was moving not toward that "philosophy"
but away from it. This appears in that very letter on "The Vale of
Soul-Making" [18] which some admirers have recently held up as a
main evidence of Keats's poetic progress and potentiality. Here he
sees the world as "a place where the heart must feel and suffer in a
thousand diverse ways" in order that "Intelligence" may evolve
therefrom the diverse personalities of men. But he misses the central
mystery of Personality, deeper than its diversities—the moral and
creative mystery. His "system of spirit-creation," as he calls it, omits
the creative battle of Satan and the Son of God in the human spirit.
Here Keats shows his utter need of Milton and, at the same time, his
utter divergence from him. He has lost the *epic* clue that he had
touched a year earlier : "High reason and the love of good and ill."

[18] April 28, 1819.

Hyperion, begun and cast aside in the intervening twelvemonth, was moving toward the humanitarian evolutionism of the letter on "The Vale of Soul-Making." The serene loveliness of young Apollo in this great fragment was designed to supersede by a sort of natural evolution the troublous grandeur of the Titans of which it was born. Keats found no essential conflict, no ethical difference so to speak, between those two levels of beauty. Both were

> Manifestations of that beauteous life
> Diffused unseen throughout eternal space.

Alas, "that beauteous life," considered in its full context, wears a Wordsworthian air. 'Tis Wordsworth Keatsianized, but Wordsworth still! It is our too familiar friend, the life "that rolls through all things"—and that rolls flat all epic actions! Therefore though the poem has its own lovely value—a serene but warm beauty rising through the dark changefulness of life and opposing "to each malignant hour ethereal presence"—it certainly could never have been developed into an epic story. And in trying to recast it a year later into the more congruent form of a vision, Keats moved still further away from the ethic profundity and surging strength of Milton, moved away from the Elizabethan mode of imagination. At the same time he came into a fateful confusion of ideas, which appears particularly in lines 145-215 of *The Vision of Hyperion*.

This passage, which is too long to quote but which the reader should have before him, has two conflicting motives. On the one hand, in reaction from his own romantic verse (his "feast of summer fruits"), Keats finds himself gripped by the notion of humanitarian sympathy.[19] This notion had been pursuing him relentlessly, as one finds in his *Letters*, as a result of the sway of Wordsworth; and now he half decides that none can be great poets

> But those to whom the miseries of the world
> Are misery, and will not let them rest.

On the other hand, as he must have felt in the depths of his being, the last six words just quoted, though true of a social reformer, are palpably untrue of a great poet: they are opposed to that very idea of high poetic serenity which was the guiding-light of Keats himself. He wanted to be "still steadfast, still unchangeable." He knew that the right way for him to rise above romantic verse was to

[19] This was noticed by Paul Elmer More years ago in his essay on Keats.

"refine one's sensual vision into a sort of north star which can never
cease to be open-lidded and steadfast over the wonders of the great
Power."[20] Hence, in the passage under discussion, he assumes the
humanitarian garb with a marked uneasiness. He sees that it may be
worn by mere "dreamers" and by "large self-worshippers," who
cannot pour upon the world the true balm it craves; and that the
true poet is "a sage, a humanist, physician to all men."

Such, I think, is the right interpretation of this significant passage.
It shows Keats swaying between Wordsworth and Milton, unable to
follow either. It shows him caught between current humanitarianism,
which his critical instinct was very suspicious of, and true Humanism, which he did not imaginatively comprehend. No wonder that
The Fall of Hyperion, like its predecessor, could not be carried on
and remains a fragment,—a broken mirror wherein, with fear and
pity, we may catch glimpses of a young-old face

> Not pined by human sorrows, but bright-blanch'd,
> By an immortal sickness which kills not. . . .

No wonder the poet, in the deathlike temple of his vision, can find
no outlet, though he pries every way, lifting his eyes from the confused heap of holy symbols that lies immediately before him:

> Turning from these with awe, once more I rais'd
> My eyes to fathom the space every way:
> The embossed roof, the silent massy range
> Of columns north and south, ending in mist
> Of nothing; then to eastward, where black gates
> Were shut against the sunrise evermore.

If those gates could have opened at all, what forward way could
he have found? The road ahead of him was very long; and the
obstacles in it were more formidable than his own view of them, remarkably realistic as it often was, could comprehend: the inadequacy
of his associates, his ignorance of foreign thought, the superficiality
of his understanding of the great English classics. No doubt if he
had lived he would have faced these obstacles more consistently. He
would have extended the winding efforts, so notable in his later
letters, to see life steadily and whole. His poetry would have entered
upon a long period of partial stagnation and painful experiment, at
times trying doubtfully to recover its first fine rapture, but mainly

[20] From a newly discovered letter of 1818 given in Amy Lowell's *Life of
Keats*, Vol. II, page 21.

continuing the endeavour of *The Fall of Hyperion* for a mode more thoughtful. But in trying to write the poetry of our "highest thoughts" (in his own phrase) could he have carried over into it, unlike his predecessors Coleridge and Wordsworth, the power of his imagination?[21] Proceeding from all the known conditions, I cannot conceive a matured Keats writing a kind of poetry not only more intellectual, but more highly and distinctively beautiful, than the poetry of him who remains for us ever young. His genius was conditioned by an age in which poetic imagination rose early and sank soon. And that very fullness of poetic instinct which differentiates him from his contemporaries served to render his predicament more acute and decisive than theirs. It swiftly developed aims far larger than his powers and opportunities could fulfil. His poetic decline in the fall of 1819 was not accidental but real. A deep tragedy of his spirit precedes the pathos of his early death.

In this view of Keats we can understand, more fully than otherwise, the growing preoccupation of his spirit, in the period of his best achievement, with the thought of death. In one of his few optimistic moments, at the close of that period, we find him looking forward to "a more thoughtful and quiet power . . . I want to compose without this fever."[22] But deeper and more insistent in his spirit, throughout his career, was the intimation that the fullness of quiet he craved was not to be had from life. His mind turned continually to the subject of death. His mind, rather than his heart; for though doubtless there appears in Keats's case something of the familiar Romantic swinging from a thirst for too much life to a thirst for no-life, and back again, his main approach to the subject of death was through a region above precipitate desires. This appears in his remarkable account of the composition of the pathetic sonnet, "Why did I laugh tonight?", which closes on the note of death. "Though the first steps to it were through my human passions," he says, "they went away and I wrote with my mind." He had been

---

[21] Arnold, in stressing Keats's ambition for "the best sort of poetry," says finely but ambiguously: "Even in his pursuit of 'the pleasures of song,' however, there is that stamp of high work which is akin to character, which is character passing into intellectual production." No one can doubt that Keats, if he had lived, would have risen to a far higher level of "intellectual production." But this is something very different from *the best sort of poetry.*

[22] September 21, 1819.

brooding on the rarity of unselfishness among men, on the brutality
of Nature, on "the violence of my temperament continually smothered down." Longing for light upon all this darkness, he had realized
with "agony," he says, how far he was from the goal of "divine
philosophy," and had come to the conviction that though

> My fancy to its utmost blisses spreads:
> Yet could I on this very midnight cease,
> And the world's gaudy ensigns see in shreds;
> Verse, fame, and beauty are intense indeed
> But Death intenser—Death is Life's high meed.[23]

Not satisfied with the "utmost blisses" of fancy, distraught by those
dark actualities which his veracity made him face, and yet needing
high repose of spirit for the full fruition of his poetic genius, he
sought the peace of wisdom; but this being too far from him, his
spirit leaned toward the stillness of death. Such is the spiritual process
that underlies Keats's poetry of death, and draws into a symphony
its successive tones,—from early passages such as:

> But this is human life: the war, the deeds,
> The disappointment, the anxiety,
> Imagination's struggles, far and nigh,
> All human; bearing in themselves this good,
> That they are still the air, the subtle food,
> To make us feel existence, and to show
> How quiet death is . . .[24]

down to the massive atmosphere of deathly stillness which is the most
distinctive feature, I think, of *The Fall of Hyperion*:

> Without stay or prop
> But my own weak mortality, I bore
> The load of this eternal quietude
> . . . Oftentimes I pray'd
> Intense, that death would take me from the vale
> And all its burthens. . . .

Though Keats could not find an articulate communion with high
truth, he could feel the stillness of her presence, which is somewhat
akin to the stillness of death.

But his loveliest tone is pitched somewhat lower than that. It comes
when, without taking his eye from the earthly object he loves so well,
he draws back from it into a sort of intense brooding quietude, and

[23] March 19, 1819.
[24] *Endymion*, II, 153ff.

suggests in his music a yearning for a peace which in life he could not win:

> Heard melodies are sweet, but those unheard
> Are sweeter; therefore, ye soft pipes, play on;
> Not to the sensual air, but, more endeared,
> Pipe to the spirit ditties of no tone.

This is the "fair attitude" of his best complete work: the Maytime odes, *On a Grecian Urn*, *On Melancholy*, *To a Nightingale*, with their September sequel, the ode *To Autumn*. Read in this order, they always appear to me like four successive phases of a single poem: they give a complete pastoral vista of life, with a sense of hidden mountain-peaks behind. In the foreground, our passing joys and sorrows are heard in meadow and forest, along the hill-slopes and streams, in daylight and brooding darkness, in the chill rains of springtime and around the warm "stubble-plains" of fall. The scene is intimate and poignant; yet the poet views it at a little distance, with a half smile, and moulds it with the firm clearness of sculpture. One may discover here all the lines of his own bitter troubles; but these are never felt as personal to him. The eye runs out to "magic casements" opening on wonderful seas in the fringes of the scene. But beyond and above the scene, we feel, there is a region "mountain-built with peaceful citadel."

IV

THE ARNOLDIAN LYRIC MELANCHOLY

MATTHEW ARNOLD is in general so confidently clear as to the nature of his own poetry that the reader is apt to credit him when he insists upon the contemporary sources of its melancholy. But those sources will appear much dimmer as time goes on. The "two worlds" that the poet wandered between, so sadly, will doubtless be rather nebular on the rear horizon, and the carefully wrought stanzas concerning them may seem the "stretchèd metre of an antique song." The future cursory reader, when he reaches the poem *On Growing Old*, may toss the volume aside with the remark that "this old fellow carefully architectured his gloom but added, here, a gable far too quaintly obtrusive." The discerning reader, however, will be in a better position than now to find, flowing beneath Arnold's verse, a profounder melancholy than the clear Arnoldian eye itself could fathom.

Not so long ago Darwin's coadjutor, Dr. Wallace, at full tide of scientific enthusiasm, produced a book which was dedicated, in title and text, to the proposition that the nineteenth century was The Wonderful Century. Later on, from a different standpoint, he wrote a book showing the same era in very gloomy colours. His shift is symbolic of the change that is taking place in the fame of the past century. Perhaps in time it will appear the very Jaques of centuries, with a melancholy all its own, "compounded of many simples, extracted from many objects": opium, Alps, whiskey, apes, seas, hospitals, death, life, sex, democracy. Some future investigator may make a more scientific list of the things from which Coleridge, Shelley, Byron, Tennyson, Arnold, Clough, Rossetti, Thomson, Henley, Hardy, and their successors, sucked melancholy. He will observe that the same simples yielded intermittent delight. For in nineteenth-century poetry there appears, more and more, an overstrained joy dogged by an overstrained sorrow: Shelley ecstatic, leading on Shelley miserable; Browning twisting hope, and then Hardy spinning gloom.

Arnold's position in this moody company will seem, to the future eye, quite natural but also very distinctive. For his melancholy will appear more essential than that of the others,—not so fully resolvable into temperamental and temporary conditions. Unlike the other poets, notably unlike Browning, Arnold had a firm and open-eyed serenity, which he cultivated more and more. In his prose, it wins a larger and steadier swing than in his verse, adding to itself a kind of cheerfulness; but at the same time it develops a guarded elaboration that prevents the finest quality of prosaic art. In his poetry his serene mood, though not so commanding, is intimate and native. And the main charm of his verse lies precisely in the quiet, upward push of this serenity upon his melancholy; like a spring of water in autumn rising again beneath a settled pool, moving, lifting, and clarifying it.

Such is the fine flow of poetry that went on in this man's spirit. But rarely has it a complete and natural circulation in his style; continually we are aware of pipes and pressure. For, in addition to the comparative tenuity of his poetic gift, Arnold was so intent upon clarifying Hippocrene, in reaction from current confusion, that clearness became in him a process too distinct and conscious for full poetic reality,—except in the didactic and satiric mode. In this kind of verse he could be superbly satisfying, and the meditative stanzas in *Empedocles on Etna* make the reader wish he had done more of it. But under the influence of that Romantic reaction from eighteenth-century forms which is still too current today, he underestimated the poetry of ethical wit. He wanted to be very lyrical. His fondness for lyric magniloquence was larger than his aptitude for it. In his odes and elegies, the true chanting is less present than excellently imitated. Often we can feel his music in the very process of freezing into architecture, under the pressure of his insistent effort at motivational clarity.

Beneath those fine pieces, *A Summer Night* and *The Buried Life*, is a poetic experience "most musical, most melancholy,"—a profounder spring of sadness than Shelley and the others could draw upon. For in the Shelleyan mode of poetry, which is with us yet, life is felt as a single wide and shallow stream, comprising infinite varieties of emotion, but always sweeping in one general direction. Therefore emotional currents are not deeply differentiated in it, and the sense of deep oppositions, so vital in great poetry, is obscured or lost. But in Arnold's poetry, the more constant and hidden currents pull continually *against* the more obvious and momentary

currents. Our true "life's flow" is felt as belonging to a region
sharply different from that of sheer temperamental overflow.

> A bolt is shot back somewhere in our breast
> And a lost pulse of feeling stirs again;
> The eye sinks inward, and the heart lies plain,
> And what we mean, we say, and what we would, we know.
> A man becomes aware of his life's flow,
> And hears its winding murmur, and he sees
> The meadows where it glides, the sun, the breeze.

Yet here the true flow is finely indicated, rather than rendered. The
same theme is treated with humbler and more adequate art in
Palladium, where Arnold equals Clough in the latter's special field.

> Set where the upper streams of Simoïs flow
> Was the Palladium, high 'mid rock and wood;
> And Hector was in Ilium, far below,
> And fought, and saw it not—but there it stood!
>
> It stood, and sun and moonshine rained their light
> On the pure columns of its glen-built hall,
> Backward and forward rolled the waves of fight
> Round Troy—but while this stood, Troy could not fall. . . .
>
> Still doth the soul, from its lone fastness high,
> Upon our life a ruling effluence send.
> And when it fails, fight as we will, we die;
> And while it lasts, we cannot wholly end.

At the other end of the scale are poems like the *Stanzas from the
Grande Chartreuse* and *Obermann Once More*, in which scenic and
temporal motifs are elaborated. Here Arnold's art tends to be centrally factitious. For here he is most intent upon localizing his
melancholy. He spreads it out too obviously upon the surroundings,
and attributes it too largely to passing conditions, losing touch with
its deepest source.

The contemporary landscape of religion, particularly, was misleading for this poet. It drew him into a false posture, as though his
melancholy were mainly due to the decline of Christianity:

> The Sea of Faith
> Was once, too, at the full, and round earth's shore
> Lay like the folds of a bright girdle furled.
> But now I only hear
> Its melancholy, long, withdrawing roar,
> Retreating, to the breath

> Of the night-wind, down the vast edges drear
> And naked shingles of the world.

This is fine—too fine to be very good poetry. It is suspiciously eloquent. If Arnold, within himself, had ever been steadily lifted on that Sea at its high tide of humility and peace . . . not a tide shining and foaming with mediaevalistic glamour, as in his Oxford days, nor a tide sonorous with institutional and social effect, such as he always continued to desire for the good of the world,—

> But such a tide as, moving, seems asleep,
> Too full for sound and foam . . .

the retreat of that Sea would not have seemed to him so absolute, and he would not have pictured it with such complacent elaboration. He was elaborately regretful, as the romantic heart of man will ever be, at arriving too late for a spring-tide on which he was never really prepared to embark. He mourned the loss of a wondrous sea which he was not born and fitted to explore. He was a born pagan, a noble Stoic, who found himself in a position to do that which he wished his leader, Marcus Aurelius, could have done,—namely, patronize Christianity. He admired its scriptures, he defended and described its morals, he reproved its modern vulgarities : he wanted it to be gentlemanly to the end. He sanctioned its emotions, too, so long as they were properly affixed to its morality, so long as religion (in his dreadful definition of it) was "morality touched with emotion." He approved its outer heart so well that he missed its inner heart entirely. He was too well satisfied with his own fine appreciation of the courtyard of the Temple. He praised "the effusion of Christianity, its relieving tears, its happy self-sacrifice." [1] He never pressed in, he never saw the need of working in, to the region where there is no *effusion* except deity's own—the innermost sanctuary of abnegation and worship and faith. His imagination was non-religious ; it did not bow before the Reality which is involved in the great myths and comprises them. His style is always void of the true movement of religious poetry—its quick obeisance and penetration.

That is why such a stanza as the following, in which he aligns himself temporarily, and very factitiously, with the Chartreuse monks, is so badly Byronic :

[1] From Arnold's essay on Marcus Aurelius.

> Wandering between two worlds, one dead,
> The other powerless to be born,
> With nowhere yet to rest my head,
> Like these, on earth I wait forlorn.
> Their faith, my tears, the world deride—
> I come to shed them at their side.

This might be a sentimental worldling caricaturing the profound truth that is glanced at in the third line, the perennial homelessness of the Son of Man upon earth. Yet Arnold was deeply aware of this truth poetically, though not religiously. The profoundest thing in his poetry is precisely his sense of the homelessness of the human spirit in its yearning that Perfection should come upon earth. The deepest source of his melancholy did not lie between his official "two worlds," did not lie between two conflicting times, but rather between a time and an eternity. More than any other Englishman of his century, Arnold succeeded, like Goethe, in mentally envisaging the full nature of Poetry, as a living norma, ever going on before mankind. He remarkably shaped his daily life in its light, while his century was doing alternate homage to "madman and slave"—as every century, in some degree, has done and will do. In the chasm between the life of the centuries and the life of Poetry lie the deepest waters of Arnoldian melancholy; and up through them and mingling with them, deriving indeed from the same ultimate source, rises his loveliest serenity. Arnold's verse is at its best when this autumnal spring flows out spontaneously, and notably where it mixes with his love of seas and streams. One hears its music mingling distantly in the strange yearning of the tides in *The Forsaken Merman*, and in the larger melancholy of *Sohrab and Rustum*, which at the close sets so majestically toward the tranquil sea:

> Oxus, forgetting the bright speed he had
> In his high mountain-cradle in Pamere,
> A foiled circuitous wanderer—till at last
> The longed-for dash of waves is heard, and wide
> His luminous home of waters opens, bright
> And tranquil, from whose floor the new-bathed stars
> Emerge, and shine upon the Aral Sea.

But its fullest and loveliest tone comes in *The Scholar Gipsy*. Significantly enough, Arnold is here under guidance of Keats, instead of his more frequent masters, Wordsworth and Byron. The shade of the fullest poetic temperament of the century broods here upon him who saw so fully what Poetry means for human life. Hence, though scenic and temporal motifs are elaborate, they have not in this poem their usual danger for Arnold. He does not get caught in his own mental geography. That stiff and stoical region subsides in a flood of real poetic passion. The loved serenity of the Oxford landscape, and then the sad withdrawal of seventeenth-century faith, are felicitously merged in the flowing theme of the mystic scholar, which Arnold follows with a "devout energy" of art unparalleled in his other elegies and odes. If, in the last third of the poem, the theme tends to wind too long among contemporary conditions, it saves itself superbly in the two closing stanzas; flowing back through the old clear Mediterranean, "betwixt the Syrtes and soft Sicily," and recapturing its reflection of eternity. Arnold's verse at its best has the melancholy "which there is in life itself": the melancholy of life yearning toward the full life of Poetry, and still "waiting for the spark from heaven to fall."

V

GENTLE SHADES OF LONGFELLOW

There are more guests at table than the hosts
Invited; the illuminated hall
Is thronged with quiet, inoffensive ghosts
As silent as the pictures on the wall.

THE poet Vachel Lindsay, tramping and talking among the Rockies several years ago, said he considered Longfellow a greater poet than Walt Whitman. The remark was noted in a book by Stephen Graham, and smiled at by reviewers. It was indeed queerly discordant with Our Age. Doubtless it conveyed the sense of the majority of Americans who happen just now to be *in existence*. But we—by which I mean, of course, Our Age—know the difference between existence and real life: we are more keenly aware of it than any age has ever been or, probably, ever will be. "[Existence] is real, [existence] is earnest," sang Longfellow, in our translation. But we have changed all that. We know that *existence*, though very extensive—characterizing, indeed, most people most of the time—is walled off from *real life* by stone-heavy conventions. Life that is real and vital is limitless: it admits no walls, it moves in all directions, it excludes no territory . . . except existence. And just here is our paradox. Life leaps all barriers; but it cannot even crawl, inwards, over the mean walls of bourgeoisie and academe. Life is fluid and all-pervasive; but it cannot permeate the continental soil where browses "that monster, custom." Our poetic spirit includes, or patronizes and assumes to include, Walt Whitman; but it excludes Longfellow,—whose work, like existence, is quite extensive.

The paradoxical state of present American poetry has been noted by the most sympathetic critics. Rate the quality of our verse as high as we will, and still it appears too much overshadowed by its quantity. Our poetic spirit is extraordinarily widespread and lively: our distinguished poems are few. Our poets feel progressive, but they don't get very far ahead. Confusion of the paths ahead is particularly marked just now, at the turn of the quarter-century (1925). The first generation of our twentieth-century poets has matured and shown its full bent. The second generation, so far, seems—well, less certain of its ways to distinction, but still more determined to be free, vital, unconventional, unacademic. At this juncture, "the horologe of eternity," blatantly cliché, rings the academic centenary of Longfellow. In the spring of 1825 he was getting ready to throw off his undergraduate coil at Bowdoin College and to plunge into real . . . academic existence. He was fortunate, comparatively, in one respect: he didn't labour under the urgent necessity of not resembling Longfellow. In fact the total world of poetry, so far, was extraordinarily open to him. He felt free to study, translate, copy, and when possible create, at any point in that world to which his genius drew him. He was mastering languages, and ready to ransack history and geography, for the sake of verse. He was preparing a rather spirited Commencement oration pleading for a fuller recognition of "our native American poets"; while fate was preparing for him the means of rambling over romantic Europe. Unlike the English Romanticists, he was not strenuously reacting from eighteenth-century verse.[1] Nor did there loom for him the strife of "God and Nature," of knowing and feeling, which tangled the misfortunate Tennyson. The God of his Puritan forefathers, somewhat dislimned, could blend well enough with the larger notion of Life which the Transcendentalists were disseminating, and with the old or distant deities into whose presence his wide study of poetry was leading him. His doctrines and exclusions were native to him, almost undeliberated. Excepting Keats, he became the least dogmatic of the major poets of the century. In 1825, in short, the young Longfellow was preparing to get poetry wherever he was capable of finding it. In 1925, our younger poets are preparing to get it wherever they are led and permitted by the current dogma of vitality, or "vitalism"; which is all the more restrictive in that it makes a great show of being broad and free.

[1] For instance, he was not to be debarred, later, from composing *The Jewish Cemetery at Newport* in Gray's elegiac rhythm—and from making it a better poem, as a whole, than Gray's very popular *Elegy.*—"Why better?"—Because while lacking Gray's finest touches, it lacks also his pompous melancholy and sentimental egoism. It catches, through a rich local condition (a characteristically American one), a pathos far wider and more valid than that which Gray read into the lives of his ideal-stolid yokels. And it is beautifully architectured.

In Whitman, the thing was not a dogma but an original experience. It was also a natural and powerful swing of the American poetic spirit, away from the thin inclusiveness of Longfellow, toward a vivid immediacy of expression. Because we and no other nation had a Longfellow, we alone had presently a Whitman. The two are complementary, and neither, except in distorted literary history, is more characteristic of America than the other, or more organic in the development of her poetry. Unable yet to produce *great poems*, America wrote through Longfellow fine and shapely poems, and then through Whitman passages and hints of a greater poetry.

The fresh American material to which Whitman devoted himself was the matrix of his imagistic manner. He saw a new nation, vivid and strong in many particulars, but in general crude, scattering, and unformed. Similar was his poetry: in vision, large and inchoate; in manner, a resonant promenade of particular images. His style, rather than his vision, has been effectual in our twentieth-century poetry. Like the style of Pope, though for different reasons, it is divorceable from the author's temper, stimulates technical interest, and engages in the writing of verse a large number of very moderate talents. Moreover, the cult of imagism—in the widest sense of the term, as indicating a general stylistic tendency of which the so-called Imagists have been only a particular sign—recalls the neo-classic cult of two centuries ago by encouraging a needed pruning of poetic style even while producing a false grandiloquence of its own. But in our case the grandiloquence is strident instead of smooth—what an English critic, the late Sir Walter Raleigh, called "a strained effort to write strong." For really strong writing in the imagistic manner, a personality the size of Whitman's is requisite. With us, the manner has been most successful, poetically, when most delicate; as in Carl Sandburg's "wide dreaming pansy of an old pond in the night," or in any one of the lovely pastels of "H. D." Her work hints the completion of the imagistic movement and our need of fresh direction. For imagism means the abeyance of large design and full poetic ideas: in this region our poets, for the past decade or so, have been obviously fumbling.

Their firmest holds, very often, have been taken upon satire; which, on account of what Mr. H. L. Mencken calls "our disillusion," has been a pressing literary overtone of our time. Many of our most satisfying poems have been satirical or, at least, swayed by satiric ideas. This department of our verse should develop in skill and explicitness. At the same time the main body and spirit of our poetry should go free of the satirical bent. For we know that satire has a way of keeping poetry a trim little servant of prose, clothing her in the used garments rather than the real powers of house-mistress. Moreover, satire today has very much less of *poetic* possibility than it had two centuries ago. Swift in his prose idyl of the Houyhnhnms lacerated society while worshiping a positive social idea, a traditional and quite poetic "Reason" coming down from ancient times. He and his brother wits assumed that philosophy was possible, for the enlightened few at least, as a guide to the social intention of the universe, and to the right and comely life of a man among men. But nowadays, says Bertrand Russell, philosophy, except when mathematical, is bankrupt. Our wits are individualists and impressionists. They merge the great conventions of old thought with the dull conventions of the new bourgeoisie, and crack their whip at the whole circling show, like the circus ring-master, with no desire of really hitting anything. Properly, they profess no social principles at all, like Mr. Mencken: his work, in attitude at least, is the crown of the genre.[2] The increasing crowd of his imitators have the right artistic instinct . . . insofar as they are not born poets, or critics capable of helping to shape our poetry. For on the whole our present satiric strain, devoid as it is of any real social idea, is the very cul-de-sac of poetry. And our American "river of water of life, bright as crystal, proceeding out of the throne of God" is not yet so copious that we can afford to let it get drained off and bottled up in that roiled cove.

To be sure, the initial indent for that cove was made by Whitman himself. He joggled sandy social banks, giving the current places to push through, if it wanted to; but he did not stay to urge or watch it. He went on with his vision. Whether *we* will go on with it, further and further, is now the pressing question for American

[2] When he keeps concealed his Nietzscheism—his shocked kindness of heart and his faith in stridency of will—his mien satisfies the artistic eye, and the cracking play of his lash has a full rhythm. But often our wits succumb to the charm of some current hobby, thus losing their rôle and becoming the more absurd; like Mr. D. H. Lawrence circling around seriously on the back of a super-sexed life-force.

poetry, as for American life. His stylistic manner, as I said, has been carried further,—into reaches of satiric pungency, or delicate sensuous effects, quite beyond his own scope. But his vision has been left where he left it. It has been reverenced and reëmbodied, as in Witter Bynner's beautiful but rather factitious poem *The New World*. But it has not been carried forward, as the spirit of Whitman yearned that it should. One sign of this stagnant condition is that Whitman has not yet become, like Longfellow, a full subject for satire. When his blatancies are just as comic and undesirable as Longfellow's in the eyes of current writers, when his accidents are clearly marked off from his essence, then our love of him will be sound and progressive. So far, he is a fetish, and a quarry for dogma. His large tolerant neglect of old convention has become, in a thousand lesser souls, a conventional antipathy to *all* convention—a blind aversion from the convention-making power in human nature itself, which is the twin of poetry. For, blunderingly enough, that power, like poetry, seeks human integration and loves design. Whitman, while deficient in the art of design, was in spirit a lover of large design. His insistence upon the inclusiveness of his Ego was an instinctive effort to transcend the particularism of his art. After listing particulars at length, he continually felt the need for a quick ascent to the universal. But he had slight power of integrating chosen particulars in some poetic form of the universal. That power is not of a day; it is built up through long centuries, and no poet's local experience can carry him far into it. In other words, poetic idea and mood—creative thought and feeling which, merged in the poet's own experience, come out in the form of notable poems—belong to poetic tradition, conceived as a living world of achieved poetry. Thither our newest poets must be urged to turn; if American poems are not to be mushrooms in our worldly pastures—numerous, often racy enough, but small and ill-fed.

Prerequisite is that special gentleness, or gentility, of spirit that fosters devotion to the world of poetry as distinct from all other worlds. Keats had it; and Keats is a very acceptable authority today. We need his rich amity, his instinct for eluding current dogma, his devoted feeling for the best poetic ideas of the past. But his poetic thought is boyish; and his style has in it a confined and rather feverish intenseness of imagery the like of which our own poets have now cultivated sufficiently. Just as he sometimes suggests "London and neighbourhood," so there is a certain mode of American style that "commutes" too eagerly between New York and nature. Our poets often feel it incumbent upon them to be intense in their writing when they are not so in themselves, thus confuting reality by means of "realism." Intensity tends to be regarded as the sine qua non. The idea of intensity confuses our present issue. But Longfellow helps to clear it. The singular unintensity of his style throws into relief his fine art of design. In *My Lost Youth*, for instance, hardly a single image seems strange and beautiful, but the whole poem—so finely is the mood upbuilded from beginning to end of the ten stanzas—is indeed a "strange and beautiful song." Longfellow's best poems, like no other, can set us free from the current pedantry of the non-cliché. He can encourage a young poet to follow intently the whole mood and design of whatever he is writing and, in process, to use any image, no matter how conventional, that he happens really to want.

Of course, many members of the present generation are reacting from the passages of Longfellow on which their childhood was fed, and have not yet made fresh selections of their own. They loathe the piece about "the for-get-me-nots of the angels" in *Evangeline*, and miss the scene of the dead in the charity hospital during the pestilence, each covered with his temporary unowned sheet . . . "drifts of snow by the roadside." They drop *Evangeline* in toto and do not yet read the charming imagistic *Kéramos*. Longfellow, re-read, has many a passage that sufficiently meets the taste of our day,[3] even while he hints the narrowness of that taste. For instance, admirers of Carl Sandburg could find faint anticipations of him in this:

> Still is the night. The sound of feet
> Has died away from the empty street.
> And like an artisan, bending down
> His head on his anvil, the dark town
> Sleeps, with a slumber deep and sweet . . .

[3] Recently I sent copies of the first stanza of *In the Churchyard at Cambridge*, with title and author's name omitted, to a number of young college persons much interested in current verse, some of them promising poets themselves. "Who wrote this?" I queried; "I have seen it quoted . . . a new poem?"— Quite new to them, their answers showed, but acceptable as supposedly belonging to our age! I have not disillusioned them; but it is just possible that some of them will read thus far in the present essay.

or in *The Ropewalk* with its "booth of mountebanks,"—

> With its smell of tar and planks,
> And a girl poised high in air
> On a cord, in spangled dress,
> With a faded loveliness,
> And a weary look of care.

Readers of Robert Frost, author of *An Old Man's Winter Night*, should appreciate the solitary father of the Baron of St. Castine—

> And the old man rouses from his dreams,
> And wanders restless through the house,
> As if he heard strange voices call.
> His footsteps echo along the floor
> Of a distant passage, and pause awhile—

whose death has this profound simplicity: "No longer he waits for any one." The New-England austerity of E. A. Robinson recalls the sunken slave-ships of Longfellow, with their dreadful *under-water* moving:

> Beyond the fall of dews,
>   Deeper than plummet lies,
> Float ships, with all their crews,
>   No more to sink or rise.
>
> There the black slave-ship swims,
>   Freighted with human forms,
> Whose fettered, fleshless limbs
>   Are not the sport of storms.

As for the Imagists,—their neat glory is incipient, I find, in numerous passages of our neglected classic. Consider this *Dutch Picture*:

> In his tulip-garden there by the town,
>   Overlooking the sluggish stream,
> With his Moorish cap and dressing-gown,
> The good sea-captain, hale and brown,
>   Walks in a waking dream. . . .
>
> But when the winter rains begin,
>   He sits and smokes by the blazing brands,
> And old seafaring men come in,
> Goat-bearded, gray, and with double chin,
>   And rings upon their hands.

Or this ceramic churchman:

> Here in this old neglected church,
> That long eludes the traveller's search,
> Lies the dead bishop on his tomb;

> Earth upon earth he slumbering lies,
> Life-like and death-like in the gloom;
> Garlands of fruit and flowers in bloom
> And foliage deck his resting-place;
> A shadow in the sightless eyes,
> A pallor on the patient face,
> Made perfect by the furnace heat,—
> All earthly passions and desires
> Burnt out by purgatorial fires.

Or these pungent Eastern ornaments:

> Osiris, holding in his hand
> The lotus; Isis, crowned and veiled;
> The sacred Ibis, and the Sphinx;
> Bracelets with blue enamelled links;
> The Scarabee in emerald mailed,
> Or spreading wide his funeral wings;
> Lamps that perchance their night-watch kept
> O'er Cleopatra while she slept:—
> All plundered from the tombs of kings.

After Amy Lowell's *City of Falling Leaves*, read this from Longfellow's *Michael Angelo*:

> Petrarca is for women and for lovers,
> And for those soft Abati who delight
> To wander down long garden-walks in summer,
> Tinkling their little sonnets all day long,
> As lap-dogs do their bells.

Surely our nice and resolute sophistication was gently germinal in Longfellow. But if we turn quickly to the following scene, laid in *Killingworth* destitute of birds—

> A wagon, overarched with evergreen,
> Upon whose boughs were wicker cages hung,
> All full of singing birds, came down the street,
> Filling the air with music wild and sweet—

we must, of course, curl a disdainful lip. The date is out of such romantic simplicity of sentiment, for us! John Masefield, to be sure, would like that passage. The English have a way of being suddenly old-fashioned, whenever they feel so inclined. In the London literary world, revivals of forgotten writers—for instance, the poet John Clare, at the present moment—jostle elbows with the excitements of newest modes. But literary New York moves in a few grooves, and projects them through the land. The main track just now is "vitalism," and the wheels of Longfellow do not fit it at all. The following, for instance, will never do:

> Sing of the air, and the wild delight
> Of wings that uplift and winds that uphold you,
> The joy of freedom, the rapture of flight
> Through the drift of the floating mists that enfold you.

Possibly that tune of "uplift," "drift," and "mists" is polyphonically prophetic. But the thing as a whole, though it has zest, has not our special brand of zest. It is too Swinburnean; it lacks deliberate irregularities . . . in short, we smell a homely hearth-fire near at hand.

If Longfellow's poetry, on the whole, is the sheltered fireside, our present poetry is the single-flue furnace—I mean the kind that was installed recently in the old New-England house of a friend of mine. It sends up in one certain spot a gush of hottest air which is *advertised* to pervade the whole house. In reality its orbit is at once narrow and vague. One wearies of this local intensity, this pseudo-catholic inclusiveness. In the parlor one glances wistfully at the old empty fireplace. It still really belongs here, no matter how much the old home has been altered since the days when

> It bronzed the rafters overhead;
> On the old spinet's ivory keys
> It played inaudible melodies;
> It crowned the sombre clock with flame,—
> The hands, the hours, the maker's name. . . .

Those images, now "improved" away, still indicate main objects in our house of life. And though the Longfellowan flame seems to us mild, its scope and touch are certain. Instead of single-flue intensity, it has a true poetic gentility with true poetic zest.

We must re-learn the difference between life's intensity and poetry's zest. To obscure it is a crude old bourgeois error that thrives in a young industrial country, and sways—even while they fancy themselves freed of bourgeois sway—her young poets. They too may crave a quantity rather than a quality of feeling, and assume that passing intensities are the very making of poetry instead of the most uncertain of all of its raw materials. To fancy that poetry may be crammed with "real life," hastily fattened on crude vivid experience, belongs with the error of the get-rich-quick citizen who decides to buy a fine life for himself and family with much cash. Both errors are more common in America than elsewhere. So is the error of the indulgent critic who, insensibly affected by the recent diffusion of pseudo-scientific optimism, believes that our present orgy of "vitality" will certainly, as though by operation of natural law, work out to the benefit of our poetry in the near future.[4] The sequel may well be quite the opposite—as a child whose parents are trying to fatten him on an overplus of vitamines is long kept thin (according to recent pronouncements of medical science) by reason of maldigestion. The near-future need of American poetry is a fresh regimen, a better diet; and the first step toward it is to realize how thin the child still is.

To fancy that our poetry is in general more "real" than Longfellow's is to be more naïve in regard to life and poetry than he was. Our poetic mettle is not thicker. But our experiences have thickened. And therefore to remake them into poetry we have all the more need of a right poetic zest, disentangled from "vital intensities" on the one hand, and cynic disillusions on the other. Poetry has a vital and constant disillusion of her own: a keen sense that things "realistic" today are not so tomorrow, that cynic tirades and sexy flairs belong to the same transiency as the dull conventions they react from. Therewith she has a keen sense of her own eternity—her own life and designs persisting through the centuries—and a patient zest in moulding something of the passing show to her own purposes. Poetry herself is not a "realist" in the present sense of the word. She realizes the difference between herself and "real life," and believes religiously in transubstantiation. The pang and joy of this skeptical faith have always been the emotional differentiæ of poetry:

> Where are the songs of Spring? Ay, where are they?
> Think not of them, thou hast thy music too. . . .

That pang, and that following joy, belong with poetic zest and mark it off from all other intensities. They come to the poet less from his experience of life than from his experience of the *life of poetry*. Longfellow had a wider experience of that life, and a clearer gift in applying it, than anyone else so far in America.

---

[4] The kind of democratism that appears in the latest work of those two fine critics, Stuart P. Sherman and W. C. Brownell, could have been developed only in the United States. It could not elsewhere have taken such hold upon such outstanding minds. Of Mr. Brownell's *Democratic Distinction in America*, Agnes Repplier says in the course of an appreciative review in *The Forum* (March 1928): "Here and there an illuminating truth relieves the optimistic pressure. . . . None dreamed that his bias set that way."

The mildness of his style, now so much misconceived, was inevitable. It was due ultimately to the limits of American poetry, which, as still today, was not strong-grown enough to apprehend very much of America's life without losing too much of its own.[5] Only an artist of the unintensity and detachment of Longfellow could so dedicate himself, under American conditions, to the world of poetry. Moreover, his work represents a golden moment. The old narrow puritanical intensity, incapable of poetry, had faded; the new industrial-democratic intensity, disruptive for poetry, had not arrived. It is significant that the fair moment could not be seized by Emerson, our profoundest worshipper of poetry. His verse shows how naïve, impatient, and fitful, how much lacking in clear grasp of poetic mode, our American devotion to poetry can be, even when most exalted and pure—how long a way toward the heights of poetic form we have to go. Our basic need is the patient and thorough zest in poetry—a zest not to be warped from its aim by our thronging cults and gusty "vitalities"—that Longfellow achieved for us. "Achieved" is the word! His poetic gentility, so far from being in its essential nature a deficiency of the Victorian New-England school,[6] now outgrown or outworn, is a positive achievement of American poetry, needing to be continually resumed and built upon.

To be sure, the achievement had to be paid for. The price was the genteel and angelic aspects of Longfellow's style—ghostly offspring of the pioneer and the Puritan. Children of harsh parents are likely to be soft in spots, especially when submitted to an elaborate book-education. In Longfellow's verse the lineaments of the pioneering Puritan gentleman hover in the form of a genteel angel, cultivating flowers instead of clearing stumps, bringing us airs from heaven, screening off and perfuming the blasts from hell. Yet at bottom the scented style had in Longfellow the same source as in Keats,—an

[5] Mr. D. H. Lawrence in his recent book upon American literature puts the matter the other way around: our notable writers have been timid Anglo-Saxons shrinking from the mammoth life of a new continent. A still more amusing book could be written upon Anglo-Saxon literary primitivists, in gardened England, yearning for American cave-realities.

[6] As in the newest view of our literary history. This view really begins our national poetry with Whitman, disbranching us from our material sap. It is likely to make headway in certain of our colleges, in reaction from the genteel attitude of our older academics who felt with the Hostess that, though very hospitable, they "could not abide swaggerers."

exceptional desire, in a century full of harsh and cross purposes, for sheer poetic beauty of expression. He succumbed to the lure of obvious aesthetic effects. But it is to *our* advantage to think rather of his successful avoidance of *un*poetic effects. Didacticism spread its claws on every side of him; but excepting a few awkward scratches —worst of all the dreadful translation of *The Children of the Lord's Supper*—he escaped and passed on fancy-free.

His style is more given over to fancy and mood than he himself was, for his milieu was not equal to his character. The Renaissance tradition of character in beauty, of moral conduct harmonious with poetic purpose, had suffered even more heavily in New than in old England. Longfellow grew up in a community which liked its verse sentimental when not moralistic, and could not much encourage the real nobility of art. In avoiding moralism Longfellow's muse was thrown much upon sentiment and fancy. Yet he continually tried for a mode of style that would be elevated without ceasing to be poetic. Emerson under the same circumstances produced the grand style jerky. Longfellow, vowed at least to other than broken music, produced the grand style flat . . . yet not flatulent, like Tennyson's, nor moving, as the Miltonic vein of Wordsworth often does, with a sort of bumptious bounce. In *Morituri Salutamus, John Endicott, The Golden Legend, Michael Angelo,* Longfellow is bearer of a high poetic tradition which at least he will not debauch. But in particular passages he could not often attain the impressiveness which belongs to his poetry as a whole, to his entire poetic mood, which holds in solution a fine personal character. This way of looking at a poet's work is not countenanced by those who, under the sway of imagism and the élan vital, desire briskness in detail and some impersonal throb of nature in the whole. Nevertheless the firm, sweet, and laborious living of the man Longfellow, devoted to the aims of poetry and free from the cult-spirit, goes on like a stream through the whole territory of his work, and gives it a recurrent freshness of poetic appeal lacking in many artists of a more originative genius.

And surely his work has a certain shadowy loveliness quite its own,—as of a stream in a flat unfertile region, shading its way with foliage, and never stagnant, having a current always toward the sea. His melancholy, I think, is mainly that of Poetry herself in a locale where the flow of verse cannot yet be beautifully strong. At the same time his realization of his limits, and his will to do what he

.could for poetry within them, won him a clear distinction in the total history of poetry. Worshiping the epic gods afar off, he created near at hand the limpid shadowy eagerness of *Hiawatha*. He cultivated the homely romance of New England's sailing-ships and country-sides and birds of passage, and could catch the quaint humours of her religionists and sea-captains; even while interpreting for her, exquisitely, the moods of old artists and old lovely cities beyond the sea. No other poet has a style at once so homely and so cultivated. No other style has the peculiar quiet gleaming of his whenever it touches a shadow. His verse is the mild rain that sometimes goes over an austere New-England landscape in autumn, or the south wind looking for spring and turning into swaying mists along the hard coast. Regarded thus in its whole mood, his style is not a foreign importation. Its gentle sombreness is the natural outcome of a true poetic spirit growing in this neighbourhood, and having in the background a constant sense of the pioneer labour of America, so long, and so often fruitless, and fruitful mainly in material things.

He could not "hear America singing" like Walt Whitman: he could not listen so widely and so confidently to her various workers "singing with open mouths their strong melodious songs." For he experienced poetry, and life, not mainly as an outpouring but as an arduous shaping; and he felt our American need of long constructive labour in the spirit. He was spiritually realistic at the point where Whitman was a simple visionary. Whitman underestimated the length of our American road to eternity. He sprinkled our very "leaves of grass" with our pseudo-religious optimism. He was a freedman of democratic Christianity, more or less consciously wooing the primitive. Longfellow, through education and the tradition of poetry, became a citizen of a *civilized* world older than Christianity, and, more or less unconsciously, was much of a pagan. Excepting in a few angelic passages, he did not slur over the great and plain human meaning of death; and his consciousness of the continued presence of the dead is not essentially Christian. He reverenced, to be sure, the high Christian reaches of eternity, especially when in Dante's presence. But he felt the difficulty of them, and the difficulty of turning them into human poetry, in America. The spirit-region characteristic of Longfellow lies somewhere between the peace of the old cathedral and the rush of the modern street, and somewhere between the ancient pagan shrines of the dead and the fireside of the New-England home. It is, indeed, the old perennial region of the Shades; which seems to outlast, in common human affection, the highly wrought views of religious, or worldly, enthusiasts. From the viewpoint of cathedral or curbstone, it seems quite a vague and negative region. But it has a positive human meaning and, in Longfellow's verse, a native beauty. In the work of no other poet of the century does the world of the dead become so constant and so real a presence without distorting the issues of life. It is a presence that excludes the incoherent egotism of romantic mystics even while it detaches us from the egotism of our everyday selves. It blends indivisibly with personal and historic memories. It surrounds us with a cloud of witnesses who neither disturb nor illuminate our workaday life, but sustain us with the intimate sense that "such as these have lived and died." Longfellow wrote the poetry of plain laborious effort in the human spirit, refreshed by the most simple loveliness of its Shades.

A greater American poet would fuse and lift the labour and faith of America in a grander design—in a narrative poem, let us say, which would go far beyond *Miles Standish* and *Hiawatha*. But America is not yet capable of such poetry. We feel that Whitman was prophetic of it. But we cannot proceed toward it through a mode of verse which rejects, instead of developing, the avenues of character and memory opened by Longfellow; which stops its memory at Whitman and only superficially remembers him. Whitman's vision of a great national spirit and verse in America has dwindled to an Aeolian attachment of a vitalistic cult. To resume and carry forward his vision, and eventually to realize it, demands the patient zest of memory and design achieved for us by Longfellow. The vital catholicity of Whitman's spirit, if followed through, does not reject but renovates the. . . . But just here I fancy a budding American satirist breaking in: "Stop here! I get you entirely. Your whole effusion, boiled down, means just this: 'We need nowadays an integration of the spirits of Longfellow and Whitman.' But as we are showing ourselves totally incapable of digesting the twentieth century, why desire to pour into us some more of the stale nineteenth? Especially as Longfellow and Whitman would mix about as well, say, as milk and whisky."

Ah, but those two liquids, in the experience of tasteful persons born *long enough* before the present era of prohibitional intemperance, make a perfect mixture,—delectable, stimulative, nourishing. And human history is a tissue of just such integrations, or of imperfect attempts at such. The attempts succeed best in the hands of Poetry; for example, in Keats's *Lamia*, where the shades of old Dryden and young Shakespeare are blent in a new achievement. With us and Jehovah, much occupied in spinning inadequate moralisms and satiric revolts, such things are not well possible; but with Apollo, all things are possible. And as a matter of fact there are various signs that this god is now at work, though not yet very whole-heartedly, on the very pattern I have hinted. One recent sign is a remarkable little poem called *The Brown Word Home* by Miss B. K. Van Slyke. Home, as a poetic theme, has had a special flavour in America because the thing itself, in its civilized maturity, was transplanted hither and re-subjected to trial-by-wilderness. But having been over-cultivated by Longfellow, it was beaten against by evolutionary freshets, and shoved aside by Whitman's *Open Road*—"the cheerful voice of the public road, the gay fresh sentiment of the road." Home became a symbol of mere existence, a thing of slight interest for up-to-date poets of real life. Miss Van Slyke, however, has taken a fine fresh hold of it. Shades of both Whitman and Longfellow stir approvingly about her poem. It has the simple sheltering intimacy of the old American home-life; and, surging up through that, the passion of a human idea struggling to realize itself—in the wilderness not just of old New England but of universal Nature—with pain, and with peace:

> About the brown word home
> There is a thing unheard
> Like eyes that fill with unshed tears,
> Throats that speak no word.
>
> It lifts within its tone
> Complete eternity
> As does a flower all night long
> Lift up a complete sea.
>
> Who reads within its heart
> Must dwell on life and death,
> The dark and curious first slime
> Whence we arose to breath.

It tells of more than God,
    And hell is but a page;
Who has his home knows mystery,
    His spirit's heritage.

I say the word and know
    The ecstasy of pain;
It is the root, the stone, the star,
    The elemental rain.

I say the word, and flesh
    Burns with a fire of dream:
Primeval and inevitable,
    Home, the flame, the stream.[7]

Many inadequacies of style can be carried on the sweep of such a full poetic mood. It is a mood we need to ponder just now. For "home" read "America"; and take the second stanza, with its great uplifted dewdrop, as a signal for our poetry. To achieve a completeness of its own, a distinctive form imaging in little the "complete eternity" of poetry, our American poetry must be content to globe itself within the flower of its own tradition, no matter how tenuous and limited this may be. Our poetry can never "lift up a complete sea" by trying to be a world-ocean—uncontained, spreading all over the globe, going nowhere. Since Whitman, it has been tossing hither and thither in the currents of sectional and cult interests, preyed on by the winds of stale European doctrine. Just now the majority of our poets, reacting from the New-England tradition—that is, from the head and source of our own poetic life—are smugly drawing their inspirations from the spent Naturalism of the past century, which the best young minds of Europe, under the after-education of the Great War, are restlessly trying to shake off. To be sure Whitman, and more and more Emerson, are being pointed at as the sources of our present literary mood. But those two great writers had a bold naïveté of spirit which marked them as distinctively American, and with which our present literary school has utterly lost touch in pursuing cosmopolite, and cosmoplastic, sophistication. Continually one reads a new American poem which is strenuously intended to be simple and natural, but succeeds in being simply Naturalistic—so faintly is the aptitude for critical distinction diffused among our writers and their audiences. However, not much

---

[7] In *The Saturday Review*, November 22, 1924. Quoted with the permission of author and editor.

critical insight is needed to recognize the plain fact that in literary sophistication Europe, by reason of her long start, will always be ahead of America; and that in a certain large ingrained simplicity, America, when she will, can always surpass Europe. The growing use of the word "sophisticated" among our young American littérateurs as a term of approbation is one sign of our febrile Europeanism. And some of these youngsters, may God help them, fancy that their sophistic enlightenment is now discovering the true spirit of Emerson.

The proper ingenuousness of the American spirit is hard to describe. It has many modes; it may subsist beneath other qualities which seem the reverse of ingenuous. On the other hand it is not itself when it defines itself too well. Without delimiting it self-consciously, we must seek to know it, conserve it, and deepen it. It lightens here and there even in our present chaos, but only in gleams,

> And ere a man hath power to say "Behold!"
> The jaws of darkness do devour it up.

By way of compensation it appears clearly and steadily through the work of Robert Frost, and indeed is largely responsible for his distinction in poetry. Whitman and Emerson had it, each in his own way. So did Longfellow. And the salvation of our poetry at present depends largely upon our learning to find it and love it in him. If the poetry of the English-speaking race, as I believe, has now reached a point from which it cannot go greatly forward without recurring to Milton, American poetry is in a similar strait in regard to its neglected classic, Longfellow; through whom, incidentally, the way to Milton runs more clearly, in certain respects, than through any other poet of the past century. A national poetry that has become intensely eager in aim but fearfully thin in accomplishment, cannot safely neglect its most accomplished master. In America we should not neglect Longfellow at least until we can overtop *The Golden Legend* and the *Tales of a Wayside Inn*, not only in picayune jewels of expression but in human scope and in narrative power. Shall we much longer continue to imitate European decadency while spurning the doctrine of imitation when it applies to the fathers of our own American literature? While these are no more than ghosts at our poetic banquet, as suggested in the motto prefixed to this paper, our "illuminated hall" with its foreign guests must wear a rather tawdry air.

Longfellow must appear to us, at best, a "quiet inoffensive ghost" so long as we miss his American way of poetic vitality. He learned from the finest foreign literature without unlearning his native simplicity of spirit. Our Age has reversed both parts of his procedure. Our American throng of "diurnalists" or "contemporaneans" — I mean, all our writers who, whether journalists by profession or not, are totally submerged in contemporaneity—have learned the worst thing in foreign literature, its Whitmanism. This influence has swept them away from the greater Whitman; they have distorted Nature's American design in him; they have made him the extinguisher instead of the corrective of Longfellow. This spectacle has not altogether pleased our academics. But the rage of the cultivated classes, as Emerson said with America in his eye, is timid. Partly, Academe has bowed the knee to diurnalism; largely, she has made Longfellow seem far more academic than he really is. She has had an undue anxiety to show that she sees just how imitative and second-rate much of his work is in comparison with the best work of the English poets. She has an uneasy fear, at the present time, of being simple-hearted: she doth protest too much. The fact is that our academics in their way, like our contemporaneans in theirs, have achieved a fatal aversion for American naïveté. Both parties, in learning the best, or worst, of foreign literature, have unlearned their American simplicity.[8] It seems that all we, like sophisticated sheep, have gone astray and the Lord hath laid on Longfellow the iniquity of us all.

It is therefore high time for us to humble ourselves before our master-poet and learn of him. The increasing interest in American literary history on the part of our writers and scholars is an excel-

[8] That is why in America the diurnalists and the academics are drawn up with such wooden straitness in two opposing camps. Their regard for American culture and literature *as American* is not deep enough at present to make them feel that both camps form part of a single army. Of course these two parties must always quarrel with each other, as they have throughout history, for the good of the general health. But the fighting should evince more fair play on the one side, and more decision on the other, than appear at present in the American situation. The personal subserviencies through which the two camps approach each other sometimes, and through which contrary principles are softened and confused, are just another symptom of low morale. The strife should be vigorous and impersonal, for the sake of the development of the Personality of America.

lent sign; but so far it has been too factual or chatty or sectional. If American poetry is to grow toward its own completeness, our critics and teachers and poets must conceive of its past growth more largely and organically. We must win a critical but profound appreciation of its central and distinctive spirit—its American simplicity. In this spirit, Longfellow and Whitman are neighbours. In proportion as we grow above our foreign sophistication and become simply wise, those two poets will be equably and nationally accepted as the necessary complements of each other in the story of our poetry. Let us sketch the orbit of our national poetry large enough to comprise them both, as foci. Then our poetic life will take on a fuller and freer movement. We shall be better able to win something of "complete eternity" for our poetic tone, and for our home.

VI

THE WHITMANISM OF BROWNING

RECENTLY, in a huge book of clippings in a collector's library, I found a cluster of articles published in 1912 to commemorate the hundredth anniversary of the birth of Robert Browning. Next in order was a cluster paying the same honour to Walt Whitman in 1919. Glancing back and forth from one cluster to the other, I got a curious sense of subconscious iteration. I seemed to be viewing two literary nosegays made up to celebrate a twin birth. What of the intervening seven years? That, in the long travails of Nature, is a brief interval (by the way, it is also a mystic interval) between the delivery of the elder and the younger twin.

In 2012 and 2019 Browning and Whitman may appear close kinsmen. They belonged to the same sphere, though in many respects at opposite poles of it; and the further that sphere diminishes in the perspective of time, the nearer together must come its poles. At present the two poets still wear an air of strong antithesis—and no wonder! The extreme emphasis that has been placed upon the individuality of each of them, has obscured their underlying relationship not only with each other but with the whole poetic movement in which they were important factors. Both mined a rich vein of metal running through the nineteenth century: namely, the "natural" emotion of "the modern man." Whitman struck into this vein with the clumsy felicity of an inexperienced miner who gets gold soon after arriving at camp, and even while jovially contemning the regular methods of his fellows. Browning developed this vein under cover of a complex artistic apparatus elaborated by himself and seemingly designed for the mining of nothing natural. Two such craftsmen must each, for a while, seem unique. But the metal they unearthed was common, and their evaluation of it was shaped by the same historical situation. Immediate feeling—feeling largely freed from the restraint and guidance of human tradition, and vivified by fresh intimacies with Nature—had previously been sung into the foreground of English poetry by Wordsworth and his contemporaries. Browning and Whitman approached it, like second-comers to a newly-discovered country, with diminished tunefulness but intensified belief. They cultivated this type of emotion more intensively than their predecessors; and they turned away more definitively from the old principles of art and the wisdom of the ages.

In this way they marked out the main course which poetry was to follow in our own time. Browning, in spite of his now despised Victorianism, ought to have even more credit than Whitman as a grandfather of our "New Poetry." For under cover of his Victorian propriety he was able to foster, in the breast of solid British and American citizenry that was cold to Whitman, a thirst for sheer temperamentalism in art. His readers could absorb from him a determined interest in "thoughts that break through language and escape." They could be initiated, without knowing it, into the cult of successful failure—that cult of impromptu and imperfection which Whitman was proclaiming with undisguised "barbaric Yawp" in America. They could be assured that Browning, unlike Whitman, was a "truly spiritual man" even while learning from him how "pleasant is this flesh":

> Let us not always say,
> "Spite of this flesh today
> I strove, made head, gained ground, upon the whole!"
> As the bird wings and sings,
> Let us cry, "All good things
> Are ours, nor soul helps flesh more, now, than flesh helps soul!"

Whitman postponed his purposed book on the soul until he should have finished with "the body and existence." He never got around to the second volume. It was really redundant. He had already given body to whatever he knew of soul. But Browning's method was different: he *interleaved* body with soul. He insisted upon the soul,—never subtly, but emphatically and at frequent intervals. His readers could find in his poetry the kind of religion they had been brought up on. But they found it accommodated to urgent human appetites. They found Christianity with the Cross omitted. They found their old accustomed Deity, but in a delightfully modified form: He had entirely doffed His age-old preoccupation with righteousness and self-control, and was now largely functioning as a guarantor of human love-affairs:

> Since, the end of life being manifest,
> He had burned His way through the world to this.

To be sure, these lines from *The Statue and the Bust* are quite exceptional in Browning's work. Rarely did he say, or know, so plainly just what he meant! He belonged by heritage and habit to the party of St. Paul; by poetic tendency, to the opposite party, to the Whitmanian "Children of Adam." Unawares, he fed the Whitmanian fire in the subconscious regions of the Victorian Browningite. The Browningite's grandchildren, therefore, are eagerly reading, writing, and trying to write, our current literature of sheer desire.

That Browning's aversion from the wisdom of human experience was not quite so extensive as Whitman's, and not nearly so declamatory, was due to difference in circumstances rather than in mental capacities. The more one may be aware of Browning's superiority to Whitman in brains, the less ought one to praise whatever advantage he had in the matter of wisdom. For when one reviews all the fortunate circumstances of his life—his places of residence, his books, his friends—one's wonder grows that so brainy a man should extract from such facilities so very little wisdom. The wonder of the Browning-lover, to be sure, is in the opposite direction. He finds, here, striking evidence of Browning's uniqueness. He admires the sturdy individualism that enabled the poet to frequent great cities without suffering the imprint of civil institutions; to read and love classic literature without being moulded by the classic spirit; and to move genially among those who considered his thought "muddy" and his art lacking in "the eternal harmonies," without being swerved an inch from the queer paths of his own genius. Such instances, however, serve to bring out Browning's kinship with Whitman. His cities were indeed older than Whitman's, his knowledge of the classics was wider, and his friends were more critical. But his successful resistance of these heavier pressures merely proves that he was even more Whitmanian than Whitman; and the Browningite is unreasonable in refusing to be equally enthusiastic about the sturdy individualism of Whitman.

To the same quality of individualism must be attributed also that social modesty which, on a superficial view, seems widely to distinguish Browning from his twin across the Atlantic. Whitman was less modest because he was more gregarious. Only in constantly asserting his individuality could he feel vividly aware that he possessed it. Browning's individualism was so impassible that, though on a few occasions he slightly shocked society, he generally felt small need of social self-assertion. To surprised visitors who were familiar with the tone of his verse, he appeared the most modest of men, for the very reason that internally he was the most self-confident of poets. In republishing the atrocious *Sordello*, unrevised, after a quarter of a century of criticism, he remarks: "I blame no-body, least of all myself, who did my best then and since." He regarded himself and the reading public as travelling on different trains. At junctions he could genially talk with it, through the car-windows, about the weather; but he could see no gain in discussing with it the direction of their respective journeys. No doubt the persistent inability of the general reader to switch over to Brown-ing's track, lent strength to his conviction that eternity consists of a network of separate travellings, conducted at a high rate of speed.

Browning's resistance to mental influences was indeed strength-ened, unlike Whitman's, by an imposing panoply of ideas, and he was intellectually precocious. The Browningite has wonderingly pointed out that by the age of twenty-three the poet had adopted, in all its essentials, the "philosophy" that runs, or twists, through the whole fabric of his work. But patient Time has more and more untwisted that philosophy and displayed its inadequacy. Nowadays the wonder must be, not that Browning adopted it so early, but that a man of his intelligence could cling to it so long. The solution of this paradox is that Browning's mind, like Whitman's, and unlike Keats's, was really averse from philosophy. In the periphery of life, in the detail of nature and human nature, Browning displayed continually a very sharp discrimination. But when turned upon the central principles of life, his critical intelligence became blunt; when turned upon his own favorite set of ideas, it lost its edge completely.

Nature, in refusing to Browning a philosophic mind, gave him a temperament that demanded a set of fixed ideas. Here again he parallels Whitman. Each of the two, in giving himself joyously to the surge of his immediate emotions, felt the need of "some elected point of central rock," in Browning's phrase, for the waters to whirl around. Browning's elected creed was more sharply defined than Whitman's, and needed to be so, because the whirl of his emotions, superficial appearances to the contrary, was more strenuous. But the point is that each elected at the beginning of his career a sort of rough and ready creed, and continued to the end to revolve around it.

A miniature reproduction of this rotatory process was painted by Browning in the case of each of his chief dramatis personae. In the case of Paracelsus, Sordello, Djabal, Luria, and the rest, where the poet's stress (as he phrased it) "lay on the incidents in the development of a soul," what happens is not spiritual development but emotional revolution. Each "soul" revolves, in a continually widening or narrowing orbit, around a certain centre, which is always close to the poet's own creed if not identical with it. This phenomenon is most striking in Browning's aged persons. If they always evince the fire of youth which their creator never lost, they do not evince the wisdom of eld which he never gained. The much-praised Pope in *The Ring and the Book* must be pronounced, if attentively studied, a notable failure. He was designed by Browning to embody the wisdom not only of old age but of accumulated centuries. But in character he is really no older than the young graybeards who arouse our affectionate enthusiasm in *A Grammarian's Funeral*, *Rabbi Ben Ezra*, and the Epilogue to *Asolando*. The momentous decision made by the Pope regarding the tragedy of Pompilia, would have been the same if he had been twenty-six years old instead of eighty-six, and if he had never read a line of the old records he holds in his hands. His extensive analysis of the case before him is supererogatory, for in the event his judgement proves to be simply the crest of a strong wave of sympathetic emotion. That which is most vital in the Pope is Whitmanian. His creed is what Browning's had been from youth to age.

Whitman's creed was Emerson passed through the genial materialism of mid-century America. Browning's creed was Shelley passed through the popular "enlightened" Protestantism of mid-century England. Thus, though keenly conscious of originality, and of *not* uttering "the word en-masse," Browning was similar to Whitman in vulgarizing the thought of his immediate predecessor. The characteristic thought of the English Romantic movement was in its highest creative phase from Wordsworth to Emerson: Emerson's work was the noble culmination of it. Carlyle, Tennyson, Arnold, and certain others, though marked in varying degrees by the Romantic outlook, were really engaged in a reaction from it. They felt its inadequacy to meet the growing complexity of life under democratic, scientific, and industrial conditions. They saw the need of qualifying it in the light of wisdom and human history, and they called for certain restrictions upon the sway of surging desires and aspirations. Quite the reverse was the trend of Browning and Whitman. They, too, felt the growing complexity of the time; but they wished to simplify it by inundating it with a still heavier stream of individualistic emotionalism. They called for a more headlong trust in natural feelings, and a completer aversion from reflection and Tradition.

Their message in itself was a popular one—it always has been! But ironically enough (and providentially enough) it rendered its two bearers incapable of delivering it in popular form. Their zest for "life immediate" led them to improvise modes of utterance which could not have immediate appeal. Their procedure was factitiously unfactitious. Their effort for naturalness was itself unnatural: they tried too hard to let themselves go. As their inner life was a spirited flow of soliloquy, their need, as artists, was to discern its natural courses and to develop its natural banks. Instead, they just kept damming and undamming it, as boys do a stream, to make it go like anything. Often, at the fortunate moment between stagnation and muddy onrush, they won the strong, clean curve of great poetry.

They had in common a distinguished gift for the dramatic presentation of lyric moments. In such fine pieces as *I Saw in Louisiana a Live-Oak Growing* and *Oh, to Be in England Now That April's There*, our two poets are at their best and they are close together. The pity of it is that their special gift, owing to their aversion from critical reflection, remained in Whitman very rudimentary, and in Browning highly unstable. Browning, of course, succeeded in creating quite a number of short monodramatic pieces that are close to perfection, and that read like developed nodes of the Whitmanian soliloquy. Whitman should have worked to develop the dramatic concentrations that appeared, continually and fleetingly, in the stream of his impressions. Browning, on the other hand, should have learnt to stem the current of his dramatic zest, or pseudo-dramatic zest, when it began to carry him onto shoals—when it lured him to assume viewpoints, and to attempt analyses, of which he was not poetically capable. And Elizabeth Barrett's intuition was a true one, notwithstanding the Browningite's iterated indignation at her meddling, when she wrote to him in 1846: "*Now* let us have your own voice speaking of yourself."

Browning could vividly reproduce temperament, and the conquest of a weaker feeling by a stronger one. But he could not veraciously represent character, insofar as character means the bringing of temperament under any rational and ethical control. At its worst his poetry is devoted to the idea, as in *By the Fireside* and *The Statue and the Bust*, that the effects of character can be attained through sheer quantity of emotion. Continually—as in the case of Festus, Sebald, Jules, Mildred, Tresham, Djabal, Aniel, Luria, Norbert and his Queen—he dashes streaks of character upon patches of temperament in such a crisscross fashion that the result resembles a Cubist painting. The contradiction becomes glaring in proportion as the poet insists that the personage in question should be regarded as a normal human being. For example, Festus in *Paracelsus*! This charming and enlightened pastor, a lifelong devotee of moderation, is suddenly made to submerge his whole habit of thought in order to countenance the transcendent balderdash of Browning's hero, Paracelsus himself. This was when the poet had only recently attained his majority; but the fault was a recurrent incident in "the development of his soul." Twenty years later he sketched essentially the same situation in the case of Norbert in the dramatic poem *In a Balcony*. The laborious and successful statesman, represented as being much in love but not blinded by love, suddenly drops his practised insight to acquiesce in the absurd policy of his mistress, Constance, whose twisted emotionalism the poet is mainly interested in following out and analyzing.

Browning was dramatically veracious when, avoiding character in the stricter sense of the word, he succeeded in concentrating his art upon simplex instances of temperament. Accordingly, animate nature, together with childhood and other states "close to nature," offered him a rich field, which he might well have cultivated more fully. He had a larger share than Whitman of the Whitmanian dramatic sympathy with animals, and with natural objects fancifully conceived as animate. Lizards and plants are often his most effective dramatis personae; and such superb creatures as his Lion in *The Glove*—above all, his Caliban—suggest that a long visit to the tropics would have been more fruitful for him, poetically, than his extended brooding upon the old volume which served as a source for *The Ring and the Book*. In the human realm, Browning could give a fine enough etching of a temperament obtrusively different from his own,—Andrea del Sarto, the Duke in *My Last Duchess*, the Bishop in *St. Praxed's Church*. But he was most successful with personages warmly resembling himself, such as Pippa, The Grammarian, Karshish, the numerous "speakers" of semi-dramatic lyrics, the heroine of *The Flight of the Duchess*, and above all the incomparable Fra Lippo. Here he simply projected traits of his own emotional life into circumstances remote from normality, and created dramatic illusions that richly refresh us when we wish to withdraw from the tests of society and character. And it is here that Browning's art appears most clearly as simply a heightened mode of the Whitmanian soliloquy.

But it is too bad that subsequent poets, unable to reproduce the superb temperamental quality of Browning and Whitman, should continue to reproduce their vast lack of understanding. "I find earlier days are gone by, there is but one way for me," said Keats, and Poetry today for the sake of her very life-blood should say the words after him: "I know nothing, I have read nothing, and I mean to follow Solomon's directions, Get learning, get understanding."

VII

SPECTRAL ETCHING BY THOMAS HARDY

HARDY'S poetry has the careful articulation of the skeleton in a modern surgical laboratory. But also it has all the atmosphere of the skeleton in old ghostly legends: the sudden visitations, the faint shine and quaver, the lank pointings, the leisurely dissolving in gloom, the telltale streaks of gray on the dark earth and sky, the posturing branches, the summoning voices in the wind. All these are in the weft of his verse. A quizzical reader could assemble therefrom quite an array of theatrical apparitions. But at centre his work is far from theatrical. It moves with a large sincerity and simplicity. Its ghostly nimbus is a natural emanation:

> I looked up from my writing,
>   And gave a start to see,
> As if rapt in my enditing,
>   The moon's full gaze on me.

> Her meditative misty head
>   Was spectral in its air,
> And I involuntarily said,
>   "What are you doing there?"

Just as inevitable is the opposite mood, the impulse to lay bare the bony tangents of Nature with a certain harsh vigour of gesture:

> At the shiver of morning, a little before the false dawn,
>   The moon was at the window-square,
> Deedily brooding in deformed decay—
>   The curve hewn off her cheek as by an adze;
> At the shiver of morning a little before the false dawn
>   So the moon looked in there.[1]

The above passages, be it noted, are vitally related to each other in spirit. They have the same spectral moon, though in almost opposite phases: "her meditative misty head," and then "the curve hewn off her cheek as by an adze." Between these two phases Hardy's

---

[1] The third line is a too conscious premonition of the melodramatic episode that ensues in this poem, *Honeymoon Time at an Inn.*

style swings in a wonderfully complete orbit. It is marvellous etching. Often, to be sure, the curves and angles are too effortful, or the
main design is too patent. In this case there is danger of a fanciful
"window-square picture,"—a flat, arranged scene such as an aesthetic
member of a parlour company might call attention to, during a pause
in the conversation at tea: "Just see what that window is framing,
see how the morbid line of that hill" . . . and so on. But the lover
of Hardy's art looks further and senses something that cannot be
babbled about, some detail in third (or fourth) dimension, some
incalculable glimmer. A kind of weird illumination, all his own, is
never far away from his lines. It may sweep the scene at any moment, like a quiet glare of lightning, or a sunset dropped out from
clouds behind a rocky hill, or a moon suddenly growing stronger in
the mist. In brief, Hardy's poetic distinction is in the blending of
two qualities that can easily be contraries: hard etching and spectral
atmosphere.

Ghostliness is not an unnatural effect, to be sure, of ardent
dissection—a fact that has appeared very strikingly in the age in
which we live. Life refuses to be sheer bones, in spite of all our
efforts. We scrape it down, enthusiastically, to a ribby framework,
and then suddenly it takes on a curious glow; it moves off a little
and shimmers beyond our finger-tips; it has a minatory phosphores-
cence. Here is a spectre that can be conjured down only by firm
advances of the religious spirit or the comic spirit, both of which
are now in a condition of confused and animated stationariness. It
cannot be annihilated by further attacks of the scalpel: it merely
fluctuates and subdivides. Little ghosts, therefore, are all about the
edges of our scientificized age, like figures on the mist. We often
regard them in pleasant vein. We sweep an electric light along
them pooh-poohingly; without tracing their intimate relation to the
dark lantern of spiritual superstition that our age bears, as unwittingly as any age ever bore it, fixed upon its breast. This old whale-
oil utensil has nowadays a new-fashioned hood of Naturalism that
matches in hue the plain modern waistcoat. So the ancient lamp is
disguised, and can be easily overlooked; while at the same time,
owing to the sudden development of material science, we have a
pervasive awareness of advanced illumination. Hence our lights are
remarkably unfocused and confused. Such is the condition of our
most characteristic art. It tries to be very forceful, and succeeds in

being very forced. It has a delusive consciousness of "realism," of vitality, that is perhaps unparalleled in the history of the human imagination. Writers fancy themselves working near the centre of Life when really they are spinning fringes. They wish to *see* life as seen by recent science, and to *feel* it as felt by prehistoric man. They seem to themselves to be working with a high-power searchlight overhead, and a primitive fire of passion in their breasts. In reality, they are working with an electric flash-light in hand, and an old oil-burning lantern at bosom.

But this duple lighting has a right employment. It indicates a quaint arrangement of smoky browns in a fitful white ray—the effect being quite original in the history of literary art: a sort of drab ironic spiritualism. This is the quality of Hardy's verse, and of much of the finest writing of the present day. Certain younger contemporaries of Hardy whom I have in mind, are more sophisti-cated than he in the use of flickering rays and drab tintings. They have gone beyond him in play of esprit; their verse is quicker, their prose style is more subtle. The blade of their irony is more slender and flexible. Their mood, not capable of any rich gravity or gaiety, ambulates entertainingly the middle ground between grave and gay; companioned often by tenuous apparitions of the Subconscious. These apparitions are the lighter and subdivided shades, so to speak, of Hardy's sombre spectrality. His "philosophy" of life, so fixed in its pessimism, is mainly passé for his successors; not because they have found a firmer one, but because they have found *his* too heavy. They gambol away from the insistent pressure of his "Immanent Will."

Consider this "Will," this anomalous Being that stretches cadaver-ously along the background of Hardy's total work in prose and verse. He has attached names to It, often too awkwardly,—the names of God, Earth, Nature, First Cause, Immanent Will. Thus he is quite responsible for the tendency of his critics to abstract It from his fancy, weighing his "philosophy" and his "art" in different hands. In reality this Being is a *nameless* figment of his imagination, fol-lowed from youth to old age. It lends an extraordinary unity to his scene. The Thing looks inert, yet It is instinct with innumerable movements. Limbs of It grow through his stories; fibres of It twist in his rhythms, putting out sudden wry tendrils of phrase. His im-ages "retract" (his own word), leering back upon It in recognition of kinship. His best poems are sturdy shoots of It; assiduously carved, but kept in position as they grew, like a row of tree-trunks, on a moor, made into wonderful totems. Closely inspected they astonish one with their detailed harmony of design, their blending of quaint natural contours into human figurations. Looked back at from a distance, as one goes on down the road, they appear in the shifting light to quiver between animate and inanimate. They might be shafts of rock arranged there by early men for some doubtful purpose; they may wear for a moment a Druidic air. But at last they are vertebrae of the landscape—and of Being.

This Being has the mien of inevitability. For It is nothing less than the wraith of the poetic idealism of the nineteenth century. An era that opens on young Wordsworth and Shelley closes, inevitably, on Thomas Hardy. The sequel of that first fine rapture, and the reaction from it, are blended in him. His poetry means that the Romantic sphere of imaginative thought has made a complete revolution. Hardy is Shelley reversed.

He retains the Shelleyan monism in all its naïveté. Life has not for him the vital doubleness of movement that it has for a spiritual realist,—the emotional surge from below, the arduous shaping from above. Life is for him, as for Shelley, a single network of emotion, "through all the web of being blindly wove." But the glow has now faded from it: the weaving is precise and listless, the darker threads of the pattern stand out. The Shelleyan hope, however, still runs through it, a strangely luminous thread against the gloom. It shines a moment and disappears and recurs, again and again, from Hardy's earliest to his latest verse. In a recently published poem, *The Aërolite*, we find him dreaming of

> some far globe where no distress
> . Had means to mar supreme delight;
> But only things abode that made
> The power to feel a gift uncloyed
> Of gladsome glow,
> And life unendingly displayed
> Emotions loved, desired, enjoyed. . . .

That "far globe" is the Shelleyan planet, the "something afar from the field of our sorrow." [2] Hardy's paradisaic tendency derives par-

[2] The author goes on to fancy that a "germ of consciousness" somehow escaped from that radiant world and "fell wanderingly upon our sphere," making us aware of our misery. "Maybe now," he ponders, "normal una-

ticularly from the kind of romanticism that found its extreme expression in Shelley: the yearning for a comfortable harmony, social and spiritual, which wears the guise of human happiness but in which the essential conditions of human happiness are slurred or submerged. This duplicity is the thing, no doubt, that Francis Thompson felt to be "poisonous" in Shelley. It is indeed poisonous for Poetry, especially when it recurs, disguised, in a "realistic movement" that proposes, in reaction from romanticism, to face the plain facts of life. It inoculates Poetry *against* the chief facts of life.[3] It poisons the truth of poetry by sicklying-o'er the vital doubleness of life with a pale emotional duplicity. It fosters what may be called the Shelleyan apathetic enrapture,—the morbid zest for oblivion, the shrinking from deep and vital contradictions.

What hope Hardy has, then, is the Shelleyan hope. But as a whole his poetry is elegiac, and finely elegiac, of the ecstatic song of the early nineteenth century. He muses upon that song in the suggestive neighbourhood of Leghorn, Italy:

wareness waits rebirth"; the "exotic germ" of painful awareness may perhaps be ousted from our nature. But at the same time he cannot help cherishing that rare germ as the seed of a new sympathy which may possibly grow, and renovate human life. This paradox goes down, of course, to the paradisaic thirst of the primitive human heart, its longing for the sweet of life without the sour. Paradisaic yearnings had a great revival in the nineteenth century. They escaped from the ruins of religious institutions. They were freed from the restraints of old moral systems. They were fostered by the humanitarian scientific-industrial mind. They flourished in opposition to obvious materialism. And William Morris, collecting many of them into his *Earthly Paradise* in a fin-de-siècle mood, was a natural contemporary of Thomas Hardy.

[3] Hardy was of course unconscious of this aspect of his work. Indeed he liked to emphasize the lack of "tendency" in his poetry. "The road to a true philosophy of life," he said in his preface to *Poems of the Past and the Present*, 1901, "seems to lie in humbly recording diverse readings of its phenomena as they are forced upon us by chance and change." To be sure, in the preface of *The Dynasts*, 1903, he was conscious of embodying in this poem "The Monistic theory of the Universe" which has such "wide prevalence in this twentieth century." But he seemed unaware that such prevalence is due to the intricate growth of the thing in the imaginative literature of the past hundred years. Certainly he was unaware of how this theoretic Monism leads *away* from "a true philosophy of life" by restricting and prejudicing one's readings of life's phenomena.

Somewhere afield here something lies
In Earth's oblivious eyeless trust
That moved a poet to prophecies—
A pinch of unseen, unguarded dust:

The dust of the lark that Shelley heard,
And made immortal through times to be;
Though it only lived like another bird,
And knew not its immortality:

Lived its meek life; then, one day fell—
A little ball of feather and bone;
And how it perished, when piped farewell,
And where it wastes, are alike unknown:

Maybe it rests in the loam I view,
Maybe it throbs in a myrtle's green,
Maybe it sleeps in the coming hue
Of a grape on the slopes of yon inland scene. . . .

From Hardy's point of view, the poetry of a hundred years ago, like every other lofty human effort, is just a lovely apparition unaccountably shaped for a moment from the "eyeless" life of Earth. It reduces to a "tiny pinch of priceless dust," gleaming, for memory, among the dark folds of Being. And these folds are the darker for it. Such precious ore of human memory throws into dreary relief the blind veins of the universal landscape. For the universe, outside of man, has neither hope nor memory; and human history has only a phantasmal meaning. This recalls the blank horror that sometimes confronted Shelley. In the relapses of his individualistic faith, he could not stay himself upon the profound meaning that there is in the painful story of human institutions and conventions: he could find there only a "chasm sightless and drear." In this respect, also, Hardy is the sequel of Shelley. But he has none of Shelley's wailing lyric ardency. He scans the landscape with eyes accustomed to the gloom. Objects come out plainly enough in a sort of ironic twilight; and he watches them with an affectionate leer:

When I look forth at dawning, pool,
　　Field, flock, and lonely tree,
　　All seem to gaze at me
Like chastened children sitting silent in a school;

Their faces dulled, constrained, and worn,
　　As though the master's ways
　　Through the long teaching days
Had cowed them till their early zest was overborne.

> Upon them stirs in lippings mere
> (As if once clear in call,
> But now scarce breathed at all) :—
> "We wonder, ever wonder, why we find us here."

This wonder—is it not the very reflux and converse of the so-called Renaissance of Wonder? This dim whispering of "field, flock, and lonely tree" was anticipated by the admonition that the same objects gave to Wordsworth in the full "May-morning" of his joy:

> But there's a tree, of many, one,
> A single field which I have looked upon,
> Both of them speak of something that is gone:
> The pansy at my feet
> Doth the same tale repeat:
> Whither is fled the visionary gleam?
> Where is it now, the glory and the dream?

Thus admonished, Wordsworth grasped for permanent meanings in the wake of this fleeting glory. It appeared to him, in after-reflection, an "intimation of immortality"; and here surely he took hold of a deep human instinct. But the high tide of his wonder swept him on. His imagination was hard to start—"moveth altogether if it move at all." But once under way, it was liable to be carried by its own stiff momentum onto reefs of relentless absurdity. Accordingly, "the visionary gleam" came to appear to him, not just a shifty ray from our *instinct* for eternity, but "a master-light of all our seeing."[4] He blurred, unpoetically, the nature of ethical insight, the true "master-light of all our seeing." He viewed it, in blind contradiction of human experience, as the natural and necessary sequel of a gleaming wonder. He submerged it in the pour of an emotionalized Nature:

> 'Tis Nature teaching what she never knew:
> The beautiful is good, the good is true.[5]

Well, in Hardy's poetry Nature confesses her total ignorance on this score. But Nature, at least as she appears in human interpretations, is a born extremist; and having once told more than she knew, she now tells less. Because "Natural Objects" would descant to Wordsworth with the air of a moral school-mistress, they demean themselves to Hardy "like chastened children sitting silent in a school." And the voiceless questions on their lips are these:

[4] *Ode on Intimations of Immortality*, line 152.
[5] From Hartley Coleridge's sonnet on Wordsworth.

> Has some Vast Imbecility,
>   Mighty to build and blend,
>   But impotent to tend,
> Framed us in jest, and left us now to hazardry?
>
> Or come we of an Automaton
>   Unconscious of our pains?
>   Or are we live remains
> Of Godhead dying downwards, brain and eye now gone?
>
> Or is it that some high Plan betides,
>   As yet not understood,
>   Of Evil stormed by Good,
> We the Forlorn Hope over which Achievement strides?
>
> Thus things around. No answerer I . . .
>   Meanwhile the winds, and rains,
>   And Earth's old glooms and pains
> Are still the same, and Death and glad Life neighbour nigh.

The movement of these verses is perfect for what they say, and very characteristic. Hardy had a rare love of formal perfection at the very outset of his career. And he could see more clearly than his chief contemporaries, from Meredith to Masefield, just what conditions the artist has to face when he finds himself in the fag end of an extraordinary creative era. He articulated the poetic remains, so to speak, of the nineteenth century. He realized what was left to be done, and what could be done best by him, in poetic method. In his earliest verse we find him reaching away from the fading lyric vein of his century; and perhaps the following quatrain from a love-sonnet dated 1866 is significant:

> Though I waste watches framing words to fetter
> Some unknown spirit to mine in clasp and kiss,
> Out of the night there looms a sense 'twere better
> To fail obtaining whom one fails to miss.

To be sure, there are a good many passages of lovely English song scattered through his volumes. They have the limpidity and unexpectedness of a spring coming out from among bare rocks. But on the whole his style rejects the flow of the waters and follows the rugged lines of the rocks. He, as well as Walt Whitman, must be considered a founder of the irregular and imagistic kind of verse which is nowadays such a lively cult. But he is free from a certain glaring unveracity that tainted Whitman's art and that thrives today, notably in the verse printed in certain American periodicals. I mean the attempt to convey a fluid mood in a coagulated style—to thicken a shallow stream of lyric inspiration with ragged chunks of rhythm and image. The practitioners are more tuneful in *soul* than they are willing to admit in their *style*, and the result is a ridiculous frustration. Hardy admits all the tunefulness he has; but this is very little. His best verse does not so much sing its way, as carve its way, into the reader. Its thwart and angular movement corresponds exactly to the sardonic elegy of the author's mood. His art is identical with his pessimism.

To a conventional reader saturated with the dominant tunes of nineteenth-century poetry, Hardy's verse may well seem frustrate— so precisely does it convey a mood of frustration. It is indeed the fine art of frustration. It represents the untuning of the nineteenth-century universe. This is what one feels so keenly in *The Darkling Thrush*, one of the great lyrics in our language. Assigned by the author to a chill dismal evening of December, 1900, it is really an elegy for the closing century:

> The land's sharp features seemed to be
> The Century's corpse outleant . . .
>
> The tangled bine-stems scored the sky
> Like strings from broken lyres. . . .

Many lyres had to be broken before Poetry would thus turn her hand to the burin. And the unexpected songster of the scene, the thrush himself, is outlined against the cloudy twilight like a ghost of the melodious birds of Wordsworth's time:

> An aged thrush, frail, gaunt, and small,
> In blast-beruffled plume,
> Had chosen thus to fling his soul
> Upon the growing gloom.

Such laconic tenderness is perhaps the finest tone that is heard in Hardy's whole work. It comes when his irony is infused with a large pity that quivers along his sharp lines without blurring them. But his art is always in danger when his pity takes the lead entirely. For instance, while out walking on another gloomy evening, the poet is overcome with a sense of all the miseries of life, in man and nature:

> The wind blew words along the skies,
> And these it blew to me
> Through the wide dusk: "Lift up your eyes,

> Behold this troubled tree,
> Complaining as it sways and plies;
> It is a limb of thee."

He proceeds to reflect upon the troublous life of men and animals, foreign and domestic, all of whom are "stuff of thy own frame"; and then concludes as follows:

> I moved on in a surging awe
> Of inarticulateness
> At the pathetic Me I saw
> In all his huge distress,
> Making self-slaughter of the law
> To kill, break, or suppress.

Here is a *real* "pathetic fallacy": the poet extends his pity to Necessity itself. This confusion is unfortunately at the very centre of his vision; and it excludes that Greek sense of Fate which rash admirers have discovered in his writings. The Thing that presides there, so impressively, is really not Fate, but Fate's ghost. It is a remarkably lifelike ghost because of Hardy's classic constructive power. His devotion to simple, inclusive, and sombre design brings him close to the notion of Fate. But what his architectural sense demands, his humanitarianism denies. Viewing the universe as a single Being, he sympathizes with it too much to believe it capable of a really sinister policy. Inexorable deities are excluded. Often, to be sure, Hardy takes on the peculiar attitude of blaming God for human troubles while denying God's existence. But generally he likes to imagine for deity a sort of lackadaisical existence which has none of the potency of Fate, and which deserves far more pity than blame—he pities God's incapacity for pity. What a falling-off from Milton's deity who asserted, all too confidently, that "what I will is Fate." Pride goes before a fall. Hardy's god is the last attenuation, in English poetry, of the Miltonic Jehovah—

> If thou beest he—but Oh, how fallen! how changed
> From him who in the happy realms of light,
> Clothed with transcendent brightness, didst outshine
> Myriads, though bright. . . .

But I hastily repent of turning these verses so frivolously. Of course, the depth of pity and the height of awe that can be found in such a passage from Milton are impossible in Hardy's work. His gravest feeling in regard to Life is what he finely calls "a surging awe of inarticulateness"—a mixture of pity and awe in which neither emotion can have its full value. When his sympathy *overflows* upon the tragedy of life, as in *The Dynasts*, it suffers from lack of contrast and becomes thinly monotonous. It is best when strictly confined by his irony. In this case his verse is distinguished for its poise of bleak austerity and fine tenderness. It is like a gaunt and dark landscape with notes of a human voice coming over it from a distance.

IN THE DYNASTS

While the novels of Thomas Hardy have been widely admired in the United States, his poetry has been neglected. When it appeared, it was not much followed in our reviews; and it has now no public honour. In his own country it stands very high. Not long ago when Hardy the poet was mentioned in a chattery assembly of literati near London, I was struck by the hush that fell. "He towers above us all," said a young poet-critic in sententious whisper. This was testimony to the contemporaneity, as well as the excellence, of Hardy's poetic art.

His contemporaneity is significant. He may properly be regarded as the founder of the "Dark Realism," so to call it, of English and American literature at the present time. He opened that vein in his verse of the later 1860's—opened it ominously in the midst of the popular silken vistas of Tennyson. But he soon knew that the public was not yet ready for a full sight of it. The gloomy fissure needed camouflage; as the upturned earth of a new-made grave is adorned, for the obsequies, with cut flowers and branches of evergreen. Therefore he shifted from verse to prose fiction, which gave him more room for rural and sylvan circumstance. *Under the Greenwood Tree* was idyllic enough. In subsequent novels the tone darkened more and more, up to *Tess of the D'Urbervilles* and *Jude the Obscure*. But always the scenic outlines were so beautifully made that casual readers could take them for natural growths, instead of cut foliage that the author was carefully arranging around the brims of his excavations. His own interest was mainly in the morbid subsoil. And his way of penetrating to it was not properly prose-thinking but poetic divination; like that of Milton's Satan, ill content with "plant, fruit, flower ambrosial" of the upper world:

Whose eye so superficially surveys
These things as not to mind from whence they grow
Deep under ground: materials dark and crude,
Of spiritous and fiery spume, till, touched
With Heaven's ray, and tempered, they shoot forth
So beauteous, opening to the amber light?
These in their dark nativity the Deep
Shall yield us, pregnant with infernal flame. . . .

In short, Hardy's novels are too scenic and factitious. In time they
will be everywhere overshadowed, in accordance with his own declared preference, by his poems. In the 1890's, when a limited English audience was ready for his poetry, he returned with zest to his
original vein. He worked it vigorously during the past thirty years,
in one volume of verse after another, tossing up fresh ore for the
fires of our New Poetry. Streaks of his sombre metal are everywhere
in contemporary verse.

No wonder that Hardy the poet is fully honoured in England.
But why is he not acclaimed in America too? Why do not our "dark
realists" proclaim a vital kinship of spirit with him? Perhaps because
their pessimism does not aim down, like his, toward the very bones
of life. They cultivate the earthy ugliness of the surface, merely.
For after all they belong to the country of Emerson and Whitman; the
American optimism which they officially repudiate is in their very
blood. They try conscientiously to be mastered with gloom. But they
have a guilty, more or less subconscious, conviction that centrally
"all's right with the world." Which reminds us, by the way, that
Browning, the obverse of Hardy, won popularity in America more
readily than in England. His optimism found quick affinity here.
Whereas Hardy, in declining an invitation to the United States some
time ago, felt the matter thus:

My ardours for emprize nigh lost
Since Life has bared its bones to me,
I shrink to seek a modern coast
Whose riper times have yet to be;
Where the new regions claim them free
From that long drip of human tears
Which peoples old in tragedy
Have left upon the centuried years.

In my fancy, alas, the second and sixth lines of this stanza insist
on falling together with an effect half ludicrous, half ghostly. I see

as in a moving-picture a weeping procession of human figures coming
down through the centuries, dropping their tears continuously upon
Europe, until, by long erosion, the old continent's bones are laid
bare—for the sake of Thomas Hardy. Perhaps this fancy is too
wilful, irreverent, silly, but it is due, I must insist, to a long preoccupation with Hardy's works. Consider, particularly, the curious
"anatomy of the Immanent Will" in the fore-scene of *The Dynasts*.
Here the life of Europe is represented as a vast "emaciated figure";
prone and fixed, with the Alps for backbone and Spain for skull, but
animated throughout with innumerable writhing motions. Presently
the twitching ganglia are seen as swarms of human creatures. They
detach into mobs and armies, marching and counter-marching. They
fight and gesticulate swiftly, and writhe, and die. Sudden "close-ups"
are given of the leading actors. The episodes flicker from the scene
too quickly to be felt too deeply. And frequently one seems to hear,
at the rear, the drone of the movie-machine . . .

> Life's but a walking shadow, a *queer* player
> That struts and frets his *moment on the screen*
> And then is *seen* no more.

My feeling is that Hardy's pessimism even in his poetry should
not be taken too seriously. How seriously he took it himself, at
bottom, may remain an open question. But I have talked with quite
a few cultivated Americans who take it, I believe, more seriously
than he did. They overestimate his specific gravity. They miss the
full force of his strain of ironic levity. He lived among peoples not
only "old in tragedy" but old in comedy, peoples who have learned
to pass rather readily into that purely artistic mood in which "all
the world's a stage and all the men and women merely players." In
America we lack that flexibility; our puritanic business sense has
always urged us to organize our emotions, gloomy or glad, into rigid
creeds. America is the land of cults. But, by way of reaction, she
has now become also the land of the moving-picture. This new form
of art teaches the mazing mobility of all things visible, and, by
implication, the transitoriness of cults and creeds and doctrinaires.
All the world's a *film-story*! Well, such it is also for Thomas Hardy,
more or less; and from this point of view we Americans can best
come to appreciate his poetic art. His novels, slow and deliberate
in structure, cannot well convey the essential mobility, the impres-
sionism, of his outlook. But his verse, culminating in his masterpiece,

The Dynasts, shows human life as a sheer moving-picture—episodic, grotesque, pathetic, flittering, ghostly.

Just here I recall that a serious American student of poetry, with whom I was discussing this matter, asserted: "Hardy's pessimism is modern, representative, and profound; it cannot be taken so lightly as you assume." I think it can. To be sure, Hardy himself, in a way, was a serious Anglo-Saxon, full of pity for suffering humanity, and religiously anxious to tell the dark philosophic truth about life. But this is not his most veracious and successful tendency as an *artist*. The whole question centres in *The Dynasts*, and the discussion may conveniently be confined almost entirely to this work. I have heard it called a modern epic,—an epic of disillusion superintended by the Greek sense of Fate. I should like to call it, rather, an epic of pity superintended by the picturesque ghost of Fate.

The central paradox of the poem is boldly put before the reader in the opening lines:

> What of the Immanent Will and its designs? . . .
> It works unconsciously, as heretofore,
> Eternal artistries in Circumstance,
> Whose patterns, wrought by rapt aesthetic rote,
> Seem in themselves Its single listless aim,
> And not their consequence.

The pronoun "their" refers apparently to the word "designs"; though even Hardy finds it difficult, now and then, to be perfectly clear in expressing a confused idea. These designless designs recall the "patterns" of the frost upon our window-panes. And indeed, if applied only to the "magic casements" of the House of Life, the idea would be effective; but the author proceeds to apply it to the fundamental structure. Very conscious of reacting from Romantic magic, he is quite unconscious of the extent to which his mind is impregnated with it. Here he frames an epic upon it; and the frame is far too slight. Therefore the poem has a naïve but false grandiloquence of inward mode, like Shelley's *Prometheus Unbound*. In each of these two works the artist sends his eye over human history with a rather magnificent gesture; but he gives us a narrow and distorted vision of the very thing that makes the magnificence of history, namely the will. Shelley, by ethereal magic, sublimates the human will to cloud. Hardy, by reversing the magic, condenses the cloud-stuff and brings it down to a low and sluggish lake in the human landscape. The idea of Love, the great driving-force in Shelley's drama, is confused and vaporous. Hardy's main idea, the Immanent Will, is confused and stagnant. Mainly it is an hypostasis of his own sense of pity for mankind. However, it is made up of various elements: it is indebted to the Christian Jehovah and to the Shadowy Something of peasants, to Greek mythology and to nineteenth-century naturalism. But it is neither as human as a god, nor as surging as desire, nor as austere as fate. Hardy, like Shelley, has no understanding of that sublime kind of austerity which is close to the summit of the human will, and which is necessary for the sustaining of an epic theme.

The *theme* of *The Dynasts* is indeed epical. From beginning to end the poem is concerned with the destructiveness of the dynastic principle in human government, and with the last great attempt of that principle to maintain its commanding position in European affairs. In a marvellous procession of scenes, this thread is carried swiftly and unbrokenly from one part of Europe to another, from one episode to another in the great Napoleonic drama, until the whole is wound-up at Waterloo. Everywhere the dynastic rulers are shown in the act of blindly bringing on their own downfall, with Napoleon, now a dynast himself, acting as their chief scourge and minister. Incessantly we are made to feel that this process of events is determined by a Will which is above the wills of individual men, and is working-out through them Its own great purpose. Such *would* be the main effect of the drama upon the reader, if it were not heavily counterchecked by the author himself. In the choruses, he informs us that the Immanent Will, so far from having a great purpose, either for good or for ill, has no purpose at all; and, in effect, that the Immanent Will is really not a will at all. In certain choral passages[6] the contradiction in the author's thought becomes glaring. The Will is represented as at once purposive and impurposive. And when the poet, struggling in vain for an adequate image, has his "Semi-chorus of Ironic Spirits" chant as follows, to the accompaniment of "aerial music":

> Stand ye apostrophizing That
> Which, working all, works but thereat
> Like some sublime fermenting-vat
> Heaving throughout its vast content
> With strenuously transmutive bent
> Though of its aim unsentient? . . .

[6] Notably in Part First, Act V, scene 4, and Act VI, scene 3.

we know that Apollo is taking ironic vengeance upon him: his muse is dipped in "some sublime fermenting-vat . . . of its aim unsentient." This confusion of aim appears also in the characterization of Napoleon. From certain passages it is clear that the author intends him to be a genius-ridden potentate, tragically serving the transcendent Will. On the whole, however, he appears merely an efficient person—an efficiency expert, even—not tragical, nor epical. In short, *The Dynasts* is a frustrate epic.

"But," some modernist might here exclaim, "why not call it *the epic of frustration*? The very phrase 'sublime fermenting-vat,' though aesthetically open to ridicule, does convey, rather precisely, the general effect which the author aims at. He gives us a sense of all the blind and powerful forces fermenting in the universe and in human history. Milton wrote the epic of ordered creation—and made the universe too tidy altogether. Hardy, by way of variety and adjustment, has written the epic of creative disorder. *The Dynasts* represents a material and spiritual universe which, in its sheer power of destruction, is sublime."

Certainly, Life has a sublimely destructive aspect; but I think that Hardy has no real hold of it. The imagination of the ancient Hindoos had hold of it when they included in their triune deity, on an equal footing with the divinities of creation and preservation, a divine destroyer, Siva. I fancy that this conception, in one form or another, is destined to be adopted in the future by the European mind and heart. The destructive function of Life, which in Christian mythology was relegated mainly to evil or inferior powers, is now being rehabilitated in our imagination through the influence of natural science. This process has affected Hardy's work. But the process is in its early, confused stage, and has not yet produced poetic images that are sufficiently firm and elevated to approach sublimity. In other words the central image of *The Dynasts*—the "Immanent Will," the "sublime fermenting-vat"—is never really sublime. It represents a fermenting-stage of poetic sublimity. It is too late for Jehovah, and too early for Siva.

But although for this reason *The Dynasts* is confused and shallow in its inward form, it is a great human expression. It *hints* at a new epic grandeur that may take shape in our poetry in the future. And it has a wonderful atmosphere of its own. Only a shallow reader, I think, could be oblivious of its magic. Only a wrong-headed reader,

misled by the creaking machinery of the poem and his own precon-
ceptions, could fancy that its magic is entirely mechanical. Its peculiar charm rises from its very conflict of mechanism and impulse,
of conscious and unconscious tendencies in the author. Beneath its
careful surface, there goes on a ferment of obscure human powers.
The poem is like a moving-picture city, constructed with minute
attention to visual effect, in some old volcanic region of whose
nature the producer is imperfectly aware. Strange tremors of Earth
communicate themselves to its transitory walls. Vapours from natural
fissures in the ground pervade the air and affect the gestures of the
well-drilled actors. Other writers of our age have given themselves
zestfully to the intoxication of the subconscious, with which they
have a temperamental affinity. Hardy is different: he has the distinction of being a very conscious artist obsessed with the idea of the
unconscious,—of being one of the most superb architects in our
literature, devoted to the subject of Chaos.

He fails to find in the universe the architecture that he has in
himself. Unlike the leading poets of earlier ages, he is never inspired
with the feeling that his constructive power is descending into him
from above. He has no Apollo, no Muse. He is not aware of that
"human Soul of universal earth" which inspired the art of Wordsworth, giving to his "forms and images a breath and everlasting
motion." He offers up no creative prayer to creative Life, like
Milton's

> Instruct me, for Thou know'st; Thou from the first
> Wast present, and with mighty wings outspread
> Dove-like sat'st brooding on the vast Abyss
> And mad'st it pregnant: what in me is dark
> Illumine, what is low raise and support. . . .

That great brooding dove of Poetry, mystically bringing order into
Chaos, is an outworn figure of speech for Hardy. In Chaos he hatches
his own eggs. At his worst, he is an architectural aesthete devoid of
afflatus, not really much interested in life, and therefore evincing
a certain crabbed effort of style. But at his best he is poignantly
aware, though not consciously aware, of the contrast between his
own beautiful skill and the meaningless surge of life around him.
The vital turmoil engages his pity; and through his pity it awakens
in him a strange sense of kinship, at once intimate and fearful. He
neither gives himself to the confusion of life, nor turns away from

it. He keeps his eyes upon it, dreamingly. He dreams upon disorder, even while his hand is putting upon paper words of lovely order. Brooding upon an inarticulate chaos, he develops his careful patterns with an almost hypnotic sense of articulation. Thus he writes (if I may turn upon him two fine phrases of his own) with "rapt aesthetic rote" and with a "surging awe of inarticulateness." Such is the rare poetic atmosphere of *The Dynasts*.

This poem is the *epical pageant* of our age—an age of historical pageants and moving-pictures and radio-activity, of multiform small appetites and humanitarian efforts and philosophical confusion, of order in the natural law and disorder in the human law, of satire and imagistic pungency and scenic display. Hardy, like the age, is distinguished for scene and atmosphere, rather than for plot. The plot conceptions in his novels and narrative poems are incessantly mechanical and absurd. The case of Tess of the D'Urbervilles will presently appear to the general reader, I think, far more bathetic than the case of Dickens's Little Nell. The sex-theme in Hardy's writings is striking in quantity, rarely in quality. It has the smother of wet leaves burning in November; there is a vast deal of troublous copulation, and very little flame of real passion, good or bad. The kind of dilemma with which he likes to confront his silly lovers, as for instance in *A Conversation at Dawn*, would seem melodramatic to the point of insincerity if we did not remember that he is always liable to be blinded by pity, and that his irony and humour are strictly limited in scope by his deficiency of high comic spirit. But the root difficulty is that in his fiction Hardy is making plots in a plotless universe. He does in his workshop that which he believes Life cannot do in the world,—namely, build a story. He wins for his stories some incidental vitality, however, when he makes use of folk-lore, local episodes, and historical material. He wins distinction when, as in *The Woodlanders*, he throws the emphasis upon scene and atmosphere. Both these conditions are fulfilled in *The Dynasts*: it has vivid local incidents and strange atmosphere. The folk and their rulers pass and repass before us in 130 scenes each of which is so clearly drawn as to fascinate the eye, and so swift and insulated as to give us just that sense of unreality which is in the author's heart. The whole is the vivid and naïve architecture of a dream—or of a moving-picture. For indeed this poem is the literary sublimation of the art of the moving-picture.

There is something very ghostly, as I have said above, in a moving-picture: in the flickering speed, the unnatural silence of the actors, the immense yet transient emphasis upon gesture. The effect would be still more ghostly if the film, instead of stopping with the triumphant marriage of the heroine, would spin along through the years of maturity, old age, and decay. And suppose the story could be continued, by a magic camera, through death and dissolution, and could follow the human personality until it became a memory in the mind of its friends,—a memory intermittently vivid, but gradually dwindling to nothingness. Such is the way Hardy views his dramatis personae. Half of them are ghosts. The other half are evolving in that direction: each has an embryonic spectrality:

> A dream of mine flew over the mead
>   To the halls where my old Love reigns;
> And it drew me on to follow its lead;
>   And I stood at her window-panes;
> And I saw but a thing of flesh and bone
>   Speeding on to its cleft in the clay;
> And my dream was scared, and expired on a moan,
>   And I whitely hastened away.

Here the reel is exceptionally swift. At the other extreme of his art, the poet moves slowly through memory in a way that recalls Longfellow:

> When the wasting embers redden the chimney-breast,
> And Life's bare pathway looms like a desert track to me,
> And from hall and parlour the living have gone to their rest,
> My perished people who housed them here come back to me.

But in Longfellow this yearning for the dead was joined with a certain inimitable gentility. In Hardy, it is joined with a certain brooding, bourgeois verve.

His personages are dramatically active; but he broods upon them as though they were shadows thrown on the stage by the scene-set. He sees them all united in a world of death and memory. And he *loves* that region of Shades. Death is more alive for him than life. He is an inverted nineteenth-century transcendentalist. He is a disillusioned Anglo-Saxon reaching furtively toward Nirvana. Around our ugly and transient world of industrial Christianity—our world of an urgent but meaningless will (as he regards it)—he feels an invisible world of No-Will which *may* be real and permanent. But his only *intimate* touch with that invisible world is through the

memory of persons whom he has loved, or pitied. Hence the extraordinary verve with which he etches his ghostly persons of the drama.
Hence, too, their ironic subsidence, continually, into a Landscape that
seems the borderland between Being and No-Being:

> There are some heights in Wessex, shaped as if by a kindly hand
> For thinking, dreaming, dying on; and at crises when I stand,
> Say, on Ingpen Beacon eastward, or on Wylls-Neck westwardly,
> I seem where I was before my birth, and after death may be.

His Wessex may be found anywhere, given the slightest trick of
similarity, or fancied similarity, in the landscape. One summer
afternoon I was rereading his poetry on the porch of an old farmhouse in a remote part of the island of Martha's Vineyard. A south
wind was thudding the sea against the clay cliffs. Gusts of it came
round the house and swirled the grass that almost hid the decayed
headstone of a grave, in the dooryard—the grave of a young farmer-
sailor who died there of small-pox two centuries ago. Just beyond, in
a moist shrubby dip of the land, some fitful bird-voices were sheltered: the crackling chatter of redwings, the throbbing of the song-
sparrow, and now and then from a dead shrub the firm plaintiveness
of a meadow-lark. A church-spire was a faint needle above the
furthest hill. Everywhere on the treeless slopes were the stone-walls
of deserted fields. I found it hard to keep my eyes from them.
I noticed, curiously, that a louder boom of the surf would draw my
gaze from the poems and set it travelling, not seaward, but along
these old gray walls. Hidden waves of thought seemed running
between my book and them. One wall was close to me, and all its
gaunt architecture was bare in the sunlight: unhewn mortarless
boulders ranging in size from an ox to a man's head, with irregular
gaps between, but firmly poised, and carefully level at the top-line.
What a huge slow labour and balancing nicety of human hands
went into these walls! The watcher wants to push his own hands
along them and take tentative holds of the upper stones, pitting his
fingers in a sort of game against fingers unseen. These walls can
pulse with straining gestures, in the full daylight. But toward
evening I felt that the landscape was quietly laying hold of them.
They became more and more subdued to the contours of the hills.
They looked as though the old glacial thrust and subsidence that
had formed the Island itself, had been iterated in the settlers who
advanced thither and deposited these stones. The walls to eastward

of me became faintly rosy here and there in the slanting sunrays—
and so did certain vast gray boulders that squatted about the fields,
unbudged by human arms. Fingering through Hardy's pages I
glanced over his many verses on sundown:

> The black lean land, of featureless contour,
> Was like a tract in pain. . . .
>
> The day is turning ghost. . . .

The breeze, now stronger, was bringing up the edges of a deep mist;
the bird-calls grew faint; the beat of the sea advanced loudly on the
land. Presently a network of walls that ridged a hill to westward
went black and stark against the sunset. It looked more and more
like the undulate spine of some old sea-creature, with shadowy ribs
reaching down the fields. It had a sort of stationary crawl stemming
the flood of misty light and shade. It was gradually blanked by the
night.

VIII

THE NEIGHBOURLY HUMOUR OF ROBERT FROST

THE NEIGHBOURLINESS

THE very readiness with which critics have responded, since 1914, to the singular charm of Frost's poetry has withheld attention from its representative meaning. He would have been better understood if he had come upon the scene in a period of political and inward quietness, capable of hearkening patiently for the deeper undertones of song—or if like others he had been a quick-fledged genius, narrowly explicit in vision, and quivering in every feather to the jerky migrations of our time. As it is, the critics have caught the contemporary aspects of his outlook and the idiosyncrasies of his style. They have emphasized his drab "realism" and free earthy tang, on the one hand, and on the other his New-England idioms and whimsies. But they have largely missed his central mood.[1]

His work is the poetry of true neighbourliness emergent from Romantic humanitarianism. The Romantic ideal of human brotherhood, soon after beginning its voyage in the eighteenth century, had a hard time among the reefs of the French Revolution. But presently (with distinguished assistance from the United States of America) it was lifted on new tides of emotionalism. Its sails bellied with fresh winds of doctrine. Science provided it with steam—and later with high explosives. One fancied that the thing was finally wrecked in the Great War. But splashing publicists by the hundreds, and politicians (especially in America), have collected its scattered planks, and are trying lustily to raft us forward on the same old voyage. This amazing spectacle has now, of course, plenty of disillusioned onlookers. They watch it aloof with cynical amusement—but not from any firm shore. In fact, they themselves are shipwrecked humanitarians treading water. Therefore the rhythm of their laughter is rather forced and awkward.[2] Their minds have not much

---

[1] A good deal of it, however, is given in Gorham B. Munson's *Robert Frost: A Study in Sensibility and Good Sense* (George H. Doran Co., 1927).

[2] Their nature appears extremely in the character of Caligula in Eugene O'Neill's play *Lazarus Laughs* (1927). Caligula is partly a worldly cynic,

elevation above sea-level. Their general visibility is low. They bob up, and subside, in the public attention spasmodically, and do not deflect the direction of the public voyage. The general imagination is still in tow of the illusion—though, since the War, a patched and ghastly illusion—of humanitarian progress.

Poetry cannot go far ahead until the social imagination turns again toward social reality.[3] But poetry herself can take a part in this turning, and hasten her own regeneration. She can clear her own wells. Our poets should no longer allow the worn-out imaginings of the past hundred years to blur for them the supreme poetic vision of the seventeenth century. Whitman chanted at the close of our Civil War: "Be not disheartened, affection shall solve the problems of freedom yet." Milton wrote at the close of the English Civil War: "Instead of fretting with vexation, or thinking that you can lay the blame on anyone but yourselves, know that to be free is the same thing as to be pious, to be wise, to be temperate and just, to be frugal and abstinent, and lastly, to be magnanimous and brave." The first passage is the theme of nineteenth-century poetry: its social unreality is now glaring; it is a worn-out imagining. The second passage speaks to us, in our post-War era, like the voice of destiny close to our ear. Moreover, it is the theme of the greatest single poem in our language, *Paradise Lost*.

If we believe that the poetic imagination has a kind of normal orbit in history and that now, after a period of hectic acceleration, it has reached a point just opposite to where it was three centuries ago; and if we hope that it shall not long be caught in its present state of trivial stationary whirling: we must hope that it will soon swing decisively in the Miltonic direction. It must get rid of the dragging humanitarian superstition: the belief that human solidarity can be founded on emotional sympathy and material cooperation; that self-interest, with the aid of scientific magic, can be worked up into smooth mortar for Babel. This towering ruinous conceit must be left behind. Poetry must move again toward the social reality that

partly a humanitarian idealist. At the end he is shown in a sort of epileptic confusion between the two rôles. His laughter is a cackling blur.

[3] Hence the signal importance of the Humanism of Irving Babbitt, particularly in his *Democracy and Leadership* (1924), for the future of poetry. This fact, which was not noticed by many of the older "creative" writers, is now coming home to quite a few of the younger ones.

she won in the time of Milton. She can catch in new form his vision of a just and charitable Will, human but supernaturally given, alone able to subdue our Satanic selfishness and to build for us some greatness of society. This is the way ahead for poetry; but "long is the way and hard." It demands a deep-going humility that is not yet active in our literature; for our very disillusion is flown with pride. It demands that the imagination shall bend again to the vital and awful cleavage that gleams through the centre of human nature, like the track of Michael's sword, dividing our "quintessence of dust" from a Life whose ways are not our ways; turning down a good deal of the confused Wordsworthian emotion that "rolls through all things"—the multifarious Whitmanian "affection"—which our poets continue to revere when they revere anything at all, and which they think (when they think at all) may "solve the problems of freedom yet." One would therefore assume that a great movement of poetry, if it is coming, is still quite a way off.

However, there appears here and there in current verse a certain mood that is on the forward way, a mood that constitutes a vital arc in what I have called the normal orbit of poetry. It is a mood devoid of highly wrought imagination. But also it is free from the naturalistic flatulency with which poetry has been diseased for more than a hundred years. It recognizes, without cynicism, and without prophecy, the ingrained selfishness of our nature. It recognizes also what capacity we have for honest labour and kindly good sense. It distrusts the thousand cults which now obsess society and withdraws itself from all the "going ideas." It finds that society today is peculiarly barren of great poetic ideas. But it is not elegiac; it has left behind the long Romantic wail, the melancholy of the poetic soul poured forth from seclusion upon the naughty modern world. It is free also from the Romantic shout, alternating with the wail— I mean, the noisy discovery of unspoiled poetry in the fringes, or hypothetic fringes, of society,—in leaves of grass, animals, Hindoos, toughs, steel-workers, outlying rustics, and so on. Perhaps the Romantic spirit has nearly exhausted, not only itself, but all available industry and geography. Meanwhile the realistic mood that I am describing is local without being localistic. It takes firm hold of the social reality that the poet has naturally found in his own neighbourhood. The best name for it, I think, is the neighbourly mood. It seems from every consideration to be the surest and most original mood of poetry that could develop under the conditions of our time. Its chief representative is Robert Frost.

He has now a large number of readers. The great majority of them, I fancy, belong to a class that may be called speechless readers. In regard to the speech-making at a recent educational congress, a wit remarked: "A good many sensible persons are here, and silent." No doubt the same remark applies to the vociferant congress of picayune cults that the newspapers term "our age." A good many sensible persons are present who are saying nothing. They are not bowing the knee to Baalim, though they find no words to utter on behalf of the Lord of Hosts. They feel they had "better leave God out of it" (to adapt a verse of Frost's)—that is, out of the talking. They feel that the loaf of daily bread that He dropped into the public yard, at the beginning of modern democracy, has now been pecked into bits too small and dirty for clucking over. But they believe that grains of fresh old truth can be uncovered by those who scratch around quietly in their native vicinity. They are weary of a crowing freedom. They wish the freedom of their own neighbourhood.

It would be incongruous to say that Frost "gives voice" to this freedom. He vibrates to it so congruously that he has, without any vocal effort, its very tone. He shows no surprise, except what belongs in the very nature of poetry. In his work poetry is freed from the overstrained wonder of a hundred years. Not long ago the newspapers were loud with the discovery in Nebraska of the tooth of an early man, which presently turned out to be the tooth of an early pig. Current literary "realists" (to whom the reviewers have badly assimilated Frost) are full of surprises and disillusions. They crow too quickly over mistaken pearls beaked out of the unsavory soil that they call common earth. Frost shows no wonder at finding *grain* in the country, or at finding it often rotten there. He is the only real "realist." The others are still caught among the revolutionary eddies left over from the past century. They keep poking up the dregs of the great Humanitarian delusion. They react from one variety of romance to another. Frost is neither reactive nor reactionary. He has won freedom by keeping his eye more faithfully than others on the facts of human nature in the immediate neighbourhood. He has envisaged the human spirit of neighbourliness: the spirit which enables people to live together more or less fruitfully in a local community, the spirit which with all its meannesses comprises the basal values of the wider human brotherhood. This wider ideal has certainly had its effect on Frost but he does not "give voice" to it. For him it has distilled itself entirely into local terms. Hence the continual sense of breadth that the reader experiences in moving through the quaint little world, as it may at first appear, of *North of Boston*. Its creator has epitomized, intuitively, the larger world in which the ideal of human solidarity is now being put, or ought now to be put, through the plain test of local conditions. Thus by remaining faithfully local, Frost has become quite deeply representative. He has been able to catch a deeper spirit at work in our age because "the spirit of our age" has not been able to catch *him*. He turned away from the cry of "Freedom," and found Her silently at hand.

In the ways of his life Frost has shown a rare devotion to his own neighbourhood, his *North of Boston*, a district embracing northern Massachusetts and southern New Hampshire. He has been absent from it, in body, for three considerable periods. The first ten years of his life were spent in San Francisco; but very few traces of that vivid and conscious vicinity can be found in his work. At the age of thirty-seven he went to the other extreme, so to speak, of the Anglo-Saxon world. He visited England for three years: he cottaged in the west country, and was drawn into close personal relations with the energetic group of new poets who were stirring London just before the outbreak of the Great War. There he completed and published his first two volumes; and after having been ignored in America, his poetry received from the English reviewers a hearty welcome. But nothing of England entered discernibly into his work. The same is true of the State of Michigan which, later, vied with his own New England in doing him public honour and in which he lived for a while. From first to last his muse has belonged to the charmed circle, North of Boston . . . never to the charming circle, I mean the academic and urban society which has more and more wooed the poet in his middle age. He pays it sporadic, genial visits; and it seems to have fostered the satiric strain that appears in his later verse. But his poetry belongs almost entirely to the countryside, where he continues to make his home.

For twenty-five years he *had* poverty (neither "suffered" nor "enjoyed" would be the right word). In boyhood he turned his hand to all sorts of local labours. Later he supported his family by farming and school-teaching. His prime associations were made on neighbourly and not on literary grounds. Poetry was always his vocation, but it never called him to mark off his consciousness from that of his sensible neighbours. The Romantic line of division between poet and rural community, persisting since Gray and Burns, and definitively demonstrated by a number of recent poets in their conscious efforts to cross it—that line never existed for Frost. He was never "a chield amang them takin' notes." His freedom from this attitude is due in no small measure to a certain sound kind of democracy that is peculiar today to rural New England. But the point is that Frost's poetry grew up naturally during the long years of his active participation in the life of his neighbourhood.

The Puritan tradition is alive in him, as it was in his Scotch mother, and in his paternal ancestors, who, while other New Englanders were following the shifting frontier, stayed settled in the narrow confines of North of Boston for seven generations. The eighth Frost, to be sure, revolted to Democratic journalism in San Francisco. His short, brilliant, violent life left a sense of tragedy in his son, the poet. Frost was precluded from admiring those of us who

> get what little misery we can
> Out of not having cause for misery.

His father did all the reacting from New England that was requisite, and left the boy one generation ahead of the current American Muse that Shakespeare warns against:

> She that herself will sliver and disbranch
> From her material sap, perforce must wither.

Among the remarks of Frost that have got into print is this: "I believe in tradition and accident and a bit of idea bothering tradition." If "tradition," in this creed, is Father, and "a bit of idea" is Son, then "accident" is surely the Holy Ghost that proceedeth from those two. Chance was the devil for Thomas Hardy: he called it "Crass Casualty." Accident, for Frost, is more or less providential, I think. His faith in it proceedeth from the Puritan tradition bothered a bit by the idea of freedom, which is Puritanism's begotten son. He rejects the necessitarianism of official Puritan thought—also, of recent scientificized thought. On the other hand he rejects the Shelleyan hope and the Emersonian anarchy. He believes in "The Trial by Existence." This is the title and theme of an early poem of his.

Implicitly it is the theme of his work as a whole. It explains why his writing inspirits us even when it deals with dispiriting things. He maintains, in his own subdued and oblique fashion, the Puritan faith that life is designed as an incessant learning. "Accident," for him, is neither gross fate nor a way of emotional escape: it is a designed way of learning—which men may or may not follow.[4] Thus Frost has written the poetry of fine casualty in the neighbourhood.

His first book, *A Boy's Will*, in which the pieces are serially arranged to adumbrate the author's development, shows him gradually passing over from the poetry of romantic mood into the poetry of neighbourliness. The opening poems render the youth's preoccupation with the flux of his own longings and with nature's shifting phenomena. "The youth is persuaded," as the author's rubric puts it, "that he will be rather more than less himself for having forsworn the world." But from this mood of isolation the "youth" does not seek relief by swinging over into the opposite mood of vague, restless sympathy with mankind. Nor does he seek the social mud, like those post-Shelleyan writers who, unable to fly, are determined to crawl because they will not learn to walk. He finds that his forward path lies through his everyday relations with the persons who happen to be nearest him, and through everyday labours. It is significant that in *Mowing* and its sequel, *The Tuft of Flowers*, where the poet lays hold of his characteristic style, the "youth" attains a true social standpoint. "He takes up life simply," says the author's rubric, "with the small tasks." He discovers first the firm personal joy, and subsequently the firm social sympathy, which may be drawn from true labour. The sympathy he wins is not an emotional aim but a spiritual result: it is not constructed through the medium of sympathetic words; it ensues from common joy, effort, and weariness under the yoke of a common task. The initial process of it is veraciously given in *The Tuft of Flowers*:

> I went to turn the grass once after one
> Who mowed it in the dew before the sun.
>
> The dew was gone that made his blade so keen
> Before I came to view the levelled scene.
>
> I looked for him behind an isle of trees;
> I listened for his whetstone on the breeze.

[4] The reader may find this idea emerging in practically every poem in *North of Boston*.

> But he had gone his way, the grass all mown,
> And I must be, as he had been—alone,
>
> "As all must be," I said within my heart,
> "Whether they work together or apart."

Presently, guided by a butterfly, the second worker finds a tuft of
flowers which his predecessor had looked upon and spared:

> The mower in the dew had loved them thus,
> By leaving them to flourish, not for us,
>
> Nor yet to draw one thought of ours to him,
> But from sheer morning gladness at the brim.
>
> The butterfly and I had lit upon,
> Nevertheless, a message from the dawn,
>
> That made me hear the wakening birds around,
> And hear his long scythe whispering to the ground,
>
> And feel a spirit kindred to my own;
> So that henceforth I worked no more alone;
>
> But glad with him, I worked as with his aid,
> And weary, sought at noon with him the shade;
>
> And dreaming, as it were, held brotherly speech
> With one whose thought I had not hoped to reach.
>
> "Men work together," I told him from the heart,
> "Whether they work together or apart."

The following note is prefixed to the opening poem of *North of
Boston*: " 'Mending Wall' takes up the theme where 'The Tuft of
Flowers' in *A Boy's Will* laid it down." And, indeed, the dominant
motif of Frost's second volume is developed from the chord he
found in *The Tuft of Flowers*. It is the harmony—a subdued harmony—of the spirit of labour and the spirit of sympathy. On the
surface, *North of Boston* is remarkable for its representations, appearing in almost every poem, of the actual processes of human
labour. Though in this genre his canvas seems small, compared with
the range attempted by Wilfrid Wilson Gibson and other "realistic"
poets of labour, Frost's picture is far more faithful than theirs to the
inner realities of labour, and therefore, in the true sense, more
representative. To an extraordinary degree this poet has taken part
in labour,—often with his hands and always in his spirit. The con-
crete details of labour respond peculiarly to the qualities of his
genius. The artistic harmony, not unmysterious, of such a poem as
Mending Wall is due in large measure to the correspondence between

the laborious physical process which is being described and the quality of spirit, the patient sympathy, which is being adumbrated. The sympathy is laborious, so to speak, without being laboured. It has behind it the concealed inward effort of real charity. Hence it is that his dramatic conceptions grow out, with a certain inevitability and with no sharp shift of mode, from his lyric and descriptive verse. From the lyric *After Apple-Picking*, a personal expression of the spirit of labour, the reader may pass, on a continuous thread of mood, to *The Woodpile*, where a second person is distantly outlined,—"Someone who lived in turning to fresh tasks"; and thence, by natural degrees, to dramatic sketches like *The Death of the Hired Man*, where the author yields the whole scene to his created personages and their tasks. The diverse modes of the poet's art are harmonized in his spirit of patient, laborious neighbourliness.

In failing to follow out the implications of this spirit, interpreters have failed to trace the distinctive pattern of Frost's work as a whole. Amy Lowell exaggerated its dramatic sadness, and Louis Untermeyer by way of reaction exaggerated its lyric gladness. Centrally, however, it is neither sad nor glad. The burdens and limitations of the neighbourhood keep the poet from being very glad; but his faith in the latent value of the neighbourly spirit prevents him from being sad. He is more dispassionate than his fellow-craftsmen when contemplating the limitations of common life. He sees at once the meanness and the validity of old social conventions and narrow ingrained tendencies. These shackles he does not sketch cynically, like Edgar Lee Masters, though constantly he shows them clogging the spirit of human brotherhood. On the other hand he does not thrust into the imprisoned lives of his workers those sudden emotional moments and those mystic dream-comforts so frequent in the narratives of W. W. Gibson.

Inside the limits of narrow and unrelieved lives, such as that of the old lady in *The Black Cottage*, Frost likes to show the presence, dim though it be, of "the truths we keep coming back and back to." The speaker in this poem, a kindly, chattering rural clergyman, carries much of the author's conviction when he says:

> For, dear me, why abandon a belief
> Merely because it ceases to be true?
> Cling to it long enough, and not a doubt
> It will turn true again, for so it goes.

> Most of the change we think we see in life
> Is due to truths being in and out of favour.

This clinging to old truths is very different from restless yearning for the lost past. Such yearning means a preoccupation with "the change we think we see in life." But "what counts is the ideals," concludes the young man in *The Generations of Men*, "and those will bear some keeping still about." This poem gently satirizes those who "try to fathom the past" in order to "get some strangeness out of it": pretentious sentiment in regard to the past is shown retreating from an urgent love which belongs to the present. The thirst for "some strangeness," in either the past or future, is rejected by the meditative common sense of the woman of *In the Home Stretch*, in Frost's third volume, *Mountain Interval*. Her husband, in a moment of relaxation after their removal from the city to a farm, where they seem destined to spend the rest of their days, is inclined to romanticize their situation. He muses wonderingly on the circumstances which prepared this crisis in their life, and on those that may follow from it. She reminds him that he is searching

> For things that don't exist; I mean beginnings.
> Ends and beginnings—there are no such things.
> There are only middles.

A couplet from the final poem in this volume condenses one of the main themes of Frost's poetry as a whole:

> Our very life depends on everything's
> Recurring till we answer from within.

Such passages show the aptness of this poet in performing a feat rare in contemporary verse, that of giving original and vigorous expression to a moral commonplace. He has had fresh experience of those old truths which "will bear some keeping still about." His fresh vision keeps him clear of a stultifying paradox that has clung to modern poetry: namely, the singing of men's common brotherhood in a tune which defies, without really transcending, men's common sense. Since Shelley, and particularly since Whitman, our poets have often chanted, in one and the same tune, the joy of human solidarity and the joy of such a free following of one's individual temperament as would badly disrupt that solidarity. In Frost's poetry there is plenty of temperament, but it is pitched in a key consonant with the tone of true neighbourliness. Keeping his eye on "Truth with all her matter-of-fact," and with a smile at once sympathetic and corrective, the poet moves temperamental longings from the centre of life to its fringe, where they belong. He uses them to relieve, and prevents them from disrupting, the everyday neighbourhood. The urge of outward-bound desires in his personages is continually walled in. The comic heroine, if so she may be called, of *The Cow in Apple Time* is the only one of his dramatis personae who, "scorning a pasture withering to the root," is allowed

> To make no more of a wall than an open gate,
> And think no more of wall-builders than fools . . .

and the result of her zest for stolen fruit is socially unfortunate: "the milk goes dry." ("Adversity's sweet milk, philosophy," is it?)

"Good fences make good neighbours"; but also, on the other hand, "Something there is that doesn't love a wall." This two-sided text of the first poem of *North of Boston* is a main theme of the poet's whole work. Does it not represent in miniature the problem which now, perhaps more decisively than ever before, confronts society? "Walls" are indispensable, we find, and yet our progress toward human community seems sadly cramped by "walls." That this paradox is soluble in the spirit of true neighbourliness, but that the solution of it is laborious and exacting, and never complete, is what one is made to feel keenly in reading Frost's poetry. On the one hand, he displays the rank-growing selfishness that finds shelter behind human walls; on the other hand, he shows unfailing respect, continually looking out through quaint patient humour, for all walls, however mean, which have some discernible utility in the neighbourhood. But what is one to do about a wall which, except in the eyes of one's neighbour, is palpably useless? The true answer to this question— a question so vexatious in the actual world—is implicit in the spirit of Frost's poetry. It appears most plainly, perhaps, in *Mending Wall*. The new-time farmer, while helping with patient good-humour to repair the needless wall between his own estate and his neighbour's, tries to "put a notion" in the old-time farmer's head:

> "Before I built a wall I'd ask to know
> What I was walling in or walling out,
> And to whom I was like to give offence.
> Something there is that doesn't love a wall,
> That wants it down." I could say "Elves" to him,
> But it's not elves exactly, and I'd rather
> He said it for himself.

To persuade our neighbour to say it "for himself" is surely the most considerable task of all. Its exacting conditions are apparent to the farmer in *Home Burial*:

> We could have some arrangement
> By which I'd bind myself to keep hands off
> Anything special you're a mind to name.
> Though I don't like such things 'twixt those that love.
> Two that don't love can't live together without them.
> But two that do can't live together with them.

In his character-poems, from which I have just been quoting, Frost has created a New-England blank verse. His style is developed from the living talk of village and farm in the North-of-Boston region. It is homely, resonant speech. Its tones range all the way from the modest humming drawl of casual conversation to the drawling vibrancy of emotional excitement. Always deliberate, it is far removed from the urban staccato of modern literary English.[5] One needs to read it slowly and evenly, giving a full tonal value to subordinate syllables. Otherwise the blank verse will sometimes lapse into lilting tetrameter. The poet himself is far from blameless; and he can be very flat. He demands too much of us when he wants us to read as a line of blank verse this praise of New Hampshire: "She's one of the two best states in the Union." On the other hand, the following encomium of the same State takes us fully in the slow noose of its rhythm, not to mention its wild casual loveliness:

> Her unpruned grapes are flung like lariats
> Far up the birches out of reach of man.

Instead of dialect verse, Frost gives us the very dialect of New England,—the spirit, the intonation, the essential manner of her speech. The rustic Yankees in Lowell's *Bigelow Papers* use a very

---

[5] I heard a cultivated Londoner read some passages from Frost with an effect unintentionally absurd. His slurred vowels and labial uprush of intonation slaughtered the poetry he was praising. I recommended to him the study of a sentence that was spoken to me by a rural neighbour in northern New England, whom I had prevailed upon to try a dish of Brussels sprouts from my garden. I had told him that this vegetable, new in his experience, was far more tasty than the native cabbages that grew profusely in his own yard. His verdict was a single scornful octameter: "I dawn't think I set much store by tham thar Broos-sel sprouts of yourn." Every syllable stood out, slowly, and the rhythmic wave had its crest in the word "store."

pronounced and captivating dialect. How close it was, or is, to real Yankee speech, is another question. Lowell wanted his people to be racily picturesque. Frost's art is too neighbourly to have any such aim. Our neighbours cease to be neighbours insofar as they appear to us picturesque. The picturesque is romantic; and the marked development of interest in dialect verse during the past century was an offshoot of Romanticism. It points to the division, previously discussed, between poet and community. It often means that the poet is *wooing* his rustic community more ardently than he *loves* it. This attitude is in Burns. Burns is a poignant genius who lived in a certain locality. Frost is a tempered genius in whom the locality lives. Burns captures us with his passionate vigour and tunefulness, coming out now on one level of style and now on another, but always overtopping the manner of the neighbourhood. Frost charms us with his sober geniality, with the insistent modulation of his style on one level, close to the very manner of his neighbourhood. Moreover, the essence of this manner is universal. Beneath all dialects, urban and suburban, there is a plain, contemplative idiom that people use when speaking to each other, neither as strangers nor as bosom friends, but as good neighbours. Frost gets down to this idiom.

THE HUMOUR

He turns upon the neighbourhood a certain light which was not there before. It is not a high illumination, nor is it low and gloomy as when clouds are heavy overhead. It is a sort of clear gray light. It reveals no glory in the landscape; but it moves the common objects close to us and brings out a special charm that they do not show in full sunlight. Frost is so close to earth, and earth is for him so *social*, that vehement love and fear of it seem to him out of focus:

> The woods are lovely, dark and deep;
> But I have promises to keep,
> And miles to go before I sleep. . . .[6]

He tosses half of a laugh at a certain "runaway from nature" for whom "the wood's in flux"—

> He knew too well for any earthly use
> The line where man leaves off and nature starts,
> And never over-stepped it save in dreams—

[6] This and most of the subsequent quotations are from Frost's fourth volume, *New Hampshire*.

and the other half at "the new school of the pseudo-phallic, mewling and puking in the public arms." He points comically toward the real-phallic in *Two Look at Two*, where, over a broken wall on a mountainside, a pair of human lovers come face to face with a buck and doe, each couple looking questions at the other. He notes how commercialism is loosening our American hold of the soil. He can't be fully at ease with a boyhood friend who had grown so rich that "his farm was 'grounds' and not a farm at all"; and a certain brook smothered by a city becomes for him a feverish human symbol. He loves New Hampshire (a state of mind rather than a state) for all the things she doesn't sell. In summers, however, he wants her mountain-tops higher,

> To tap the upper sky and draw a flow
> Of frosty night air on the vale below.

Winter, indeed, spreads all through his poetry, with fringes of chill spring and late autumn. At the same time he rejects the kind of gloom that so many "realists" are aiming at nowadays, and sets over against it "the need of being versed in country things.". . . "For them there is really nothing sad." He cultivates cold and meagre soil, not to get a dark emotion out of it, but from a humorous-creative delight in whatever can manage to live there. His birds, for instance, neither assemble in lovely chanting groves, as of old, nor warble in bleak solitude like Hardy's thrush "upon the growing gloom." They gather quite naturally on a muddy road when a snowstorm has driven them from every other foothold. For the ordinary person, nothing can be less inspiring than the heavy snowfall that brings winter back upon the middle spring of New England, breaking branches and checking shoots that are late enough already: it seems the very distillation of all that is aimless in life. This time, however,

> The road became a channel running flocks
> Of glossy birds like ripples over rocks. . . .
> Well, something for the snowstorm to have shown
> The country's singing strength thus brought together,
> That though repressed and moody with the weather
> Was none the less there ready to be freed
> And sing the wildflowers up from root and seed.

The reader who finds a deliberate cheerfulness in lyrics like *Our Singing Strength* is as far from the Frostian humour as when he finds a deliberate depression in drab narratives like *Place for a*

Third. The neighbourhood in this poem is indeed a drab "product of life's ironing-out." [7] Here death seems life's main interest—if one is looking at New-England life from the viewpoint, for instance, of Amy Lowell's *Overgrown Pasture.* The community seems mainly interested in getting itself decently buried. Its dutifulness and its economy are ironically exercised, simultaneously, in the question of proper graves and grief. But, catching aright the humour of the poem, one sees that Laban's procedure in regard to his dead wife is more convincingly romantic than bereaved Romeo's. Laban is a gray, Yankee Romeo who is neither tragic nor comical. In his concern for the last resting-place of his Eliza, he is an exponent of the poetry of the neighbourly spirit. In fact, the whole dull neighbourhood wins a real stir of poetic life from its "glimpse of lingering person in Eliza." This glimpse (which the poet might well have developed a little more fully) broadens down into the region of neighbourly humour, between laughter and sadness, from which Frost's "singing strength" comes.

In *New Hampshire*, his humour is more marked than in his previous volumes. Yet it was entirely slighted in two prominent reviews of that book, one on either side of the Atlantic. [8] Each side of the Atlantic, for different reasons, desires American humour to be characteristically American, like our "movies." And Frost's humour is quite un-American in its slowness to "register," in its very quiet and gradual way of "intriguing" the reader. Even so, it would seem strange that intelligent critics could peruse with brows entirely knitted a book that was written with a constant smile. The explanation seems to be that our current literary taste, while alert for smart satire or picayune intensities, is rather obtuse to the deeper and quieter kinds of humour. Effervescence is demanded, and the literary market is absorbing an astonishing quantity of poor champagne. Frost's humour, however, never quite bubbles; when it tends to do so it loses its own fine distinction. On the other hand, it never quite

---

[7] It recalls to my memory a gaunt and patched Maine farmer whom I once stopped to talk with beside the road. When I tried to find out what leisure time he had and what he did with it, he pointed with interest to the family graveplot on a nearby slope (the least unkempt spot on the farm that a passerby could see) and said: "I shan't get rest worth speakin' of till I'll lie up yonder."

[8] *London Times*, July 24, 1924, and *New York Evening Post*, March 22, 1924.

subsides. It is a ripe northern whisky. To imbibe his work slowly and completely, with decent intervals for meditation between drams, is to feel his humour gradually seeping through one's whole system. One vibrates from tip to toe with soundless laughter. And the vibration recommunicates itself to particular passages. In other words, many a passage of his verse that at first looked flat and colourless—or sadly or redly coloured, from reflection of obtrusive objects in the atmosphere of our age—now shows its right hue, and sparkles quietly back to us, a vital tawny-gray.

We need to reanimate, in this age of literary cults, the old wide sense of the word "humour," denoting a central and fluent mood. It would help to set us in a tide of life free from forced laughter, from hot little coves of emotion, and from ragged little rocks of factuality. Frost's mood is the humour of one who, like Emerson and Whitman, will not commit himself to anything short of Life itself; but who, unlike them, will not cultivate life ecstatically, either in soul or soil. His work is devoid of grandeur but free from grandiosity—the kind of grandiosity which, continually shifting its modes so as to conceal itself from itself, has pursued poetry from Wordsworth to the present time. Frost has realized that Romantic *energia* in all its forms and disguises is quite off colour today. "Nothing gold can stay," he sings; like his own Oven Bird when "the highway dust is over all":

> The bird would cease and be as other birds
> But that he knows in singing not to sing.
> The question that he frames in all but words
> Is what to make of a diminished thing.

He perches not far from soul and soil. Between those two houses of life he will be a good neighbour: kindly, shrewd, withdrawing, humorously watchful of right values in everyday intercourse. He calls himself, half seriously, a "sensibilitist"; and one thinks of Montaigne. He is really the humour-poet of our time, and the reviewers have generously recognized him—as everything but that.

His persistent solitariness of mood, for instance, has been misinterpreted. His is the sort of loneliness which insists that Life itself is not lonely but neighbourly—neither intimate nor aloof. He constantly gives us a part mystic, part comic, sense of Life standing-off a bit from life and assessing it, in right neighbourly fashion. He recoils from explicit judgements, as apt to be too mental and committal. He will give us hell, or heaven, only in friendly hints. As for hell: in rebutting the charge that he condemns New Hampshire life in particular, he is drawn to confess that he has written his books "against the world in general." He thinks the world has in it enough "fire and ice" (desire and hate) to compass its own destruction by either means, and enough blather to obscure its own great needs:

> Better defeat almost,
> If seen clear,
> Than life's victories of doubt
> That need endless talk talk
> To make them out.

In short, human life is considerably hellish. As to its heavenly tincture:

> blue so far above us comes so high
> It only gives our wish for blue a whet.

He admits, though he refuses to assert, that he wants to make something of whatever "fragmentary blue" he comes across on earth. The fragments are insufficient to inspire him with any enthusiasm, but sufficient to make him "want life to go on living." So long as it goes on, he doesn't wish to fly off, since he "doesn't know where it's likely to go better." He refuses to get tangled in this mazy world of ours; his mind tends to "let go of it"; but

> nothing tells me
> That I need learn to let go with the *heart*.

This ambiguous humour is rendered with extraordinary power in *The Census-taker*. The speaker comes to a decayed woodmen's hut in a vast cut-over mountain region:

> An emptiness flayed to the very stone.
> I found no people that dared show themselves,
> None not in hiding from the outward eye—
> And every tree stood up a rotting trunk
> Without a single leaf to spend on autumn,
> Or branch to whistle after what was spent.

When the wind has slammed the door of the shack nine times, he enters, as "the tenth across the threshold":

> The stove was cold—the stove was off the chimney—
> And down by one side where it lacked a leg.
> The people that had loudly passed the door
> Were people to the ear but not the eye.

> They were not on the table with their elbows.
> They were not sleeping in the shelves of bunks.

This "house in one year fallen to decay" has a melancholy as valid as ever Byron at his best elaborated from the ruins of the old world; but of a very different quality. One feels here America's wide desire of ordinary persons and ordinary labour. Yet her vast busy scene is thrown into poetic distance; and we can imagine it, in some future century, allied with the places

> Fallen to ruin in ten thousand years
> Where Asia wedges Africa from Europe.

At the same time the poet regards the scene with a sort of half-smiling irony. He makes us feel that Poetry wants our life "to go on living," but that she is far from being satisfied with it and committed to it. If, as quickly as we have become a numerous noisy nation, we should "shrink to none at all,"—she would express a melancholy regret even while turning, with a certain humorous relief, to life elsewhere. She is like the owner of the forsaken woodpile in *North of Boston*: "Someone who lives in turning to fresh tasks."

Frost's attitude is thus quite different from another kind of ambiguity prominent in present literature. One moment a poet will submerge himself energetically in some ugly aspect of the democratic-industrial world; the next moment, for needed relief, he will fly to alien beauties; or he may swim in a rather uneasy mid-region of mingled satire and yearning. This region is more animated but less satisfying than the ironic humour of Frost. He keeps to his highway, never disappearing headfirst into marshy places, nor hailing an aeroplane. His impulses in either direction are very marginal, especially in his later work. The flyaway theme that pulsed in *A Boy's Will*, and sent some echoes through *A Mountain Interval*, becomes in the *New Hampshire* volume (as hinted in one poem) *An Empty Threat*. At the same time the pathological element that appeared in *North of Boston* (in *Home Burial*, *A Servant to Servants*, and *The Fear*) is left behind. Or rather, it is transmuted by the poet's growing humour; as the reader may see in two of the *New Hampshire* poems. I refer to *Paul's Wife*, with its humorous-pathetic Pygmalion of the lumber-camps; and to that dramatic masterpiece *The Witch of Coös*, with its rare mingling of genial and shivering humours, the genial predominating. In this story, the skeleton of a murdered man

moves about with "the faintest restless rustling" in the home
guilty fancies of Mrs. Toffile Lajway. It "carries itself like a pi
of dishes" up from the frozen cellar to the creaking attic of he
everyday life. The mystery is too humorous to be pathological: it
moral and personal.

An atmosphere of natural mystery, coming down like a thi
snowfall that settles into the earth with scarcely, here and ther
a hint of covering, belongs to Frost's humour. Drab everyda
objects—Mrs. Lajway's chandelier, button-box, and window-shutte
—maintain their own quaint contours, sharply, while faint lines c
incidence begin to relate them to an upper air. The mystery, i
large measure, is the mystery of human Personality. Always the
is some one "in hiding from the outward eye." Moreover the perso
ages who talk and gesture in the foreground, vivid though they l
for a while, have about them a certain tentative and momentar
air,—eminently in the sharp little sketch, *An Old Man's Wint*
Night. In *Snow*, which seems to me the most remarkable amon
Frost's longer poems of persons, the central figure, Brother Meserv
is transient as the gust of storm that opens the dialogue,

> a fresh access
> Of wind that caught against the house a moment,
> Gulped snow, and then blew free again.

On his way home at night he has had to take refuge awhile in th
farmhouse of the Coles. Their regard of him is not so cold and blin
as the driving snow's, for it is opened and warmed a little b
humour. But to them he is less a person than a repugnant type,—th
conceited pastor of a "wretched little Racker Sect," who "seems t
have lost off his Christian name":

> That sort of man talks straight on all his life
> From the last thing he said himself, stone deaf
> To anything anyone else may say. . . .

Yet beside the lamp in the sitting-room—while the snow climbs th
sash, looking as if

> Some pallid thing had squashed its features flat
> And its eyes shut with overeagerness
> To see what people found so interesting
> In one another, and had gone to sleep
> Of its own stupid lack of understanding—

Meserve becomes for the nonce a real individual. At the same time his own words give us a sense that he is only *one of Life's* ways, and that Life has many ways. Presently he goes out into the darkness and snow again, and the Coles feel that they have been "too much concerned":

> But let's forgive him.
> We've had a share in one night of his life.
> What'll you bet he ever calls again?

Frost's persons are too near him to be ghostly; but they do not live with him as relatives and house-mates. He has no more thought of letting them into his inmost concerns than of repulsing them when they pause on the road by his field for a chat: "No, not as there is a time to talk!" They are his neighbours. His mystic-humorous view of them is entirely subservient to his neighbourly spirit. He drops hints of a real religious outlook, such as poetry may regain in the future after a period of severe critical purgation; but the hints are faint. On the other hand he is free from the confused mysticism of naturalistic poetry—from the dubious Emersonian Over-soul and the current Under-soul that It helped to hatch. He is humorously wary of twisting, soulfully, the hard autumn-facts of earth. He glances into mystic avenues of the Soul, and turns away. He re-approaches his neighbours with a deepened sense of his and their elusiveness, as in *The Lockless Door*, and with a more pungent humour for meeting them while there is still "a time to talk."

He finds their labours and their working-ways somewhat less transitory than themselves; also peculiarly expressive of them and, beyond them, of life that wants "to go on living." Hence the rare inward beauty of his poetry of human work. Any object shaped or even testingly touched by human hands has an idiomatic fascination for him. He keeps turning it over and over, loath to leave it till he has caught all its smell of mortality. Wild nature has small part in his verse. Deep in the forests he likes to find a telegraph-wire in summer, and in winter a woodpile with "runner tracks in this year's snow looped near it." He loves to watch a human way develop, if it *can*, through obstinate material. Baptiste in *The Axe-Helve* is Poetry and Hand-labour at one in the effort of finely shaping a piece of tough-grained hickory; at the same time he becomes an individual, a neighbour, shaped out from the human mass through his own work. *A Star in a Stone-Boat* touches at the inward beauty of work through a profoundly humorous image:

> Never tell me that not one star of all
> That slip from heaven at night and softly fall
> Has been picked up with stones to build a wall.

The ordinary farm-labourer, in the act of thus utilizing a meteorite, would not recognize its real nature. Therefore a labourer who is also a poet must rediscover it:

> From following walls I never lift my eye
> Except at night to places in the sky
> Where showers of charted meteors let fly.
> Some may know what they seek in school or church
> And why they seek it there; for what I search
> I must go measuring stone walls, perch on perch.

But Frost will no more idealize work than anything else. He loves the human shaping of places and objects; but he is almost as much interested in finding them deserted, given over to "the slow smokeless burning of decay." A full humour evades fixity. It is amusing to note how much this poet "doesn't love a *wall*," even while he pats fondly the stones that have been laboriously dragged to it in stone-boats and shaped into it by hand. He likes broken and deserted walls. He finds in human work, after all, the transience of the persons who do it. Moreover, he feels how much of human effort is either uncreative or capricious: we like "to plough the snow," he notes, when we happen to be feeling bitter "at having cultivated rock." A great deal of it is too mechanic for warm personal interest. In this regard his story of *The Grindstone*, the grindstone of rural boyhood, becomes a rich apologue:

> It stands beside the same old apple tree.
> The shadow of the apple tree is thin
> Upon it now, its feet are fast in snow.

He intimates that he could drive the grindstone hard in youth, when Time bade. But on the whole he finds his loitering more fruitful. He writes, indeed, *the poetry of loitering*—very different from the Whitmanian *loafing*. In one poem we find him pausing in the midst of late chores, with his head between the stars and the barnyard, to take a long-distance look at human labours on the one hand, and "the infinities" on the other. He ponders the case of a nearby farmer who had burned down his own house to buy with the insurance money a great telescope; which thereafter was locally christened "the star-splitter" because it revealed to the neighbourhood two or three stars where only one had been before. The result:

> We've looked and looked, but after all where are we?
> Do we know any better where we are,
> And how it stands between the night to-night
> And a man with a smoky lantern chimney?
> How different from the way it ever stood?

Yet he believes the costly rusticated telescope

> ought to do some good if splitting stars
> 'Sa thing to be compared with splitting wood.

Each of these two modes of effort helps to throw the other into true focus, doesn't it?—so long as the poet commits himself to neither. Modern science, for this poet, is merely an extension of human work. It is a way, not of cleaving the Eternal Mystery, but of splitting wood!

As for cleaving the Eternal Mystery—why, It is cloven in itself. It is divided against itself in a way that baffles our chopping reason but invites the working of our better will and purer sense of beauty. It appears to us as eternal appetite under eternal control. This divine temperance, imitated so poorly in our world, is better imitated by Poetry in hers when she is true to it. When untrue to her proper motion, Poetry makes the wrong cleavages: she splits our nature in scientific or sentimental directions and misses the essential division. A sense of that mysterious division goes through the work of Frost and is clearly established in his latest volume, *West-Running Brook*; in such pieces as *Riders* or *Sitting By a Road in Broad Sunlight*, but most notably in the title poem:

> What does it think it's doing running west
> When all the other country brooks flow east
> To reach the ocean? . . .

The reader may reflect that, for a century past, poetry has been loud with waters, "a land of streams" indeed, Shelleyan streams, eagerly flowing east toward the ocean—trying to make short-cuts to Eternity. These rash currents have short-circuited, so to speak, the human experience of Eternity. So that for poor William Morris, coming as he did in the last febrility of this multitudinous flowing, there was a strange emptiness in "the dread eternity," as he called it,

> In whose void patience how can these have part,
> These outstretched feverish hands, this restless heart?

In Frost's work, this void and fever have been left behind. There is a fresh patience and humility bred of a fresh and plain recognition of the truth that the stream of our life, though "made in heaven," is dark—dark from the very fact of its current—and flows west, though with a significant wave to the eastward:

> The black stream, catching on a sunken rock,
> Flung backward on itself in one white wave,
> And the white water rode the black forever,
> Not gaining but not losing. . . .
>
> Speaking of contraries, see how the brook
> In that white wave runs counter to itself.
> It is from that in water we were from
> Long, long before we were from any creature. . . .
>
> It is this backward motion toward the source,
> Against the stream, that most we see ourselves in,
> The tribute of the current to the source.

The poem has a lovely and profound originality. It recalls Vaughan's *Waterfall*; it interchanges a clear signal with the great seventeenth-century faith; but it is far from, and free from, the manner of that age. It lacks of course Vaughan's rich assurance and bright rapture. But it is free from the spiritual and poetic turgidity of Vaughan's time; and it faces the difficulties of faith that have arisen since then. It meets and stems the current of modern "Nature" with a plain strength and charm. My extracts, above, convey small sense of its complete charm. It is cast in the form of a homely, whimsical dialogue between man and wife in a scene which they love and which, one feels, loves them. It has the right humour for our time.

The Frostian humour is peculiarly important for America. No other of our poets has shown a mood at once so individual and so neighbourly. The comparative thinness of American literature, its lack of full social body and flavour, is due to the extraordinary interval between our artistry and our national life. Our nation is widespreading and unformed, tangled in raw freedoms and archaic conventionalities. Our poetry, now responding to and now reacting from our national life, tends to be rather banal, or rather esoteric—in either case, thin. Frost's work is notably free from that double and wasting tendency. His own ambiguity is vital: it comes from artistic and moral integrity in rare union with fluent sympathy. His love is so chemically combined with good sense that the reader cannot isolate the one from the other. His neighbourly humour is on the curve toward the richer American poetry of the future, if that is to be.

IX

MILTON AND THE PRESENT STATE OF POETRY

POETRY today has "a short uneasy motion," like the Ancient Mariner's ship at the equator when the "Polar Spirit" below was reluctant to resign her to the charge of the "Angelic Power" appointed to bring her toward home. Our poetry, in England and America, has a pervasive but jerky animation. Perhaps never before has poetry been so widely eager and experimental and, at the same time, so shortly tethered. It seems agreed that she is trying to escape from the spirit of the nineteenth century. Victorianism, recently regarded as the main enemy, is now seen to be simply one cohort of the nineteenth-century legion. Nor does the opposition between poetry and science, or even between poetry and industrialism, hold any longer the centre of critical attention. Many who are interested in poetry today, feel that she has properly a life of her own, a life which, if it is strong in its own strength, will know how to deal with all extraneous forces, how to assimilate to its nature all things that time can bring. That is just the point. We feel that the past century, in spite of its series of distinguished poets, had within the very movement of its poetry something hostile to the full course of poetry—some Polar Spirit, acting as a cold backward drag beneath the surface.

IMAGISM

But the Polar Spirit is still with us, under the keel, even while we deprecate him. This circumstance would seem to demand special attention before we can clearly go ahead. Poetry is always in danger of engaging herself, unawares, to some or other non-poetic spirit. She has this price to pay for the ambiguous medium she uses, human words. Stone, for the sculptor, is always the same in nature, and its use for paving-blocks and house-corners does not affect its possibilities for him (unless he is a Cubist). But words never remain the same, and their meaning is largely determined by other than poetic uses. They squirm and shift like the flamingoes that served as croquet mallets in Wonderland. The poet, from the viewpoint of the modern citizen, is a dreamy Alice persistently trying to reverse them and keep their heads down. But the poet sees the situation the other way round. Words are fine birds that the citizen tucks clumsily under his arm, confining their use to what he calls the real business of life, which turns out to be only an afternoon game.

May we not say that words are the joint creation of two great human powers, poetry and science,—if we take each of these two terms in its widest possible sense? Our diction is bodied by science and fledged by poetry. It tends to be bodily possessed by science: that is, its main use is for logically organized thinking, in biology, ethics, theology, history, industry, Behaviorism, domestic science, and all the other fields of more or less mental effort. The Fine Arts are under no necessity of entering these fields; they stroll the sidelines, gathering impressions of the game and embodying them in materials drawn from surrounding nature. But Poetry, coming from a region beyond, must enter violently into the kingdom of words. She must make her way onto the grounds and take such part in the game as will induce the regular players to recognize that words are not mere implements for batting definable objects toward definable goals; that, for the full exercise of their nature, they must be allowed to hop and fly considerably; and that this procedure, even if it deranges the rules of the game somewhat, supplies life with a profoundly needed enlivenment. But the poet pays a high price of admission to the game. Something of the very spirit of his work must be left outside the gate. In taking a hand in the poetry of life, he loosens his hold on the life of poetry.

Feeling this danger, the poet swings off continually to the sidelines, taking aid and comfort of the Fine Arts, and shaping his phrases under their influence. He thus enriches the sensuous quality of his words; but he fails to retrieve the essential life of poetry: indeed, the Arts may hide it from him. For the common phrase "Poetry AND Art" is not just a crude Philistine convenience: it records a fundamental distinction of human experience. This needs to be recalled in the face of certain recent criticism which, in a rather veiled fashion, repeats the old error of assimilating poetry to the Fine Arts. It would be nearer the truth if we should say bluntly that poetry is not an "Art" at all. "Art" incorporates mental designs in *material* media.[1] Poetry symbolizes everything in words, and incorporates nothing. It is Merlin in his invisible prison, communing with all that pass and joining hands with none. We recognize this unbodied omnipresence when we speak of the poetry of a scene, of a painting, of someone's life, of life itself. We recognize it just as surely, if less obviously, when we discuss a poem's colour, music, and the like—attributing to poetry those properties that she inspirits but does not actually possess.

Poetry is the spirit of all Art withheld from all the proper media of art. She is the mother of the Arts, with a larger genius than her children and less talent. She cannot equal them in completeness of particular designs, because she is dedicated to the complete design of human nature. To pursue this afar off, to catch something of it in words, is her peculiar glory. But the effort is very exacting for poet and reader. It wearies us. We indemnify and amuse ourselves by trying to assimilate poetry to the Arts. People take a special satisfaction in sentimentalizing the relation between poetry and music: poetry, in reverse of the truth, is made to appear as a child endeavouring hopelessly to express in words the thing that music really conveys. Such is the idea of Browning's Abt Vogler, with his pure nonsense about the "fourth sound" and "the star." But when the life of poetry is fully awake within us, we feel, with Keats, that music is "yearning like a god in pain"—yearning to come down from its narrow heaven into the strenuous catholicity of words.

In recoil from the ways of Art, poetry recurs to life. Thus the "artistical" and "vitalistic" tendencies of poetry, as we may term them, are closely involved together: one leads into the other. They are simply two phases of a single effort, the effort of poetry to free herself from alien methods, and to find her way ahead in human words. This effort has been extraordinary during the past hundred years, owing to the extraordinary development of scientific thought and the appropriation of language, more and more, for scientific purposes. Hence the phenomenon of Imagism. The term applies particularly to a recent poetic cult. But the thing itself goes back beyond

---

[1] *Oral* poetry, like music, uses the medium of sound. But this medium is instantly *dematerialized* by the articulate meaning of the words. Hence some recent theorists have urged that "pure" poetry is sheer tone—in plain terms, sound without sense. This theory is illustrated in a good deal of contemporary verse.

the opening of the nineteenth century, and shows the two aspects described above. Imagism, in its widest meaning, is the fervid attempt to win for verse new vitality from modern life and, on the other hand, to offset the scientific trend of words by evoking all their sensuous and artistic possibilities.

Wordsworth, reacting in youth from the stereotyped art of the eighteenth century, wanted to plunge poetry into the language of common life. Though he modified this aim later, he never really relinquished it. But ordinary language had become immensely rationalized, since Shakespeare's time. Moreover, young Wordsworth, Coleridge, and Shelley, looked at ordinary life through the spectacles of the scientificized philosophy of the eighteenth century. By way of adjustment they steeped their eyes in the belladonna of Transcendentalism. The net result was that the vision of these three poets could never cease to be theoretical. Keats felt that this side of his older contemporaries was untrue to the art of poetry. By way of reaction, and much under the influence of sculpture and painting, he evolved the most deliberately sensuous style in our language. He wished to be "more of an artist," as he advised Shelley. Recently a French scientist claimed that the sense of sight can be reached through the nerves of touch, and that blind persons can be taught to see with their skin. Keats might have said the same. His work is a kind of glowing sculpture that makes the finger-tips see.

In the end he severely criticized his own style: he longed for words of "high philosophy." But the artistical tendency was carried on, in one way or another, by his successors. It appealed to young Tennyson, dreaming in his "Palace of Art." It keenly appealed to Browning, who was a lifelong devotee of the arts, particularly music and painting. The one deeply affected his poetic outlook; the other, his style, which became a kind of staccato painting. He was far from desiring to revive the eighteenth-century "picturesque" manner discarded by Wordsworth. His contemporary, Turner, would as soon have tried to revive the contemplative grace of Reynolds' portraits, instead of painting his own "Rain, Steam and Speed." That thirst for motion which was to mother the invention of moving-pictures, was strong in Browning; his poetry is moving-picturesque. In this respect he may be considered the grandfather of present-day verse; and critics of Amy Lowell's affectionate biography of Keats need not have been surprised at her assumption that Browning was the greater poet of the two. His method leads on from Keats toward Miss Lowell and her contemporaries. His manner, like theirs, is a sort of friendly combat with science. In earliest manhood he had faced the idea of Evolution. He and his admirers liked to point back to his *Paracelsus* and to feel that young Browning had so entirely comprehended the main trend of science that he did not need to bother with it further. All the more, then, did his "subconscious self" resolve to rescue *words* from the growing reach of scientific thought. After *Paracelsus* his style became a plangent effort to thrust our language from the hands of the drab, coherent, modern understanding. His immediate successors, devoid of his vital energy, retreated from the arena, and sheltered poetry under Art. Browning had worshipped music without letting it affect his verse very much—as a man may be more religious in sentiment than in conduct. But Swinburne and Lanier, not to speak of Poe, practised the rhythm of verse like musical virtuosos. Rossetti devoted his fine mind to the marriage of poetry and painting, and surprised his acquaintances with his vast ignorance of scientific ideas. Morris, strenuously rescuing the decorative arts in the age of machines, wrote a kind of verse that, as he admitted, could be justifiably parodied as "upholsterers' poetry." In his vision of the Island of the Hesperides in *The Golden Apples*, language turns into a lovely scroll-work and mural design. The "shadowy isle of bliss" that he built "midmost the beating of the steely sea" was the region where a group of smaller poets set up their so-called Ivory Tower of decadence, as the century closed.

To break away from that island tower, to plunge again into life, was the first aim of our New Poetry when it came into view some twenty years ago. It resumed the original impulse of Wordsworth. It reacted from the "poetic diction" of the nineteenth century and turned to the language of ordinary life. But ordinary language had been still more heavily invaded, since the time of young Wordsworth, by scientific concepts. Hence the unprecedented stress that the New Poetry has placed upon sensuous and emotional immediacy. This quality, however, belongs more to the Fine Arts than to verse. Therefore in our time the artistical tendency of nineteenth-century poetry, which I have traced so sketchily above, has been revived and widely extended. It runs through scores of poets and hundreds of versifiers. Tactual and visual effects, as in Keats, are pursued espe-

cially; at the expense of euphony, since this was overdone by Tennyson and his followers. Wallace Stevens exclaims:

> At the sight of blackbirds
> Flying in a green light,
> Even the bawds of euphony
> Would cry out sharply.

The image loses a good deal of its *poetic* loveliness in being pursued for its own sake, to make us "cry out sharply." A similar image
came casually to Shakespeare while he was pursuing a rich poetic
idea:

> The ornament of beauty is suspect,—
> A crow that flies in heaven's sweetest air.

And no doubt a certain ancient writer was so much occupied with the
thought of the light of the divine nature coming down into low and
dark human nature—"Whereby the dayspring from on high hath
visited us"—that he could thus write in one line, unintentionally,
a great poem of the dawn. What a quick beauty of surprise and elevation and hope! Lola Ridge in her latest book of verse has this:

> Dawn is like a broken honeycomb
> spilling over the waxen edges of the clouds that drip with light.

What a captivating combination of visual and tactile effects! Yet
if these two passages on the dawn should get running together in our
fancy, we would remember that the loveliest things in poetry cannot
be seen or touched: "The dayspring from on high . . . hath dripped
upon us like a broken honeycomb!"

Certainly the "bawds of euphony," as Mr. Stevens calls them,
have been progressively silenced—that is, the Tennysonian bawds.
But new bawds have taken their place. New tricks of euphony and
cacaphony (these two terms being simply heads and tails of a single
coin) have been minted prolifically by our poets, and by the most
advanced musicians: poetry is here at work in the same shop as
music. "Naturalness" and "subtlety," to be sure, are claimed for
the new poetic rhythm. But its effects are often natural to something
other than poetry; its subtlety is less poetic than plastic or auditory
or visual. In short, the contemporary movement in verse, while aiming at a new vitality, has arrived, considerably, at a new artisticality.
Poetry has bowed, more subserviently than ever, to the Arts. Her
best excuse is that language has become more subservient than ever
to industry and science. She is trying to rescue her medium, human

words, from the clutches of the commercialized and scientificized citizenry.

Our time is thus witnessing the finale of a process that first became prominent in Keats. Toward the end of his short career, while longing for a completer kind of poetry than he or his contemporaries had produced, he became painfully aware of an opposition between reason and feeling—in himself and (though he was scarcely conscious of this) in the very spirit of the nineteenth century. He remarked, emblematically, that natural science had spoiled the rainbow even while in his *Lamia*—"so rainbow-sided, touched with miseries"—he was weaving all its tints into verse, disillusionedly. In similar mood, the other day, Mr. Stevens saw the "gesticulating lightning mystical make pallid flitter." This, by a kind of pale violence, rescues the lightning for us from the laboratories where it is now being reproduced mechanically for purposes of scientific study.

Mr. Stevens' work is finely twisted filigree on ebony backgrounds. At the opposite pole of contemporary verse, one would say, is the fertile and popular John Masefield. Yet if we eliminate those aspects of his work that have only a passing appeal, we find that his distinction, too, is merely stylistic. He has a new sensuous experience of a West England countryside; and of the ocean, like his own "Dauber," the would-be painter of the seas. He gives us, as Professor O. W. Firkins put it congruently, the excitement of "plough and prow" in "loam and foam." In proportion as he attempts a more deeply human excitement, he sinks from artist to practitioner, from animated scene to scenic melodrama. Much the same is true of the other recent "Realists" who, in reaction from the Ivory Tower, have devoted themselves to common life. Their interest in it is more artistical than real. They sympathize indeed with the joys and troubles, especially the troubles, of the workingman; but they have very little insight into his working life and character. They use him, sometimes with ludicrous incongruity, as subject-matter for racy and picturesque verse. Otherwise, they chronicle his ways with that determined dullness which is now called realistic. The fact is that these poets, unlike many ordinary persons, are not much interested in ordinary life. It seems to them pathetically dull because they themselves are pathetically deficient in the poetic thought that penetrates to large human meanings beneath drab detail and routine. They are mainly averse from thought. What they really want is minstrel excitement. Like Browning, they seize upon exciting moments, and represent them often with valid and original art. Their best art is an imagistic snatching at the emotional surface of life. Here they join forces with that other series of poets, including Mr. Stevens, who, making no attempt to connect with common life, regard poetry as mainly the fine art of rhythm and image. Moreover, each successive group of poets that has come into prominence during the past ten years has shown, roughly speaking, an increasing trend toward sheer Imagism, and away from intellect.[2]

In general, it seems that the combat that went on in Keats, between style and thought, has been ended by the disqualification of the second combatant. Thought, the life of thought, has been relinquished to science and semi-science. Amy Lowell in her advocacy of Imagism said that poetry must now face a universe of which natural science holds the key. In that case, poetry is intellectually outside, and the door is firmly locked against her. In any case it appears that Apollo has abandoned the human mind, temporarily; while he recoups the sensuous quality of language by devoting a hundred minor poets to the human nerves,—an imagistic hecatomb.

That is one side of the story. If it represents the dominant trend, our New Poetry is bound to eventuate, presently, in a mere and conscious fine art. When its sturdier impulses have worn out, and its extremer vagaries have worn off, it will reduce itself to a conventionalistic art of grotesquerie. This will serve as complement to the conventionalized art of euphony, which attained its peak two centuries ago, when Ned Softly worried about the smoothest order of words in his verses:

> I fancy when your song you sing,
> You sing your song with so much art. . . .

His descendant, Ned Roughly, will soon have at his disposal a hundred recognized devices for sputtering out his vital reactions with regular irregularity. His verse is achieving a curiously conventional unconventionality.

But our New Poetry, on its other side, recoils from such a sequel. It has a longing for real life, life that escapes forever from artifice.

---

[2] To be sure, quite a few of the newcomers, wishing to avoid the emotional naïveté of their elders, have tried to banish sentiment and to develop an intellectual manner. But its texture is too slight to be called thoughtful.

During the past twenty years, perhaps more than ever before in the history of literature, the word "life" has become the chief staple of poets and critics. "That ye may have *life*, and have it more abundantly," is the favourite Biblical quotation; and the other day a Western critic commended a certain poem very highly for being "just a great gob torn from *life* and flung onto the canvas." Between these two extremes, a legion of examples could be ranged. The meaning of the omnipresent word "life" is diverse and confused, as everyone admits. By way of compensation, it is supposed to have a certain juicy thickness. But this is quite delusive; like the depth of muddy water from a flooded stream, swirling over a flat countryside. I remember the excitement, in boyhood, of launching a boat on such a "lake," as we called it; but the ship was soon badly grounded, and our voyaging was mainly oscillation. The word "life" today, at least from the essential standpoint of poetry, has a very shallow denotation. The vast array of non-poetic uses that it has subserved during two hundred years, have worn it thin. Our present poets have desperate recourse to it in a more or less conscious reaction from their own artisticality. Poetry, now badly caught between her two old friendly enemies—the artistical and the vitalistic tendencies—swings choppily from one to the other. This is a partial explanation of the phenomenon noted at the beginning, her "short uneasy motion." The Imagistic imagination has developed for itself a sharp dilemma.

THE WORDSWORTHIAN CONFUSION

For this situation, not much help has come from the investigative-psychological critics so numerous of late. They have illumined many by-ways of the poetic imagination. But their premises have been too largely moulded by that very nineteenth-century outlook from which poetry is trying to extricate herself. These doctors are better at anatomy than at diagnosis, though their diagnoses are better than their prescriptions. Moreover, their method tends to assimilate poetry still further to the Arts. For it throws into relief those artistic phenomena which are more or less subject to analytic and technical treatment, but which are not deeply characteristic of verse alone. Another group of critics refuse any serious attention to contemporary verse. "*Chicago* is singing!" I heard one of them exclaim, disposing of the whole Illinois group in a single groan. But Chicago is the capitol of a modern state of mind; and poetry, lobbying there assiduously, has at least a serious design upon the future. These critics, however, assume that the future of poetry is determined by "historical" factors almost entirely outside her own control: the "spirit of the age" must change before poetry can do so. But this is another nineteenth-century delusion, deposited by the scientific flood, and fostered into wide growth by so-called "history of literature." A true *history of poetry* would take its cue from the opening verses of St. John rather than from history. It would recognize that poetry has a life peculiarly her own, in all parts of the world, from the beginning until now—a life distinguishable from the ways of Art on the one hand, and from the "forces of history" on the other; affecting these, in its ebb and flow, at least as much as it is affected by them. At the present time there is crying need of a criticism proceeding from that standpoint, a criticism thoroughly equipped but devoted to poetry alone. Coleridge and Arnold, as critics of poetry, suffered from the fact that they were interested in too many other fields. They responded to the discursive kind of catholicity that marked the nineteenth century. And in most of our critics who have any substantial background, that attitude persists—just at a time when poetry herself has become abnormally affected by other fields. The learned physicians reinforce the disease.

Our need of a distinctively poetic criticism is felt by a third type of critic, now prominent in our periodicals. He knows that poetry has a life of its own; but, excepting its contemporary phase, he knows little about it. One wonders how he managed to acquire so much ignorance of it. But one suspects that he knows much more than he shows. He conceals his knowledge of the history of poetry: partly because he is journalistic, by profession or by profession of faith; partly because he is reacting from the scientificized study of literature in our colleges. At all events he is resolved to be unacademic, vital. Vivid and intimate impressions of current poetry are what he wants, and he often writes them effectively; though, as copies of a painting are usually less effective than the painting itself, his art suffers from identicism. He clings, pattingly, to the neck of Pegasus and is carried everywhere, doubling and circling. Yet now and then he lifts his head to urge, with Balaamic violence, the need of forward mileage. He feels that, when so much poetry is going around, there ought to be more great poems. He wonders at the discrepancy between achievement and gait. His attitude is significant. It indicates a public desire for a more vital poetry. On the other hand it shares the uneasy ambiguity that pervades the tone of our poetry itself. Accordingly, when this type of critic gives constructive advice to the poets it is not very clarifying. It generally amounts to this: "You are very much alive, but you need more life."

Rather, they need *more life of poetry*. Certainly those poets in the past whom we recognize as vital, whether their art was great or small, were in love with "life." But formerly the main intention of the word was different. I think it may best be conveyed, today, not by "life" but by "Personality"—if we take this word not in its Romantic aspect but in its fullest meaning,

> As alone, there, triumphs to the life
> All the gain, all the good, of the elements' strife.

Ben Jonson, in the ecstasy of his *Charis*, is celebrating neither an individual person nor the life of the universe, in the modern sense; but something between these two and above them. It is human nature, but conceived as personal. It is Personality, but conceived as universal. It lives through persons, but is more than they. It is shaped through "the elements' strife," [3] yet comprises and transcends that strife. It is a single entity, yet its life is twofold, deriving at once from below and above. Here is the vital paradox that baffles our understanding, but animates poetry. It is solved in true "ecstasy" —not just a sweep of emotion, but the attainment of a quiet station above our ordinary lives—as in Donne's well-known poem on that subject. Though turning upon an episode of love, his verses labour to describe that which is the very life of poetry. "This ecstasy," he says, "doth unperplex and tell us what we love":

> We then, who are this new soul, know
> Of what we are composed and made:
> For the atoms of which we grow
> Are soul, whom no change can invade.

Old and always new; made of "atoms" and yet "begotten not made"; involved in change but quiet above it . . . prose is inapt for this impersonal Personality, this Person of persons, that poetry loves. For this is that of which her words *are*. Her patterns are partial copies from Its full pattern. Her pursuit of this, through the

---

[3] The word "elements" in the usage of Jonson's time refers, of course, to both physical nature and human nature.

ages, is her historical life. The *Iliad*, the *Aeneid*, the *Divine Comedy*, the *Lear*, the *Paradise Lost*, the *Faust*, are a series of full-length *glimpses*, each from a different standpoint, of the design of Personality. The sequence of these works is not casual, nor merely occasioned by "the evolutionary forces of history." It is poetry's indigenous effort at self-realization and self-recovery. Each great poem signals back to its predecessors, with a recognition at once genial and critical. This lofty heliographing depreciates for us the intervening landscapes of history; we see that poetry is "a criticism of life." But we see, too, that Personality is a criticism of poetry; and that poetry is a criticism of Art. A supreme painting may be perfect in its way; but a supreme poem, in its very way, is imperfect. It has within itself, as a cause of its supremacy, as an essential part of its art, an awareness of the inadequacy of its own design. The criterion, one must insist, is not derived from the Arts, but from the art of Personality; in the practice of which quite a few individuals have been great and none complete. Poetry is an imitation of the whole art of Personality.

Therefore the current phrase "poetry of individualism," which even intelligent people use, points to a great degradation of poetic thought. "Poetry" and "individualism" are in reality opposed terms. Every true poet knows that when he succeeds in writing well he ceases to be an individual: he loses his life to save it. He ceases to be possessed by his individual experiences; he re-possesses them, in a new and impersonal way. Yet he becomes impersonal only toward that which is experienced; not, like the scientist, toward *that which experiences*. He knows that the experience is personal. He continues to have personality; or rather, Personality, more than ever, has him. But this fundamental truth of poetry has been obscured by the rush of scientific and humanitarian ideas concerning human nature. "Personality" has been badly assimilated to "individuality."

This grand confusion, as it deserves to be called, was prepared by eighteenth-century thought, and deeply established in English poetry by William Wordsworth. A potent individual, rather than a great poetic person, he was sincerely able to obliterate for himself the distinction between these two types, and to obscure it for others. Doubtless a vast and necessary work will some day be written on the subject of his influence on English and American literature. The real extent of it is veiled by the fact that his poetic manner was censured by his chief successors even while they were being moulded by the power of his life and mind. They saw the flaws of design in his work, but not its inmost duplicity of spirit. They preserved this inward duplicity and handed it down to the present age. Shelley conserved it effectually by submitting it to a sea change, and distilling it into a rapturous atmosphere which is still shedding dews of confusion today. Keats, while his sound poetic instinct recoiled from Wordsworth's method, fancied that his insight was perhaps an advance upon Milton's—a fancy that sadly hampered Keats in his attempt to recapture the poetic truth, the poetic life, of the Renaissance. Emerson, the loftiest intellect of the century, filled his early journals with complaints of Wordsworth's poetry, but ended by accepting it for the truth of its vision, of which he was curiously uncritical. So was Matthew Arnold, the leading critic. Wordsworthian confusion was critically reinforced by him. He admired the critical ability of Wordsworth's prefaces, read his verse as a confessed Wordsworthian, and in his own thinking was far more Wordsworthian than he knew. Large and wary stepper that he was, he declared his intention of waiving Wordsworth's "philosophy," and of judging his work from the purely poetic standpoint. Actually, he judged it too largely from an *individual* standpoint; and what he waived was a critical analysis of Wordsworth's poetic outlook. Such analysis was just then profoundly needed. It would have had a beneficent effect upon the development of our poetic thought. Arnold's failure to undertake it, to provide at least a firm clue for it, is one of the notable failures in the history of English criticism.

Yet Arnold was right in his feeling that Wordsworth has "more of life" than any contemporary or successor in English poetry. That statement, made in 1879, needs iteration today. Our feeling today that "Wordsworth withdrew from life," as a recent schoolbook puts it, is an important evidence of our increased confusion in regard to the nature of poetry. Really, he launched vigorously into life, as he experienced it. He opened up that considerable bayou of life, that region of individualistic experience, which our poets are still exploring to its utmost picayune coves, even while disclaiming its prime discoverer. That region has now been pretty well exhausted: there is a restless desire for a way out and onward. But the way is obscured by the delusion that we have already found it, that we are breaking through to a full stream of "life" from which Wordsworth withdrew. Rather, we are still caught in his revolving current. The most animated little whirlpools that our poetry is making, belong to the outer edges of that current, and owe a good deal of their animation to its slow but powerful motion. The situation would be clarified if our schoolbooks and teachers and critics would point out that Wordsworth withdrew, not from "life," in the modern sense of the word "life," but from the life of poetry.

He opened up a fine poetic byway, and made it seem a highway. It would indeed be a highway if, according to the faith of Arnold and other Wordsworthians, it were made "of joy in widest commonalty spread"—if the way of Wordsworth's joy were both high and common. But this is not the case. The quality of the Wordsworthian mood is such that when it wins a real elevation it loses its "commonalty."

A common and elemental joy does indeed run through the work of Wordsworth, as it does through human history, like a powerful underground river. It is a thing that nourishes the blind roots of human life. It supplies an unseen, inexplicable motive for living when all superior motives seem parched and barren. It is

> A pleasurable feeling of blind love,
> The pleasure which there is in life itself.

Partly it belongs to solitude, as in the introductory passage of *Michael* from which I have just quoted: it is a man's lone and dumb satisfaction in the labour that keeps him alive in midst of the kindred forces of nature with which he is struggling. But more importantly it derives from a sense of human fellowship in human effort. This sense, though at first elementary and crude, a thing "that blindly works in the blood of all," opens the way that leads up from a merely primitive joy in life to a real human happiness,—and thence maybe to a kind of peace that seems almost superhuman. Such an ascent is dimly involved in the theme of *Michael*; it is prefigured, but it is not poetically made. The same ascending process, now clearly seen and firmly developed, is the theme of *Laodamia*, written some fourteen years later. But here the style is too rigid and the treatment too narrow. The poet's mood has reached an elevation beyond *Michael*, but only at the expense of its common touch.

The pathos of *Michael*, one of the greatest and most characteristic poems of our modern era, is deep and common. It culminates no doubt in the verse that Arnold loved: "And never lifted up a single stone." Yet I think an unbiased reader must feel in this verse and its context an artificial or, at least, a too deliberate blankness that does not belong to the finest simplicity of poetry—the simplicity, for instance, of the closing lines of *Paradise Lost*:

> They, hand in hand, with wandering steps and slow,
> Through Eden took their solitary way.

This illustration, to be sure, would fail of its effect if the reader should claim that he has always felt too much of artifice in the powerful antithesis here used; but then I would consider him a Wordsworthianized reader! The word "solitary" over against "hand in hand" is perfectly simple, considering its sublime suggestion: Adam and Eve's lingering sense of the loss of something divine in their *new* human companionship. Their pathos is in the truest sense tragic. It is active. As we took part sympathetically in their fault, we take part no less in their active efforts to escape or meliorate the grief of it. And these efforts are all gathered together in the phrase "hand in hand" in the closing lines, of which we may say what Arnold says less properly of the line from *Michael*: "it is expression of the highest and most truly expressive kind."[4] The pathos of Michael lacks the highest kind of poetic expressiveness because it lacks *agency*. The old man, in regard to the cause and effect of his trouble, is largely inert. In this respect he is the ancestor of all those urban and suburban sufferers in present-day poetry who are over-whelmed by external circumstances; or by appetite so irresistible, or unresisted, that it appears to belong organically to circumstance. Their stories are often called tragic. But Wordsworth rightly called his piece "a pastoral poem"; and he gave his hero, in labour and defeat, a nature akin to rocks and trees. The poem turns upon an elemental capacity for suffering which goes along with an elemental capacity for joy, for "the pleasure which there is in life itself." That power of sufferance, "pagan" and "stoical" as we call it for lack of proper terms, is below all creeds and civilizations. It is too primitive to provide by itself the greatest poetry. It is so primal that it provides a real poetic strength. If Wordsworth had concen-

---

[4]Addison thought the two last lines of *Paradise Lost* should be omitted (*Spectator*, No. 369). His reasoning is delightfully expressive of himself and his time; but it obliterates the power of Milton's climactic master-touch.

trated more upon its primal quality, his poem would be still stronger.[5] As it is, the appeal of this poem is deep and common, without being really tragic.[6]

That is how *Michael* appears in the light of the standard that Wordsworth set for himself in *Laodamia*. Here he wins a higher level of Personality, though he has lost his poetic flow, the mysterious flow that signalizes poetry as the art of Personality. Potentially the woman Laodamia is more richly human than the man Michael. In a periodical that lies before me, the heroine of a recent novel is said to be "triumphantly sexed." Well, so is Laodamia. Just as distasteful to her as to any recent heroine, is the sound moral advice that the gods have sent her:

> And Thou, though strong in love, art all too weak. . . .
> Learn, by a mortal yearning to ascend
> Seeking a higher object. . . .
> The depth and not the tumult of the soul. . . .

The shade of her dead husband, Protesilaus, responds to her prayer like a sort of homely Messiah, incarnating for her the higher ecstasy and peace which her inmost being yearns for, but which she fails to grasp. Here is the vital paradox, the doubleness of Personal life, that makes great tragedy and moves at the centre of poetry as a whole.

No wonder this poem cost Wordsworth, as he said, "more trouble than anything of equal length I have ever written." His creative power was declining even while his instinct as a great poet was impelling him toward the centre of the life of poetry. Subconsciously he was far from being fully satisfied with *Michael* and the other characteristic works of his great period. An unacknowledged criticism of them appears in such poems as *Laodamia*. Here, significantly, he chose as his subject an ancient classic myth, and strove to give it "a loftier tone," as he said, than the ancients had done. Just in this way, by such critical heliographing between the past and present

---

[5] For example, the primitive power of the story is weakened by Michael's conventional references to the Christian God. They do not occur at the end of the poem, where the old man's need of divine comfort is sorest, and they should have been omitted from the middle. (Of course a Wordsworthian could explain that Michael outgrew them!)

[6] The important distinction which is touched on above is admirably developed in P. H. Frye's *Romance and Tragedy* (Boston, 1922).

stations of poetry, the life of poetry is at once conserved and developed.

But such was not Wordsworth's attitude in his great creative period, which was finished by 1810. Not only did he reject the Christian and classic myths as subjects for verse: he discarded, with them, the central way of poetry; and he did so unawares. His sense of travelling a highway, when he was actually on a byway, accounts for the strain of false grandiloquence in his style. It appears especially when he is contemplating his own poetic mission, as in the famous closing section of *The Recluse*, "On Man, on Nature, and on Human Life." Certainly the passage has a real elevation of spirit. The poet declares his emulation of Milton. He feels that he is taking hold of English poetry where Milton left it and carrying it along, in a new direction, but on the same high level. Insensibly, however, he is declining from that level and trying, at the same time, to maintain it by loftiness of stride. I don't mean to suggest the full absurdity of a man stepping high in going down stairs. But surely the blank verse has in it a kind of bumptious bounce.[7] One reads it with a curious mixture of affectionate respect and risibility.

In reference to Milton's *Paradise Lost*, Wordsworth chants:

> Urania, I shall need
> Thy guidance, or a greater Muse, if such
> Descend to earth or dwell in highest heaven!
> For I must tread on shadowy ground, must sink
> Deep—and, aloft ascending, breathe in worlds
> To which the heaven of heavens is but a veil.
> All strength—all terror, single or in bands,
> That ever was put forth in personal form—
> Jehovah—with his thunder, and the choir

[7] A very explicit example, if desired, may be found in the passage beginning "I, long before the blissful hour arrives" (lines 809-24). The poet announces his intention of proclaiming "how exquisitely" the "individual mind" and the "external world" are fitted to each other; and how wonderful is the "creation" which they achieve together. This has always been an *important* theme of poetry, and can never be the *main* theme. It is "exquisite" (in Wordsworth's own word) rather than "noble" or "high." Yet he makes it a source of "noble rapture" (line 815) and gives it the climactic position in his "high argument" (line 824). Really, it forms an anticlimax to what precedes. The poet tries to bolster it into epic significance by means of awkward parentheses (lines 817-23). Hence the curious angular strut in the movement of the passage.

Of shouting Angels, and the empyreal thrones—
I pass them unalarmed. Not Chaos, not
The darkest pit of lowest Erebus,
Nor aught of blinder vacancy, scooped out
By help of dreams—can breed such fear and awe
As fall upon us often when we look
Into our Minds, into the Mind of Man—
My haunt and the main region of my song.

Of course, the "Mind of Man" is the "main region" of all great poetry. But Wordsworth proposes to represent it in verse more simply and directly than his great predecessors had done. While maintaining the nobility of the old epics, he will reject their traditional methods and images. He will draw his own images from the common sights and sounds of nature, from the joys and sorrows of ordinary people, and from the story of his own development, as in *The Prelude*, which he was now composing. He will use words "which speak of nothing more than what we are." He will omit the supernatural machinery of classic and Christian mythology,—the heavens and hells, the gods and demigods. Just here, however, we come upon one of the most remarkable ironies in the history of poetry. Wordsworth at this time was creating for himself a new supernatural image, a modern myth; or rather he was re-creating for modern poetry an ancient mythical concept. It was familiar to the early Greeks; it came down through the ages, on the edge of the main stream of tradition; it won new prominence in the eighteenth century and was versified by Pope. In Wordsworth, it moved to the centre of the modern imagination:

A presence that disturbs me with the joy
Of elevated thoughts; a sense sublime
Of something far more deeply interfused,
Whose dwelling is the light of setting suns,
And the round ocean and the living air,
And the blue sky, and in the mind of man;
A motion and a spirit, that impels
All thinking things, all objects of all thought,
And rolls through all things.

Certainly these are not words that speak of "nothing more than what we are." They mean that the common objects to which the poet was devoting himself were inadequate, by themselves, to convey his "sense sublime," his sublime yearning. He was groping through them for "something far more deeply interfused"—for an image that could retain the exaltation of the epical Joves and Jehovahs, and yet seem "a simple produce of the common day." Thus he arrived at the mythical spirit or life "that impels all thinking things . . . and rolls through all things."

Wordsworth quickly left behind him the *obvious* pantheism of this passage and was much irritated at orthodox persons who charged him with that belief. We need not return upon the nineteenth-century quarrel between poetic pantheism and orthodox "pot-theism," as Carlyle called it. The significant point is that the poetic imagination became obsessed with the notion that the life of the universe consists of a single kind of energy. Generally speaking, that notion has served as the very axis of poetry whenever poetry, during the past hundred years, has had decided momentum. We may say that the "motion" or "spirit" that "rolls through all things" has rolled through the nineteenth century and into the twentieth; gaining in speed and quantity (not quality) like a snowball rolling down hill. It won new substance from evolutionary science and élan vital from new philosophies. It has assumed all sorts of curious forms without losing its identity. In one form or another it rolls around in present-day literature, verse and prose. It wabbles throughout the general mind. Collegiate atheists, who regard the Christian and other deities as outworn myths, are inclined to condone, if not to accept, the myth of a single impersonal life that "rolls through all things." Of course, the thing has had the value of breaking open, so to speak, the smug personifications of conventionalized religion. That, apparently, is the "sociological" function of this old myth in human history. But when it extends its sway beyond its proper field, when it persists after its function has been sufficiently fulfilled, when it comes to be regarded as a sort of scientific reality instead of a myth that belongs in the outskirts of poetry, then it means a fearful stultifying of the human imagination. For this image of a single impersonal life crushes toward each other the very poles of human Personality. It reduces and blurs those mighty oppositions in our nature between which the true world of poetry revolves. And it may do so while maintaining an appearance of real magnitude, of sublimity, as in the poetry of Wordsworth.

He had, as he said, a "sense sublime," a sublime emotional tendency. But he had not a sublime imagination. The passage in *Tintern Abbey* cited above, and later and better passages in the same general vein, have beneath them a *feeling* for what is greatest in human nature. But they do not shape up that feeling and establish it in adequate images: they fail to body forth "the *forms* of things unknown." Young Shakespeare in the passage in *Midsummer Night's Dream* from which I have just quoted, had also a "sense sublime." He had sublime yearnings that glanced "from heaven to earth, from earth to heaven." But unlike Wordsworth (at about the same age) he was not trying to weave together his heaven and earth—"all thinking things, all objects of all thought"—into one sublime image. A critical and humorous modesty kept whispering to him the limitations of his own imagination,—indeed, of the human imagination in general. Along with his ecstasy he was able to remark that

> The lunatic, the lover, and the poet
> Are of imagination all compact . . .
> Such tricks hath strong imagination
> That, if it would but apprehend some joy,
> It comprehends some bringer of that joy. . . .

Wordsworth, who had found for himself a fresh and deep joy in life, was solemnly endeavouring to "comprehend some bringer of that joy." He mistook apprehension for comprehension; or at any rate his imaginative comprehension was far behind his "sense sublime," and he had no proper awareness of the discrepancy.[8] Therefore what the Wordsworthian calls the "sublime" passages in his work have a general inclination, at the least, toward an inflated grandiloquency. They miss the true epic loftiness which their author desired and which he felt he was more or less attaining. His best passages have his quiet mystic power, his lofty wonder, his serene sympathy with human sorrow, and his joy that passes along our heart with "tranquil restoration." But they do *not*

> breed such fear and awe
> As fall upon us often when we look
> Into our minds, into the mind of Man—
> My haunt and the main region of my song.

MILTON'S IMAGINATION

An image that does take hold of the opposing depths and heights of Personality is given by Milton at the beginning of *Paradise Lost* in his invocation to the creative spirit. Let us put beside it a quite

[8] Such awareness, as I said above, is an integral part of great poetic ability and charm.

parallel invocation from Wordsworth, in which the life that "rolls through all things" appears at its best. Thus Wordsworth:

> Wisdom and Spirit of the universe!
> Thou Soul that art the eternity of thought,
> That givest to forms and images a breath
> And everlasting motion, not in vain
> By day or star-light thus from my first dawn
> Of childhood didst thou intertwine for me
> The passions that build up our human soul;
> Not with the mean and vulgar works of man,
> But with high objects, with enduring things—
> With life and nature—purifying thus
> The elements of feeling and of thought,
> And sanctifying, by such discipline,
> Both pain and fear, until we recognize
> A grandeur in the beatings of the heart.

Thus Milton:

> And chiefly Thou, O Spirit, that dost prefer
> Before all temples the upright heart and pure,
> Instruct me, for Thou know'st; Thou from the first
> Wast present, and, with mighty wings outspread,
> Dovelike sat'st brooding on the vast Abyss,
> And mad'st it pregnant: what in me is dark
> Illumine, what is low raise and support. . . .

Something like this, surely, is what we see when with "fear and awe," as Wordsworth says, we look "into our minds, into the Mind of Man." We see a chaos of desire, and above it a nameless power, or potentiality, of light and order. Milton's image, like the mystery of Personality itself, is at once single and twofold: "with mighty wings outspread, dovelike . . . brooding on the vast Abyss." The "vast Abyss" and the "dove-like" presence are inseparable. They have no meaning, no poetic and human meaning, apart from each other. We are aware of the chaos in us because of something different that moves upon it, making its "darkness visible." At the same time, because of our chaos—"outrageous as a sea, dark, wasteful, wild"—we recognize our higher nature as simple, luminous, shapely, peaceful, *small*, small in human quantity, but in its power to "illumine," "raise," and "support," wide perhaps as the abyss itself. Hence Milton even while calling it "dove-like" sees, through the shadows, its *"mighty* wings outspread." Presently in the great passage on his blindness, his physical blindness and the great blindness that there is in human nature, he invokes the same power as a "Celestial Light" that shines inward and can irradiate "the mind through *all her powers.*" In fact, throughout the whole background of *Paradise Lost,* in one way or another, he maintains his original image with its two-fold implication. His "empyreal Heaven," for instance, is not represented as a thing apart. He elaborates its manifold relationships with all that is beneath it. It is first shown to us, with sublime art, as the complement of Chaos.[9] We come up to it as it comes down to us. We draw near to it "with tumult less and with less hostile din," as it draws near to us with its "sacred influence of light." In fact this "empyreal" splendour is a part of our chaos that has been transformed. It is a region conquered and built out of "the wasteful Deep," in sequel to the invocation

> what in me is dark
> Illumine, what is low raise and support.

It is only against this imaginative background, and in their proper relation to it, that the great figures of Satan and the Son of God emerge in their true poetic meaning. Of course, the nineteenth-century tendency to detach Satan from the story and make him a symbol of contemporary dogma is just as non-poetic as the older tendency to treat the Son in that way. If the Son is quite mechanical when regarded as the deus ex machina of Protestant salvationism, Satan, as a hero of revolutionary naturalism, is worse: he moves with a melodramatic strut. Poetically, neither of these two personages has any great meaning apart from the other. The complementary fashion in which their stories are woven together provides the very organism of the poem and, I think, its greatest passages of verse. The two are never brought face to face, never exchange a word. Yet when either of them is present, we are made to feel the need and the nearness of the other in the background. When both are absent, the background itself is alive with reflections of them, with the conflicting influences that radiate from them. For example, those influences impregnate the very atmosphere of the Garden of Eden from the moment of its first appearance to us.

Fully to feel the poetic omnipresence of the Son, the modern reader must overcome his infantile predilection for Satan and open his imagination to all suggestions of the other figure. He must

[9] *Paradise Lost,* II, 1034*ff.*

realize that all the various titles applied to deity in the course of the poem converge upon the Son; that they are just as synonymous, in effect, as the various titles applied to Satan; and that any one of them may serve to call up the whole image of the Son when He is not actually present. By subtle and incessant touches, of conscious or unconscious art, Milton really submerges the other members of the triune deity in the figure of the Messiah. Be it noted that Jehovah is represented, in general, as a mere chairman introducing the Son. The dullness of the presiding officer's remarks,—which may possibly have been quite as evident to Milton as to the enlightened modern reader,—is quite relevant. Moreover, it has the effect of throwing the ensuing speeches of the Son into glowing relief. Really, the "Almighty Father" is represented as a narrower being who passes into the larger nature of the Son and forms a subordinate part of It,—namely, Its sheer might. This is the elementary aspect of the Son, contiguous to the nature of Satan. Therefore it is emphasized in the background of the first two books of the poem, where Satan has the foreground preeminently. The modern reader delights in Satan here; yet his *poetic* delight is very limited unless he sees, with Milton, the greater image of the Son already taking form in the background. Its main outlines are suggested in the first fifty verses of the poem, before Satan is allowed to appear. The "one greater Man" destined to restore human happiness (line 4), the "Spirit" inhabiting the upright heart and brooding upon chaos (line 17), and finally the "Almighty Power" by whom Satan was "hurled headlong flaming from the ethereal sky" (line 44),—these three are synonymous for Milton and suggest, in a significant sequence, the three aspects exhibited in the course of the story by the Son. This great nature pervades the poem like light itself—the Light which for Milton is Its chief symbol.

But obviously it has not pervaded the imagination of the modern age. In other words, modern readers have not yet accepted the main theme of *Paradise Lost*. Milton would probably declare that they deny the very existence of his poem *as a poem*. While delighting in particular features of it, they are cool or hostile to its whole conception, which they assume is not poetically vital. This assumption has been fostered by four agencies: by classicists who have treated the poem as mainly an imitation of the ancient epic; by romanticists who have distorted its native epic purpose; by Christians, like Dr.

Johnson, who have lauded it all too efficiently as a moral document; and finally by the modern stoics who, reacting like Arnold from the Puritans, have admired its "grand style" in disjunction from its great meaning.[10] When we reflect upon that array of obstacles we may be inclined to admit that *Paradise Lost* has so far been running an obstacle race; and if we believe in its singular greatness as an English poem, we may also believe that its influence during the first two centuries of its career has been very meagre compared with what it must be in the future if our poetry shall again find the highway.

As for the fourth obstacle mentioned above, the plain fact is that the Arnoldian view of Milton slurs the passionate conviction of his tone. In reality, his "grand style" is not just the product of a "noble nature poetically gifted" applying itself to some or other great subject. His grand style is the vesture of a certain grand conviction. Arnold makes the Miltonic style seem quite factitious—like a magnificent sea-weed flourishing on dry land. Properly its movement, its "bridled excitement" as he calls it, is not separable from the tidal movement of the poem as a whole; and this tide flows from the great human truth which has captured Milton and which he is working out, pretty successfully, in the total scheme of his poem. In other words, the unexampled union of peace and strenuousness in his style, comes from his unexampled belief in "Satan" and the "Son of God" as the prime facts of human nature. Poetically, if not theologically, he experienced these two facts as inseparable. Hence the surging dark fire, so to call it, that goes through the first two books of *Paradise Lost*. We all feel it, but surely we miss its full intensity if we attribute it mainly to Milton's stylistic art engaged upon a fortunate subject. Really, it derives from the rush of his imagination towards the full opening of his thought in Book III, and from the presence of the Light of Book III in the background of Books I and II. Satan is "proudly eminent," in the well-known passage in Book I, not just in contrast with his legions around him, but because in Milton's conception he rises like a dark tower against the Celestial Light on the horizon. It shines about him dimly: "his form had not yet lost all

[10]An excellent critical summary of eighteenth- and nineteenth-century views of Milton is given by James Holly Hanford in his essay on "Milton and the Return to Humanism" (*Studies in Philology*, vol. 16). The new and truer view of Milton which certain American and European scholars are now engaged in developing, is of great importance for the future of poetry.

her original brightness." The "original brightness" is not just reminiscent. It is anticipatory of the Celestial Light of Book III, in the centre of which is the figure of the Messiah.

Satan, to be sure, bulks larger in the poem than the Son; he is a dramatic and quickly captivating figure. But this does not mean that he is Milton's real "hero," that Milton fell in love with him in spite of Milton; nor, above all, does it mean that Satan is a greater work of poetic art than the Son. He bulks larger in the story of *Paradise Lost* because he bulks larger in the story of mankind, today and yesterday. The great human appetites directed by human intellect, trying for human happiness and missing it, trying again and again in new guises, age after age—that spectacle, whatever else we may say of it, is hugely dramatic. Satan plays a more *striking* part than the Son in human Personality, of which this poem is a veracious imitation. His Titanic size, brought out by Milton on every possible occasion, appeals to the most elementary kind of Satanism in our nature, our love of giants, which clings to us from the cradle to the skyscraper.[11] The figure of the Son, on the other hand, is never allowed to appear gigantic or dramatic. In the course of the poem there are plenty of occasions on which Milton must have been tempted to exert his stylistic art in that direction if he had been less in love with the truth. The truth is that the highest power that appears in human Personality, the power of creative or strenuous Peace, if so we may term it, is not in itself extensive or dramatic, though its effects may be so.[12] It may overcome the world, and yet it is not of the world. It is greatest in the very thick of human affairs, says Marcus Aurelius, even while it creates in the midst of those affairs a kind of retirement from them. This indicates the quality of Milton's image.

[11] If not, nowadays, to the grave. However, a vast democratic mausoleum, erected for public use near a vast American city, was recently advertised in the newspapers. A friendly allusion was made to the Egyptian pyramids.

[12] Milton carefully distinguished this strenuous Peace from the attitude of Mammon and Belial, which he represents with appropriate dramatic vividness:

> "Thus Belial, with words clothed in reason's garb,
> Counselled ignoble ease and peaceful sloth,
> Not peace; and after him thus Mammon spake. . . ."

Denis Saurat in his remarkable book, *Milton, Man and Thinker* (1924), identifies the Son of God with "Reason" and neglects His higher significance, His embodiment of what we may call "the human peace divine."

The Son has a certain aloofness in the midst of the mighty business of Milton's story. His voice comes quietly at the very centre of all the tumult and magniloquence of that vast universe. His speeches in their very tone and rhythm are congruent with his title of "omnific Word": they come from that region within us which is at once most peaceful and most creative. In the episode of the creation of the universe, the introductory speech of Jehovah is used to convey the material sublime, the external magnitude of the coming Creation; thereafter the Son conveys the very spirit of it. Jehovah swells to the dimension of the great forces and materials of nature: "Boundless the Deep, because I am who fill Infinitude," and so forth. The angelic chorus makes a fitting response.

> So sang the Hierarchies.—Meanwhile the Son
> On his great expedition now appeared,
> Girt with omnipotence, with radiance crowned
> Of majesty divine, sapience and love
> Immense; and *all his Father in him shone*.[13]

The clause that I have italicized brings out the natural emphasis of the passage. The Son retains his mysterious simplicity and separateness. Power in Him is always inward and radiant. The sheer *immensity* of his power is conveyed, never through his person, but through the various symbols with which he is "girt," or which attach to him in one way or another in the course of the poem. His figure is made to seem curiously small in comparison with the gigantic creatures and objects that surround Him. The poet without actual description suggests for him an ideal and yet normal human form. This treatment culminates in the episode of the creation of Adam in Book VIII. With a fine restraint and beautiful pertinency, the poet intimates that the creator of Adam—of noble and typical humanity—is the Son in sublime human form. The figure is visionary and genial, yet touched with austerity. The dreadfulness of the Son, here kept in abeyance, is displayed in the crucial episode of the poem at the end of Book VI. In this episode the Son uses the strength of Satan, so to speak, in overcoming Satan, who is now more than ever the embodiment of chaotic passion organized by intellectual power. Yet even here the Son retains his suggestion of humanity and, above all, his peace. His destructive power, which is conceived by Milton as a subordinate but essential part of his creative and re-creative

---

[13] *Paradise Lost*, VII, 192*ff*.

power,[14] gathers head slowly, reluctantly, during the first half of the poem, and breaks forth here like a storm, and passes away, without affecting the peace above it. The *meekness* of the Son, in the great old sense of that word, is always maintained at the centre. His powers spread out from him, through the Miltonic universe, like vast shadowy wings which belong to him and yet, in respect of their *mere* vastness, do not belong to his essential nature. He is a presence "with mighty wings outspread"—yet "dove-like, brooding on the vast Abyss."

For this image, for this kind of myth, the modern imagination has substituted the mythical life that "rolls through all things." The suburbs of poetry have been enriched with fresh and subtle images from external nature. But the very citadel of poetry has been undermined by the rejection or dehumanization of old images saturated with the meaning and mystery of human nature. The mischief lies in the Wordsworthian supposition that the reaction from the classic and Christian myths is a *poetic* reaction. It is no more poetic, and no less temporary, than the debasement of pagan myths by the zeal of the earlier Christians. Poetry does not react from her own images. She keeps them alive and transforms them, gradually, in accordance with her shifting emphases. Milton's imagination was formed upon the revival of the pagan myths in the Renaissance and the attempt to blend them, vitally, into the myths of Christianity. This attempt, of course, was only partially successful because the Christian stories were still regarded, more or less, as scientifically true. But the attempt was on the highway of poetry. It must be resumed and continued. The Greek deities came alive for Keats more than for any other poet of the past hundred years because, as one finds in his Letters, he was wary of the baleful individualism of the age and was struggling, though blindly, toward a renewed vision of the mystery of passion and peace in human Personality. The sequel of his effort was Tennyson's endeavour, very weak but very significant, to resume the figure of the "Son of God," under modern conditions, as an image of the shaping peace at work in our chaos:

> And what I am beheld again
> What is, and no man understands;

[14] As in *Paradise Lost*, VII, 602*ff*.

And out of darkness came the hands
That reach through nature, moulding men.[15]

When one comes to think of it, the "Son of God" is the chief image
that emerges from two thousand years of European poetry. It cannot
be simply shoved aside and left behind.[16] It can be carried on and
modified in the light of other images, derived from Greece, the
Orient, the countryside, the factory-town.—In short, the mythical life
that "rolls through all things" rolls along the by-paths of poetry
and the highway of poetry ahead of us passes through the centre of
Milton's poem.

SHAKESPEARE AND MILTON

The highway passes also of course through the work of Shakespeare; but not the nineteenth-century Shakespeare, who is still with
us, the Shakespeare supposed to be endowed with a poetic vitality
far surpassing that of Milton. This common belief is perhaps the
main barrier today between us and the fresh poetic outlook that we
want. The nineteenth-century lust for the unconscious and spontaneous element in poetry, which has now developed into a morbid disease, battened upon Shakespeare. It is a real misfortune for us that
he left us so little information, and that Milton left us so much
concerning the poet's attitude toward his own work. Shakespeare's
silence on this score and Milton's loquacity, which are pretty well
accounted for by extraneous circumstances, have both been taken too
literally, with the aid of a too literal scholarship. A sublime unconsciousness in regard to his own creation has been read *into* Shakespeare and *out* of Milton. In this respect the two have been thrown
into a contrast so heightened, and even violent, as to be incredible
especially when common sense whispers to us that whatever a poet
says, or does *not* say, about his own work must be taken always with

[15] Of course Shelley and Browning were also addicted to the Greek and
Christian myths, respectively. But they blurred their inmost meaning
Shelley turned the pagan gods into Romantic mists, and Browning turned
the Christian ones into mouthpieces of Browningism. However, in the super
epilogue to Book I of *The Ring and the Book*, Browning approaches the
insight of Tennyson in the stanza quoted above.

[16] To be confident that it has been left behind already, one must need
be a devoted "—ologist" of some sort, like Harriet Martineau, who recorded
the following "fact" in the year 1855: "The last and noblest of the my-
thologies (Christianity) is about to vanish before the flood of a brighter
light"—this brighter light being "a true science of human nature."

a good many grains of salt. The fact is that if we simply put along-side each other the best passages in Shakespeare and Milton, the same quality of consciousness and unconsciousness is evident in both. Nor is the result different, I think, when we compare a great Shakespearean play as a whole with *Paradise Lost*. Shakespeare, if we lift him out of the Romantic cult of Shakespeare and interpret him in the light of the world's best poetry, may be assumed to have been normally conscious of what he was doing when he wrote *Macbeth*; as Milton was normally *un*conscious of what he was doing when he wrote *Paradise Lost*.

The opposite assumption about Milton, owing to the false antithesis between him and Shakespeare, has of course fostered the view that the whole form of *Paradise Lost* is mechanically imitative. The poem has been regarded partly as an epic inferior to Homer's, and partly as a religious vision inferior to Dante's. It derives, indeed, from both of those forms; but essentially it is a new and independent form which Milton created with a vital unconsciousness of what he was doing. Milton gives no adequate account of this new form in all that he has to say about his "heroic poem," as he terms it. He never gives it an adequate name. In lieu of such a name, we may call it a symbolical epic. The point is that Milton was trying, whether he knew it or not, to find a new form of poetry in which a strictness of epical outline could be made to serve the purposes of an intensely symbolic imagination. He wished to write a poem in which "more is meant," very much more is meant, "than meets the ear." But he did not wish to write a loose allegory, like that of his immediate master, Spenser. His reining-in of his imagination, his effort year after year to achieve a compact and reasonable form for his poem, had the effect of intensifying the symbolic quality of his style. His poem, as a whole and in detail, is intensely suggestive to the reader just because Milton did not immediately aim at suggestiveness but at form. On the other hand, he did not first build the poem and then lay-on the style as he seems to say, infelicitously, in that too conscious mood of his which we are apt to take too literally.[17] To compare *Paradise Lost* with *Comus*, which is really an early forestudy for it in both thought and style, is to realize that in the very act of shaping the concept of his symbolical epic he was developing his style

[17] As in *Paradise Lost*, IX, 20.

toward the right manner for it. He fed on thoughts and images that "voluntary moved" the right "harmonious numbers," and also the right stringent and passionate numbers. A great labour of premeditation underlies his "unpremeditated verse." He built up his poem, he built up his spirit, toward the Muse that "deigns," as he says,

> her nightly visitation unimplored,
> And dictates to me slumbering or inspires
> Easy my unpremeditated verse.

More signally than any other English poet, he ascended into spontaneity through meditation. Today many writers are descending into spontaneity through a kind of visceral abandonment of the region of meditation. Of course this is an ancient process. But today it is being pursued very extensively and dogmatically as a professed means of *renewing* the imagination. The truth is that the troubled stream of spontaneity flowing down through nineteenth-century literature has now disintegrated into a kind of oily mist, obscuring the heights of spontaneity. Milton, therefore, is the one English poet above all others who should be studied today by those who are interested in a real renewal of poetic imagination. He is the great proponent of such renewal. If Shakespeare, in a way, exhausted the poetic imagination, Milton renewed it. He accomplished the thing that poetry at its best is blindly striving toward today. With a free and comprehensive attitude toward tradition, he created a new form of poetry. And he opened the highest, the most powerful, source of poetic spontaneity at a time when certain poets were already laying the groundlines of the neo-classic conventionalism of the eighteenth century. That is worth noting in view of the conventionalized unconventionality which threatens to be the firmest result of the present situation of poetry.

Yet the spontaneity of Shakespeare, at his best, has the same quality as Milton's and was attained in the same way. We need to get rid of the legendary opposition between these two poets. The modest Shakespeare was worshipped by the poets and critics of the past century in a way that would have astounded him, if he could have reappeared on the scene. Emerson's friend, Bronson Alcott, discovered in Shakespeare a supreme religious vision. And Charles Lamb was being very temperate when he declared that at a sudden reappearance of Christ we would kneel—of Shakespeare, stand up. He did not record the proper modern posture for receiving a visit from Milton,—

flight, perhaps, flight into "the intense inane"! If Shakespeare should enter the room, no doubt we would all stand up; but in that case Shakespeare himself would feel very uncomfortable.[18] Nor would his spirit be pleased with Carlyle's claim that Milton's imagination compared with his own (and, by implication, with Carlyle's) was quite mechanical. For the amazing flexibility of the Shakespearean spirit, which the nineteenth century tried vainly to reproduce, was centred in critical modesty. Shakespeare, unlike many of his worshippers, had a clear sense of the limits of his own extraordinary scope. And he would be the first to recognize in Milton a consistent height of poetic power (including poetic spontaneity) that he himself could not achieve.

However, through the agencies of theatre and library and school and college, there has risen between us and Milton a colossal inflated figure of Shakespeare. The attempts of Shaw and other iconoclasts to prick that figure are prophetic. But so far these sharp darts have not availed. They have pierced the colossus only in its fringes, in "the cloudy border of its base":

> For the loftiest hill,
> Who to the stars uncrowns his majesty,
> Planting his steadfast footsteps in the sea,
> Making the heaven of heavens his dwelling-place,
> Spares but the cloudy border of his base
> To the foiled searching of mortality. . . .

Shakespeare's lungs would crow like chanticleer at this grandiose image of himself. Arnold's sonnet, produced in the middle of the past century, marked the high tide of Shakespeare-worship. But after the poet-critics came the college professors of English literature, "planting *their* steadfast footsteps in the sea."[19] Their combined efforts have served to hold in place a vast shipload of uncritical admiration. However, "there *is* a tide in the affairs of men." The ship must put out to sea, and "the loftiest hill" must retreat toward the horizon. When our poetry is released from its present shallows, an important circumstance of its forward voyage must surely be a rather general effort to see the work of Shakespeare in true perspective.

[18] He seems to say from his tomb to the throngs at Stratford-on-Avon: "Good friends, for Jesus' sake forbear. . . ."

[19] One thinks of the delightful books on Shakespeare by Professors Dowden, Raleigh, and Bradley. They steadfastly carried on the canon of Shakespearean infallibility.

But so far, on account of our exaggerated individualism, the general imagination is still enslaved by the verisimilitude of Shakespeare's individual characters, and by the magical flow of style in which they move and breathe and have their being. For instance, we may patronize the *Tragedy of Othello* because of what seems to us its naïveté. But we are still naïvely fascinated by the marvellous "psychology" (as we now call it) of the leading personages. We are really not much interested in the work as a whole. We may feel in its tone a certain radical inconsistency—which is due to a restless sense of contradiction on the part of the great poet who is here trying forcibly, but not quite successfully, to confine the scope of his imaginative thought to a kind of mental spotlight. We may go further and feel that there is a violent improbability at the very core of the action, that the play contradicts its own kind of probability. I am not saying that this is surely the case. The point is that such difficulties, though supremely important in their bearing upon the whole value of the work and, indeed, of Shakespeare as a poet, can be generally felt without being brought to the forefront of general interest. For our interest has not yet decisively risen from Shakespeare the creator of wonderful images and individuals, to Shakespeare the creator of whole poems. A modest foundation for such a view of him was laid down by eighteenth-century criticism, but presently the Romantic deluge swept over it.

In the wake of that flood, a certain degree of exaggerated skepticism was sure to come. The "vast-flowing vigour" of Shakespeare, which still captivates the many, has been satirically questioned by the few. To what extent is it a real flow of imagination, and to what extent is it sheer rhetorical ability? That vital question has won a certain prominence through the recent study of Shakespeare as a popular Elizabethan playwright. But this study has had the effect of throwing his rhetoric into false relief by deprecating his poetic conceptions. Investigation has dug up all his stage-tricks, all his shallower motives, to the last knuckle-bone, and has spread them on the table before us. We are invited to watch the assembly of them if we wish to see the *real* Shakespeare rise again before us in his habit as he *wrote*. At this séance, the Arnoldian Shakespeare—

> Others abide our question. Thou art free
> We ask and ask, Thou smilest and art still . . .

is denied admittance. We are to understand now that the real Shakespeare does abide our question, and that he is far too practical a person ever to be loftily "still." And surely the dreaming Shakespeare of the earlier nineteenth century, devoted only to the magic evocation of Hamlet, Falstaff, Lady Macbeth, Dogberry, and the others, is a romantic illusion. But we cannot be satisfied to replace that ghost with a dramaturgic skeleton active on wires. We should all the more be driven toward the great poetic person who is behind these two lay figures: I mean the Shakespeare who in each of his better plays is indeed trying to "body forth" a firm poetic conception—an idea that is "more than cool reason ever comprehends" and yet is shaped by reason. He may take hold of his central idea rather blindly, and work it out more or less brokenly, with plenty of rhetoric and stagecraft in the interstices. But it is there, and it forms the main source of poetic value in the play. It is the very fountain that supplies the flow of his imagination when this flow is neither illusory nor trivial. And his conceptions deepen and clarify as his work proceeds, up to *Lear* and *Macbeth*.

So far, the effect of these two plays in *shaping* the modern imagination has been comparatively slight. The shaping ideas at work in them are averse from the main trend of modern imaginative thought. *Lear* has been called a "glorified nursery tale"; *Macbeth*, a "glorified melodrama." And this is a fair summary of the modern view of them. It is accepted at heart by a good many lovers of Shakespeare who would reject it with their lips. They do not feel that these two plays, *as whole poems*, entirely overshadow their predecessors, *Hamlet* and *Othello*; whereas they do feel in them a decided decline of individualistic appeal. Yet the two later tragedies are Shakespeare's profound criticism of the two earlier ones. They convey his conviction that in *Hamlet* and *Othello* tragic passion was "sicklied o'er with the pale cast of thought," of psychologic brooding; and that such elaborate and subtle protagonists as Iago and Hamlet—such "young intellectuals"—had to be dispensed with if the play was to be the thing, if he was to achieve a kind of tragedy that would be sublime in its total effect. The *Tragedy of Lear*, with its simplified characters and quick storm of passion, is the escape of Shakespeare from the stifling confinement of *Othello*. It is an escape into larger veracity. Hazlitt felt this when he said that in *Lear* Shakespeare was "fairly caught in the web of his own imagination." More exactly, Shakespeare here *escaped* from the web that had hitherto enmeshed him: he worked himself free, by meditative effort, and could then freely follow the higher flow of his imagination. He had been "benetted round" with subtleties; and now, ere he could make a "prologue to his brains," they had begun the play. In *Hamlet* and *Othello* he was not deeply in earnest regarding the whole story. Hence the note of quizzical virtuosity in those plays, coming out especially in passages where the main theme is broken or obscure. Certainly there are plenty of lapses in *Lear* and *Macbeth*. But the author's mind does not play around them; his higher imagination overrides them, preoccupied as it is with the whole theme.

The theme of Shakespeare's chief tragedy, *Macbeth*, is essentially the same as that of *Paradise Lost*: the battle of the lust of power against the power of Peace. This theme appears of course in Shakespeare's previous works, appears increasingly, we may say. But here he pulls it, almost violently, to the foreground, and applies himself to it with an unprecedented rigour of concentration, as though it were all in all—as though he had suddenly come to feel that this theme, and this only, could satisfy his vision on the last height of his journey. Hence the unique symbolic quality of the style of *Macbeth*. The intensity of the author's vision packs his lines with symbolic images.

These images, with the hearty cooperation of modern individualism, lend the play its melodramatic flavor on the stage. The speeches of Macbeth and his Lady are not spoken "trippingly on the tongue"; their lurid psychic qualities are dwelt upon and played-up by the two distinguished histrionic artists who take the rôles and absorb the attention of the audience. We like to concentrate upon the morbid psychology of the "hero" and "heroine"; and as this feature in itself is not a sufficient source of the terrific style of the poem, the thing as a whole must strike us, when honest with ourselves, as something of a sham battle, "full of sound and fury signifying" . . . nothing too much; signifying, in our reflective moments, that the human individual "struts and frets his hour upon the stage," and then rolls off, perhaps, into the Force "that rolls through all things."

The fact is that we view Macbeth under the aspect of Iago and Hamlet. Rather, the dramatic poem *Macbeth* should be viewed as the converse of the dramatic poem *Hamlet*, in its whole mode of conception and style. *Hamlet* is dramatic-psychological. *Macbeth* is dramatic-symbolical. Macbeth himself is a symbolic character in a manner,—not merely in a degree,—that is quite foreign to Hamlet. If the play *Hamlet* is nothing with Hamlet left out, the individual Macbeth, on the contrary, is nothing without the whole action of the play. We should let him draw back into that. The terrific images that run through his speeches should be taken, not mainly as the expression of his own mental "complexes," but as emblems of a thought beyond the reaches of *his* soul. We should bring to bear upon him the same kind of imagination, the symbolic imagination, that created him. In other words we need in the case of Macbeth essentially the same kind of approach as we need in the case of his great successor, Milton's Satan. We need to view him in the light of the whole idea of the poem.

In simplicity of outline the *Tragedy of Macbeth* is no doubt quite classical; but its symbolic quality is mediaeval. *Hamlet*, on the other hand, is a mediaeval story merged in a modern monodrama. The blend is suggestive, captivatingly so; but on the whole, in spite of all the sympathetic labours of modern exegesis, it is plainly not accomplished. Shakespeare himself, unlike his worshippers, is not in full earnest about it. He patronizes the mediaeval aspect of his plot:

> So have I heard, and do in part believe it;
> But, look, the morn in russet mantle clad
> Walks o'er the dew of yon high eastern hill.

He is still enraptured with the fresh light of Nature that had dawned in his time upon things mediaeval; his mind delights to range the whole tangled scene of human motives, without much concern for causeways leading through. The speech of Horatio just quoted is a fair enough token of Shakespeare's general attitude, before *Macbeth*, toward the mediaeval mode of imagination. In *Macbeth*, however, he throws himself into this mode with a kind of conviction which would have made him smile in the 1590's when he was evolving *Hamlet*.

Macbeth like *Paradise Lost* has that magnificent blending of the mediaeval and the classical which Renaissance poetry at its best was able to accomplish. It indicates the highway of modern poetry. It means a real union of two different modes of the imagination: large strictness and symbolic intensity. The poet's imagination moves in a full, strict orbit, like a planet around its sun. He feels, at every point in the movement of his story, the pull of his central idea—if we take the word "idea" in a rather Platonic sense, as denoting something that belongs to the whole mind, to the imagination and the intellect at once. The idea, even when the poet seems to be going away from it, throws its light upon every episode. The episode may revolve completely on its own axis; the poet may devote to it the intense individual scrutiny that we call modern—for example, in the scene of Macbeth and his dagger just before the murder of Duncan; or the scene of Satan and his serpent, just before the murder of the innocence of Eve! But the rare power of each episode comes from the centripetal pull exerted upon the poet by the "idea" that dominates his poem. He is so occupied with the particular human situation before him that he cannot descend to *mere* symbolism. He is so *pre*occupied with a great human idea that he cannot prevent it from descending into his images. It sheds through them a light indeed "that never was on sea or land."

Poetry is not purely poetic when she is very conscious of possessing that mysterious light, as in the early nineteenth century; nor when, by way of sequel, as at the present time, she consciously pursues the glimmer of the subconscious. The symbolic quality of the two great poetic episodes mentioned above is, at its best, superconscious. Macbeth's dagger is a "dagger of the mind," and Satan's serpent is a serpent of the mind, in a fuller sense than the poet consciously intends. The human mind itself is present above the puppets, the human mind in its most awful dilemma. Here is "the torture of the mind in restless ecstasy" between human appetite at its greatest and the *unrecognized* power of Peace which alone can subdue such appetite and temper it to human happiness,—that power which is "in Heaven and Earth the only peace found out for mankind under wrath," as Milton phrased it, speaking better than he knew.

Macbeth, of course, is "mankind under wrath," decidedly. The power of peace, as I have called it, has no scope in his story. The Satanic powers take large possession and make the very air murky. In Milton's Eden, evil enters along the ground "like a black mist low creeping"; in *Macbeth*, from the very beginning, it hovers "through the fog and filthy air." The obvious reason is that Shakespeare was writing a romantic drama and that the Satanic side of life, being romantic and dramatic, had a natural fascination for him and his audience: it was good stage material. But this does not account for the peculiar greatness of the poem: for the stringent tone of conviction, the fearful logic of imagination, with which it develops and displays the power of evil desire. On this subject a great deal of severe meditation had been done by the man Shakespeare before he could write *Macbeth*. Shakespeare the man and Shakespeare the poet have been curiously separated from each other of late. The Romantics made him a prodigy of imagination; later the antiquarians displayed him a shrewd man of business. Recent esthetes, making the most of this division, have liked to fancy him as shaking off his citizen nature entirely when he plunged into his artistic dreams. But the plain fact is that Shakespeare's nature was uniformly centred in his rare faculty of judgement. He applied this to his economic affairs on the one hand, and on the other to the affairs of his imagination; though he was impelled by the conditions in which he found himself to set aside his judgement, often, in his writings and never (so far as the records show) in his business. But he did not set it aside in composing *Macbeth*. He brought all his judgement to bear, finally and strenuously, on the subject of wrong desire.

The fact is obvious enough to the minds of normal readers and spectators. But it is denied by persons who, under the influence of modern artistical dogma, regard Shakespeare's attitude here as a mere dramatic make-believe; and by those who, going to the other extreme, find him uttering his own despair of humanity through the mouth of Macbeth: "Life's but a walking shadow," and so on. This passage, in relation to the whole action of the play, if we will only attend to that as clearly as Shakespeare attended to it, conveys his judgement not only of Macbeth but of the effect of uncontrolled desire in human Personality in general. Therefore it is not true that Shakespeare's attitude in this poem is just the sequel of the bitter sense of evil that appears in the earlier works of his tragic period. Through those works, to be sure, there runs a series of speeches in which the author, stepping aside somewhat from the story in hand, utters himself with a kind of acrid vividness on all the ills and evils "that flesh is heir to." But that series of speeches is not continued into *Macbeth*; that sort of utterance is here left behind. Here Shakespeare surmounts his own sensibilities. He rises above "the thousand natural shocks" to an intense vision of the spiritual nature of evil. He sees it as uncontrolled appetite, enlisting the imagination, and frustrating human happiness and peace. He is preoccupied, as never before, with the immediate effect of evil upon the nature of the evil-doer himself. Therefore he loses the acrimony with which he had previously regarded the trouble brought by the evil-doer upon others, "the spurns that patient merit of the unworthy takes." The ills that Macbeth inflicts upon innocent persons are viewed by Shakespeare with a certain equanimity. He is engrossed by the tragic deterioration of human Personality within itself. He sees, preeminently, that the person whose will is wrong has only a dim and sentimental perception of his own inward condition. Therefore the fearful irony of the play centres in the fact that Macbeth puts a merely external and sentimental interpretation upon a conviction which Shakespeare himself, in the whole course of the action, is applying to the inmost region of Personality: "We still have judgement *here*."

Certainly those critics are right who have found in Shakespearean tragedy the sense of a "spiritual order" or "a living system of moral law," or whatever it may be called, that judges human actions. Critics who deny this should also deny the very sense of tragedy with which Shakespeare induces us to contemplate the sea of human passions. There is no real thunder in a sea that has no shore. Certainly, there is a good deal of theatrical tempest in the Shakespearean tragic hero: "bursts of horrid thunder," "groans of roaring wind and rain," and "tears that drown the wind." But through it all the deeper tone is heard, the sound of the ground-swell of human passion against the shore. The shore had been made firm for Shakespeare by the great revival of ethical thought in the sixteenth century. Sometimes, no doubt, he took his stand upon that shore with a kind of citizen satisfaction, adorned with facile poetic sentiment, which too much pleases the citizen today and very much irritates Bernard Shaw and the whole brood of anti-citizens. But we should take note that the civilian smugness that appears in Shakespeare's work is the complement of its romantic passionism. Because he stood so safely on the shore, he could be easily delighted by the sheer spectacularity of storms at sea. This phenomenon reappears at the present time in our parlour cave-men (and -women). They, however, bite the hand that fed them: they disdain the civilian morality that

provided them with safe ground upon which to indulge the morbid
passionism of their literary fancies. After all, the simplicity of
Shakespeare's attitude toward conventional standards belongs to the
simplicity of a great poetic nature. He took these standards into his
imagination, and grew upon them and above them. If he was youth-
fully conventional when he wrote

> Though justice be thy plea, consider this:
> That, in the course of justice, none of us
> Should see salvation. . . .

he was nevertheless on his way to the intense conviction of his greatest tragedy, which has for its motif the same thought in sublimated
form:

> We'd jump the life to come. But in these cases
> We still have judgement here. . . .

His best attitude toward the "spiritual order" seems to be a kind
of Stoical faith, divested of Stoic pride and touched with Christian
intensity, but not very much illuminated with the Christian sense
of Peace. It was not in his nature, not in the nature of his dramatic
work, to take any large hold of the idea of the highest human peace,
the "peace found out for mankind under wrath." But in the *Tragedy
of Macbeth* he could not lift his mind to envisage the greatest wrath
of human passion without lifting it, at the same time, into the very
precincts of the power of Peace. His conception of the story demanded that this power should be dreadfully close to the scene and
yet dreadfully obscured. Hence the peculiar greatness of the play.
The unexampled tenseness of its atmosphere does not come ultimately from the sense of impending evil, but from the sense of
impending Peace. Heaven *does* "peep through the blanket of the
dark to cry, Hold, hold." Macbeth, at first, has a very strong sense
of the things that belong unto his peace. He is not conceived by
Shakespeare as an individual who was made by nature abnormally
simple, or worldly, or temperamental. That view reduces the play
to piecemeal, and fails to account for its total effect on the normal
reader. The play simply does not hold together unless we recognize
the author's concentration upon Macbeth's will, his "free will."
Macbeth is conceived as a quite normal person who, by fearful acts
of his will, makes himself abnormal. We watch him forcing his
imagination into the service of his great desire, and away from the

things of his peace. Then when the desire is fulfilled, and nothing really threatens his success from without, we hear him say:

> better be with the dead
> Whom we to gain our peace have sent to peace,
> Than on the torture of the mind to lie
> In restless ecstasy.

In Milton's Satan the same despair, rendered in a style proper to a symbolic epic, opens upon an infinite vista:

> Which way I fly is Hell; myself am Hell;
> And, in the lowest deep, a lower deep
> Still threatening to devour me opens wide,   _
> To which the Hell I suffer seems a heaven.

In both cases the sequel is the same: "only in destroying I find ease to my relentless thoughts," as Satan puts it. In both cases the speaker becomes a symbol of the most awful irony that there is in human nature: the incessant effort to achieve our happiness—or our vitality,[20] if we prefer the contemporary term—in ways that conflict with our peace and lead to chaos; and then, our conceited effort to be at home in chaos, to move naturally in it as though it were our native element instead of the thing which in our heart of hearts we most hate and dread.

Shakespeare had come to feel that irony to the full when he wrote *Macbeth*. It is a theme that is best developed in dramatic form, and it is more convincing to our emotions in *Macbeth* than in *Paradise Lost*. On the other hand the theme of Peace, on which that irony depends, is non-dramatic and calls for the form of *Paradise Lost*. The dramatic symbolism of *Macbeth* is on the way to the epic symbolism of *Paradise Lost*. It is fair to claim that the master trend of Shakespeare's genius, beginning, let us say, in the years when he wrote *Richard Third* (an early forestudy for *Macbeth*), was toward the kind of poetic art we find in *Macbeth*; and that this trend was part of the whole development of the Renaissance spirit toward the kind of poetic art we find in *Paradise Lost*.

[20] Maxim Gorky in a paper that has just come before me says that literature today needs *both* vitality and happiness: "The man of the present day is particularly in need of a vigorous spirit. . . . Meanwhile, life is a song which, although not always in tune, is sung in chorus by the whole human world. The song is: the prayer for happiness." (*The Saturday Review*, December 24, 1927.)

This development has been obscured by the modern fondness for merging poetry in Art and, on the other hand, for over-stressing the influence of "historical forces" on the history of poetry. Thus the "historical force" known as Puritanism has come to be represented as the deadly opposite of Art and poetry. Arnold did much to foster this view by throwing the idea of poetry and culture over against the idea of moral conduct, and by associating the latter with puritanical ugliness and narrowness. To redress the balance, he insisted that "conduct is three-fourths of life"; and in his later years, sensing the spread of decadent naturalism, he urged that "a poetry of revolt against moral ideas is a poetry of revolt against life." But unfortunately this great critic himself was too much swayed by naturalism. He departmentalized human nature, as the naturalistic classifiers were doing. He insulated morality, and admired it! He made it seem, not a vital and ever-present quality, but a necessary and not highly interesting quantity,—"three-fourths" of the tree of life, the hard wood stoically upholding the fine shoots and leaves of poetry. Well, let us rather say that morality (in the inner sense of the word) is only one-quarter, or one one-hundredth, of the total bulk of that tree. It is the living sap. The foliage cannot dispense with it. When budding authors dam it back into the woody citizenry, they achieve but a hectic vitality, which soon turns limp. That is why the lively poetic movement of the opening twentieth century appears now a red leaf—

> the last of its clan
> That dances as often as dance it can.

It is not just "a poetry of *revolt against* moral ideas . . . of revolt against life." It is a poetry *insulated* from that which is the very *life of poetry*. This conviction, or something very like this, has dominated the work of our two chief critical thinkers since Arnold, Irving Babbitt and Paul Elmer More. Not so widely imaginative as he, they have nevertheless penetrated more deeply than he into the truth of the human imagination. They have explored and charted that central region which he approved and skirted: the region where the moral intellect and the imagination are deeply at one. Modern poetic thought must pass through this region before we can have any great rebirth of poetry. That fact becomes clearer every year. Yet the very idea of poetry continues to be balefully opposed to religious and moral thought. In America, patricularly, the blinding reaction from Puritanism persists.

The Puritan movement (so the legend runs) unhorsed poetry in the middle of her great career in the English Renaissance. She flourished in the time of Shakespeare, and then this Joan of Arc, captured by English Puritanism, was badly seared, if not burned up, in its grim fire. But the legend lacks the kind of plausibility to which it pretends. Joan topples too suddenly into the fire, and the fire itself is unbelievably hostile. A truer myth would be this: the fire of poetry, descending unaccountably upon "the forces of history," took up into itself the force of Puritanism. The fire came down upon the crude English altar, consuming the stones and the sacrifice and even the much water that Elijah's followers poured there by way of insurance against all earthly flames. The poetic spirit in the English Renaissance—that is, in its most powerful phase since the great Age of Greece—comprised *all* the energies of life, fostering them and feeding upon them. These energies were so diverse and wide-ranging that the poetic art was in danger of losing itself in diffusion. At the same time its very capaciousness enabled it to develop, within itself, a strong critical faculty. Poetry became critical of its own diffuseness, and strove for concentration. In other words, the severe concentration that appears in seventeenth-century verse must be regarded, primarily, not as the result of "religious and moral factors," but as a natural development that poetry, at the height of its power,—and because of the extraordinary height of its power,—was able to accomplish within its own proper realm.

Hence the transition of Shakespeare from the extraordinary diffuseness of *Hamlet* to the extraordinary concentration of *Macbeth*. *Hamlet* is a more or less moralistic poem. At regular intervals, almost, the poet salts his romantic story with moralizings upon human life; whereas his ethical intention in the play as a whole is vague and wavering. In other words, *Hamlet* has something of that criss-crossing of romantic and puritanical sentiments which is so popular with the Anglo-Saxon citizenry. In the wide surface of *Hamlet*, Shakespeare held up a mirror to "the very age and body" of his time. In *Macbeth*, his effort of concentration led him to penetrate to the deeper thought and conviction of his time: the conviction "that we still have judgement here"; the thought of the irony of human desire at war with human peace. This outlook on life, which grew from the very fullness of experience that characterized the Renaissance, may properly be called Puritan (not "puritanical"). In *Macbeth* we see the poetic fire descending upon and taking up into itself the thought that the Puritan mind, at its best, was engaged in building. The continuation and completion of this process is Milton's *Paradise Lost*. Shakespeare's transition from *Hamlet* to *Macbeth* was on the crest of the general movement which, going forward in English poetry between (let us say) 1580 and 1660, carried the symbolical epic from the unexampled diffuseness of Spenser's *Faerie Queene* to the austere concentration of *Paradise Lost*.

Spenser's immense poem is devoted to that Elizabethan notion of "the Complete Gentleman" which permeates the work of the first half of Shakespeare's career and is consummated in *Hamlet*. The character of Hamlet may be regarded as an attempt to bring within the bounds of human and poetic probability the many-sided type of personality which Prince Arthur was designed to represent, but which, in Spenser's hands, lost itself in an amazing array of multiplex symbolism. The poetry of the Renaissance in general is pervaded by the desire to represent the full nature of Man beyond and above the natures of individual men. Spenser set out, really, to illustrate all the known qualities of human nature through a vast panorama of episodes and personages loosely centring in the ideal figure of Prince Arthur. He wanted to show "what a piece of work is man" by showing him "how infinite in faculties"! The same desire was active in Shakespeare when he wrote *Hamlet*, and induced a procedure essentially the same as that of *The Faerie Queene*. He wrote a loose series of dialogues and soliloquies centring in the figure of Hamlet and representing, with immense gusto, one quality after another of human Personality. The series, as it runs along in Shakespeare's imagination, is really endless. At many points in the play we feel that he might easily have inserted additional passages.[21] As it was, the play had to be reduced extraordinarily to come within the two hours' limit of his stage. And Goethe's remark about Mercutio would better apply to Hamlet: Shakespeare was forced to kill him (and by a poor melodramatic device) or he would have killed the play.

---

[21] For instance, when Hamlet says to Ophelia, "I am very proud, revengeful, ambitious" (Act III, scene 1) we should be glad to hear more on that matter: we feel that Shakespeare has *thought* more.

Prince Hamlet, as successor of Prince Arthur, benefits from the compression demanded by the dramatic form. Yet in the dramatic Hamlet, as in the symbolic Arthur, human representativeness is weakened by multiplicity. That, apparently, was the opinion of Shakespeare himself: the form of his next great work, *Othello*, means an abrupt revulsion from the discursive method of *Hamlet*. *Hamlet* in its whole nature and method is the brilliant finale of Shakespeare's many-sided development as a writer during the earlier half of his career. Presently he may well have looked back upon it as a somewhat nondescript tour de force. Certainly, the mysterious complexity of Hamlet's *individuality* was a by-product for Shakespeare: he is obviously quite nonchalant in regard to that heart of mystery which modern individualists have tried to pluck out. His own great wonder, when he wrote this play, was for the "infinite faculties" of the piece of work called man: it was this, rather than the peculiarities of Hamlet, that haunted him between the scenes. The fact is that the amazing array of human qualities assembled in this poem does not focus, or focuses very loosely, in the figure of Hamlet. The rays shoot beyond him and never meet. They run out toward the large and shadowy circumference of human Personality; which, with a distinct sense of bafflement, Shakespeare was pursuing in the play as a whole.

He learned by this glowing experiment that the pursuit was vain or, at least, that the highway of poetry, and especially tragic poetry, leads toward the centre rather than the circumference of human nature,—not toward the "infinite faculties" of Man but toward the vital division that goes through the very centre of his being, whereby his awful greatness and his awful meanness appear, inseparably: "in apprehension how like a god—and yet . . . this quintessence of dust." Certainly this inner division, as well as the circumferential view, is conveyed in the *Tragedy of Hamlet*: it is close behind the greatest passages in the play. We are shown the very dust of human nature, its "bestial oblivion" stirred only by the "dream of passion"; and, along with that theme and above it, a theme of "godlike reason" and stoic elevation runs throughout the poem to Hamlet's closing words, "The rest is silence." [22] Yet this vital doubleness of Man's

---

[22] Hence the fine shock of surprise and reminiscence in these four words. They glance *upstream*, as well as out to sea, from the muddy flat where the current seems to be ending. They remind us that the divine silence

nature, if so it may be called, is kept in the background of *Hamlet*. It moves forward in the next two tragedies.[23] In *Macbeth* it holds the front centre of the stage. In *Paradise Lost*, it is shown to be the centre of the universe—of the universe as it came to appear when for a century it had been enveloped and searched through and through by imaginative thought in the full tide of its power.

In short, *Paradise Lost* is not a puritanic subjugation, but a Renaissance fulfilment, of poetic passion. Its deficiencies are expressional, as Milton himself suggested:[24] he gave inadequate expression to his great theme. But he was equally right in his conviction that the theme itself, the whole conception of his story, was thoroughly poetic. It was simply a final concentration of the theme that had become more and more prominent as the poetry of the Renaissance, in its effort at an adequate representation of Man, passed from the circumference to the centre of Man's nature. The conflict of human passion and human peace was present, vividly enough, to the eyes of young Milton in the work of his master, Spenser.[25] Yet if Shakespeare, as he passed on toward *Macbeth*, was aware of the extraordinary diffuseness of *Hamlet*, Milton, as he searched and waited year after year for the theme of his "heroic song," must have come to feel something like chaos in *The Faerie Queene*. No wonder he rejected, after consideration, the story of Arthur for his own poem. The fact is that he had to make his way with fearful difficulty through the poetic chaos of the Renaissance,—

> Taught by the Heavenly Muse to venture down
> The dark descent, and up to reascend,
> Though hard and rare.

to which Hamlet now gives himself, was often *heard* behind his volubility in the course of the drama.

[23]At the same time the notion of the Complete Gentleman retires. It is not too comical to say that the Complete Gentleman makes his final appearance, so far as Renaissance poetry is concerned, in Milton's Adam. Taine had a tincture of the truth when he said that Adam is an English gentleman divested of his clothes. But the point, of course, is that Milton uses the notion only to subordinate it effectually—except in the eyes of barbarous readers.

[24] In the introduction of Book IX.

[25] Notably in Book I of *The Faerie Queene*. In Spenser's Una, romantic and religious tendencies are blended with a kind of incongruity that must have been offensive to the maturing Milton. Yet the figure of Una, when imaginatively most profound, is the antecedent of Milton's Son of God.

The "Heavenly Muse" taught him by means of the troubles of the middle period of his life. His diversion from poetry at this time, which has been deplored by Romantic commentators, was poetically fortunate. He had to confront in his own life every aspect of human chaos, domestic, religious, political; every faculty of the shaping power within him had to be strenuously exercised; before he could shape his great poem with utter conviction. He had to have personal experience of the great religious and moral energies that go into the shaping of Personality, and he had to experience them as poetically beautiful. At the very heart of his poetic vision is the fact that, for him, poetry and morality were neither confused nor separated. Since his time, Addisonian writers have tried to "make morality fashionable," and Whitmanian writers by way of sequel have tried to make it unfashionable. But Milton's aim—at least in that deep unconscious region that we admire so much today—was never didactic, moralistically or unmoralistically. His aim was to represent, in the form of a symbolic epic, the mystery of the inward shaping of Personality. He was speaking humbly and impersonally when he said that any man who would write a true poem "ought himself to *be* a true poem." But the fact is that the new kind of poem he was aiming at, demanded that he should shape his personal life more strenuously than any poet had ever done. The vital theme of the Renaissance, which he was drawing forth from confusion, was such that it had to be lived out signally in his own life before it would assume signal form in poetry. It demanded that he should feed his great eyes to the full, and then shade them. He had to "*feel*" that "sovran vital lamp" which was at the very centre of the wide confused radiance of Renaissance poetry,—the mystery of the great human passions transcended by a great human peace. The thing that Shakespeare saw in lightning flashes, appearing and disappearing, is steadily *felt* through all the alternations of Light and Darkness in the vast scene of *Paradise Lost*: how Man is the "quintessence of dust" [26]—and yet "in apprehension how like a god" when he apprehends what belongs unto his Peace.

[26] The Biblical simplicity with which Raphael mentions the creation of Adam from "dust of the ground" (VII, 525), after all the magniloquence of the preceding creation, has in it a profound solemnity that seems the outcome of the whole previous treatment of the subject, in Greek as well as Christian mythology.

Milton's poetic journey was indeed "hard and rare." It should be regarded as the crucial episode in the story of European poetry since ancient times. His poem had to be shaped out of an imaginational chaos,

> a universal hubbub wild
> Of stunning sounds and voices all confused.

The poetic voices that Homer heard were few, clear, and simple. But the Homeric world, to which Milton sometimes looked back with a kind of restrained yearning, was now gone forever. The "ancient symmetry" had been broken open, so to speak, by the primitive energies of northern Europe on the one side and, on the other, by the vast spiritual yearnings of the Orient. European Personality in the Renaissance was a vital, seething chaos. Dante saw it all in static, mystical perspective. Shakespeare, moving in the midst of it, experienced it as a multiform dramatic vision. Milton, "standing on Earth, not rapt above the pole," loved first of all the tempered simplicity of the ancients; but also he had in his nature something of the Dantean inwardness and the Shakespearean dramatic energy. His primary vision, therefore, was of the beautiful shapeliness of human nature when this is seen, as by the Greeks, in its simple universality, behind the mists of all passing distractions and distortions. But he sought more and more for its inmost mode; and he saw this, not as something static, but as an incessant drama. His theme is really the continuous creation of human Personality from within; in other words, the mystery of the creation, destruction, and re-creation of vital human happiness. He subordinates human society, and makes Man appear as a single Person. He reduces to its simplest terms the vast social complexity that had grown up in European civilization since Greek times. In place of the Homeric simplicity of the outward life, he gives us a Miltonic simplicity of the inward life, bodied forth in a symbolic story. In Homer, the upper and nether gods take part in the social conduct of Man. In Milton, they take part in the endless shaping of his nature. In Homer, the social life is divinely important and interesting; but the gods "descend to meet." In Milton, the social life is relatively small, but the gods achieve a good deal of essential deity. Milton's poem is no less *inevitable* than Homer's. It was the natural outcome, not only of the English Renaissance, but of the whole life of European poetry hitherto.

PARADISE AND DRAMA

The myth of a human paradise is European and indeed universal rather than Greek or Christian. In one form or another it always has been and always will be the favourite human story—whether the paradise is supposed to reside in the Hesperian Isles, or the Garden of Eden, or the "intense inane" of Shelley, or the "one far-off divine event" of Tennyson, or the state of the aesthetic cave-man which is popular just now. It images that quest of happiness which is the main theme of human life and therefore of poetry. But the myth itself, like the human quest of happiness, is predominantly idyllic. It means a withdrawal, in one way or another, from the real conditions of Personality. Milton preserved its idyllic quality in the "bowery loneliness" that so enchanted Tennyson, "the brooks of Eden mazily murmuring." But at the same time he tried to make his paradise emblematic of the real happiness that men have found, by experiment, to be achievable though precarious: a rational, temperate fullness of life, sustained always by an abnegation that is clearly and cheerfully undertaken. The dominant tone of *Paradise Lost* is one of healthy cheerfulness, in the best sense of this bitterly abused word. Incidentally, Milton anticipated our current wisdom by having Adam and Eve lose their Eden by reason of their failure to recognize and to control a "suppressed desire."

His emphasis upon the *real* quality of human happiness deepens as the poem proceeds. First, he brings the earthly paradise and the heavenly paradise into a bold parallelism to convey his faith that the nature of true happiness is the same whether it is viewed under the aspect of time or under the aspect of eternity. Then, the whole paradisaic *scenery* is thrown more and more into symbolic distance. Its idyllic nature fades. No one who reads the story poetically, allowing full effect to those features on which Milton, consciously or not, lays the emphasis of his poetic treatment, can miss the conviction with which he dooms and abolishes the merely idyllic paradise. He leaves the old Garden of Eden far behind. The author dismisses himself from Eden with Adam, and in speaking the following words to Adam he speaks them to himself:

> Only add
> Deeds to thy knowledge answerable; add faith;
> Add virtue, patience, temperance; add love
> By name to come called Charity, the soul

> Of all the rest: then wilt thou not be loth
> To leave this Paradise, but shalt possess
> A Paradise within thee, happier far.

This passage is not a mere moralizing after-thought, tacked on near the end of the poem. It is a clear winding-up of the clue that runs through the whole story. To miss that clue is to leave the quarrel of Achilles and Agamemnon out of the *Iliad*. In Milton's imagination, from the very beginning of the poem, a real paradise, a real human happiness, is hung precariously just above Chaos and "not unvisited of Heaven's fair light." Not merely is it *open* to the inroads of Satanic passion from below, and to Messianic visitings from above: its very creation and its continued existence are represented as derivative from those great opposing powers, in their never-ending conflict. The battle of Light and Darkness has its moments of relaxation, very charming moments in Milton, but it has no ending. His conviction is that we discover reality only by taking a vigorous part in that battle, on one side or the other. Insofar as we fight determinedly against the Light, we achieve real misery and despair, thereby learning, for certain, that the Light is more powerful than the Darkness: hence the magnificent realism of Satan in Milton's treatment. Insofar as we battle on behalf of the Light, we achieve happiness, with illuminations of peace. But this happiness has no reality for us—I should like to say, no Personal reality—apart from the constant effort through which it is achieved. The battle has no real ending. The notion of its ending in time, or of its abrogation in eternity, has no hold on Milton's imagination. He plays with the notion, theoretically and idyllically. But he does not allow it to come anywhere near the apex of his poetic thought.

In short, Milton abolished the Garden of Eden; or rather he pushed it with affectionate austerity into the outer suburbs of poetry. That, in our heart of hearts, is precisely the thing we hold against him. That is the ultimate ground of the vague feeling of aversion with which many persons today regard his poem. It glances, with unexampled realism, into the very nature of all paradisaic apples, golden or rosy—and we shrink from such prying:

> Where the apple reddens
> Never pry—
> Lest we lose our Edens,
> Eve and I.

The nineteenth century revived and pursued idyllic dreams that Milton left behind. The sequel, for him, was *paradise regained*; but for us, today, it is a clear case of paradise lost. The sense of disillusion in imaginative literature at the present time is not, mainly, the result of the advance of science, as one hears people say. Wherever the disillusion has any real depth, as in the work of Thomas Hardy, it is the direct sequel of the delusive notions of human happiness that began in the eighteenth century to pervade literature. Hardy was the leader of an emotional reaction from what we may call the paradisaic tendency of nineteenth-century poetry.

Hardy writes satirically of Wordsworth's trust in the goodness of Nature.[27] The truth is that Wordsworth at the height of his power was caught *back* by the old dream of an idyllic paradise, while he fancied that he was being caught *forward* by a new reality. Milton had retained the old names of paradise and given them a new meaning. Wordsworth revived the old meaning and gave it new names:

> Paradise and groves
> Elysian, Fortunate Fields—like those of old
> Sought in the Atlantic Main—why should they be
> A history only of departed things,
> Or a mere fiction of what never was?
> For the discerning intellect of Man,
> When wedded to this goodly universe
> In love and holy passion, shall find these
> A simple produce of the common day.
> I, long before the blissful hour arrives,
> Would chant, in lonely peace, the spousal verse
> Of this great consummation. . . .

This passage is unconsciously reminiscent. Eve, too, was tired of traditional Eden and wanted to make the thing realistic, "a simple produce of the common day." She had a fresh experience of Nature and, like Wordsworth, she worshipped the experience; she thought it opened the way of Wisdom.[28] In effect she proposed to apply "the discerning intellect of Man"—and woman—to "this goodly universe" in a mood of "holy passion." This seemed to her the highway to human happiness. Later she underwent a change of mind. So did

---

[27] "Some people would like to know whence the poet whose philosophy is in these days deemed as profound and trustworthy as his song is breezy and pure, gets his authority for speaking of 'Nature's holy plan'" (from *Tess of the D'Urbervilles*).

[28] *Paradise Lost*, IX, 795*ff*.

Wordsworth. He decided that Nature was a "bounded field," and not a medium of real happiness except for persons whose will had been purged of evil by a power above Nature:

> But who is innocent? By grace divine
> Not otherwise, O Nature! we are thine.

This might be the cry of repentant Eve! But it is the voice of her poetic grandson in 1834, calling *others* to repentance for their false trust in Nature.

But he called in vain; like Prince Arthur, combatant in the service of Truth, searching for Holiness who was hidden in a dungeon beneath the earth in the realm of Natural Pride! He called, but "no one cared to answer to his call." The younger poets scolded the master for having retracted his vision. And indeed that earlier vision was too alluring,—the ancient Garden of Eden disguised in modern foliage,—rechristened into Real Nature:

> Tempting region *that*
> For Zeal to enter and refresh herself,
> Where passions had the privilege to work,
> And never hear the sound of their own names.[29]

Shelley's work, of course, is the main exemplar of that region, and of the acute melancholy developed by the blind idyllic quest of happiness. In the end the melancholy won its inevitable triumph, as in the poetry of Thomas Hardy, which is a kind of darkened idyll. His rare quality of irony is due to the fact that his work is at once the result and the rejection of the paradisaic trend. The thing is in him too—yet he officiates at its funeral. Hence his mood of funereal delight. Finding no paradise in life, he discovers a faint kind of paradise in death,—a region of Shades who are not happy but take a curious satisfaction in not being able to be unhappy. This is the region of Shelley's "intense inane" descended from beyond the blue and settling ironically beneath the brown.

If in this way Hardy's work marks the closing of a poetic era, in another way it seems to look forward to a new poetic era, namely in its dramatic representation of human passions. Wordsworth was so deficient in dramatic power that the fact became apparent even to himself. It was very apparent to others. Byron, the opponent of Wordsworth, was also a powerful writer and advocate of dra-

[29] *Prelude*, XI, 228.

matic poetry. In the next generation this kind of verse endeavoured in various ways to reassert itself, notably in the work of Browning, who admired Byron and disliked Wordsworth. In our own time it is significant that almost all the outstanding poets have shown a marked dramatic vein. Meanwhile the stage-drama, which was dead a century ago, has been revived. Today it is obviously trying to pass over from the prosaic and sociological cast of Bernard Shaw to a poetic treatment of human passions. Mr. Shaw himself has leaned in this direction in his recent and very moving drama, *Joan of Arc*. Not long ago I heard one of the younger playwrights explain to a public audience that the newest drama is trying to recapture the dramatic passion of the Elizabethans; and he read with much gusto the closing scene of Marlowe's *Faustus*. I can still hear his rendering of Faustus' lines:

> O, I'll leap up to my God! Who pulls me down?
> See, see where Christ's blood streams in the firmament!
> One drop would save my soul—half a drop. . . .

Half a drop of Elizabethan "blood," passion, might indeed save the soul of our present drama. But the terrific passion of Marlowe's scene derives from the difference that Faustus feels between his own "blood" and the uplifted blood now far beyond his reach,—between the passion that rushes toward hellish misery and the Passion above passion that quietly "streams in the firmament." Behind all the turbulent rhetoric of Marlowe's drama there is something of real heaven and real hell conflicting in the soul of Faustus. Human passions are not highly interesting poetically unless they are effectually hostile, or effectually conducive, to human happiness. In other words, passion is highly dramatic only in relation to the real idea of human happiness. That idea was working strongly in the poetry of the Renaissance, but not in the poetry of the nineteenth century. Certainly it was present, but it was present weakly or didactically, not with imaginative power. Apparently the literary movement of the past hundred and fifty years is distinguished, above all recorded literary movements, for the multitudinousness of its imaginations and the tenuity of its imaginative happiness.

Is not this the ultimate reason for the inadequacy that we feel in the dramatic poetry of Byron and Browning? They scarcely direct our imagination to any firmament or shore bounding the sea of emotion that they conjure up before us. The other day, sitting in the modern Palace of Art, I saw a moving-picture of waves, nothing but waves. No sky-line visible on the screen, no land, not even a piece of bulwark—no "loved mansionry, no jutty, frieze, buttress, nor coign of vantage" where the imagination could have a "procreant cradle"! Just a conjuror's ocean! Something of the same curious feeling of unreality creeps through us during a long session with Byron or Browning. Yet—if our reading is not directed by contemporary dogma—we get that feeling more decidedly from Browning than from Bryon; and we get it definitively from most of the dramatic poetry of the present time.

Byron, in spite of his blighting egotism, is closer than any subsequent English poet to the dramatic passion of the Renaissance. Therefore the neglect of him today is one barrier between us and it. Why is so great a poet so greatly in the shade? A number of reasons suggest themselves. But the main one is simply that fashions in egoism change very rapidly and insensibly, and have done so especially during the past hundred years,— a period distinguished for protuberance and intricacy of Ego. The nineteenth-century *genus* of egoism is still with us; but the *species* has shifted from Byronic to post-Whitmanian. The essential quality of Byron's individualism, his revolt from the gods, is ours too. But his rejection of men as well as gods, his aversion from paradisaic humanitarianism, withdrew him from what proved to be the main current of nineteenth-century emotion, flowing down from Wordsworth to (let us say) Vachel Lindsay. But now that this current is stagnating and we are going round and round, we have the opportunity to look back with fuller appreciation at that "strong swimmer in his agony," cutting his solitary way *across* the stream. Our disillusion may enable us to see more deeply than the intervening generations have done, into his. We may see that our own species of egoism, while no less melodramatic behind its mist of sham sophistication than the Byronic species, is even less favourable to great dramatic writing. In short, the work of Byron can become a real aid to us, a relay station forwarding our attempt to signal back to the Renaissance drama. Byron at the least is "simple, sensuous, and passionate." Moreover, though he had no firm grip of the central dramatic standpoint, the idea of human happiness, he had some grip of real spiritual misery. Behind his smoke-screen of Satanism, there is something of the real Satan, "in shape and gesture proudly eminent." He could lend assist-

ance to those present-day writers who are attempting, with complete
lack of success so far, to create dramatic characters who are convincingly unhappy.

Byron, at his best, is convincingly miserable. Browning, at his
best, is never convincingly happy. His life as a man was healthy,
full-blooded, and cheerful. But as many friends observed, notably
Mrs. Browning, there was an ominous divorce between his personality and his poetry. The fact is that, as a poet, he never recovered
from the influence of Shelley, to which he was heavily exposed when
young. He had no relish for Shelleyan sadness, but through Shelley
he absorbed the joy-faith of Wordsworth. He remarked to his wife
that he would not cross the room to pick up a bottle containing the
condensed essence of Wordsworth. But the vaporized essence of
Wordsworth was contained in the Shelleyan atmosphere in which the
very lungs of his poetry were formed. He preferred to take his
Wordsworth in Shelleyan form. He learned too young the creed that

> happy will our nature be
> When love is an unerring light
> And joy its own security.

Being at once a healthy and an obstinate youngster, he made up his
mind, once and for all, that love, at least in poetry, gives *always* an
unerring light if it makes a big enough fire. He went in for sheer
quantities of passion. Intensely intellectual but never wise, he ana-
lysed passion into many currents; but he never discovered the shore.
Intensely idealistic, he impelled all his currents toward Eternity; but
what he achieved was wavier waves of Time. He wrote a number
of wonderful lyrics. He contributed to dramatic poetry a great deal
of fascinating detail. But toward the development of a real dramatic
outlook, he contributed nothing but confusion.

One may say that he threw a dramatic intensity into the Wordsworthian confusion, which he had adopted without knowing it—the
confusion between our emotional nature and that higher nature in
us that bounds and controls, and may deny, our emotions. For Wordsworth, poetry was "a spontaneous overflow of powerful feelings,"
rising from "emotion recollected in tranquillity." Browning omitted
the recollection in tranquillity, and added a force-pump to the spontaneous overflow. Spasmodic intensity was his contribution to Words-
worthianism. At the same time, unlike Wordsworth, he failed to face
the radically non-dramatic element in his own nature. He decided

that his poetry was "always dramatic in principle." Mrs. Browning, it seems, tried to tell him the contrary. She claimed that she knew his innermost being so well that she could "hear him think." His thoughts did not sound, to her stethoscopic ear, "always dramatic in principle." The truth is that *in principle*, in innermost mode, his poetry is from first to last non-dramatic.

So is the poetry of the nineteenth century as a whole. So is the literature of the present time; for example, the work of Eugene O'Neill. William Archer said he was inclined to "call O'Neill the greatest dramatist now writing in the English language"; Walter Prichard Eaton and others have emphasized his poetic imagination. His work is fascinating, in its promise, to those of us who believe that the way ahead of us in poetry is mainly dramatic. Mr. O'Neill has a fine power of dramatic scene. He has evinced also a sincere desire for passion; but the substance of his work, so far, is largely a passion for desire. One of his representative plays is rightly titled *Desire Under the Elms*. There is no real passion under those elms: nothing but a slimy, squirming tangle of appetites. The spectacle is essentially non-dramatic. Its most arresting quality is its fantasticality. In scenic fantasy, indeed, Mr. O'Neill is at his best; witness the satirical pageant, *Marco Millions*, and that superb moving-picture nightmare of subconscious desires, *The Emperor Jones*. In the realm of dramatic conception, however, where something greater than fantasy is required, he is also fantastic; as in the Pulitzer Prize play for 1920, *Beyond the Horizon*, the plot of which does not succeed in not being absurd. In the first Act, indeed, appears a personage, Andrew Mayo, who shows some real character and promises to lend dramatic backbone to the action of the play. But presently Andrew's character is dissolved in the stream of sheer desire that flows through the story toward a Shelleyan region "beyond the horizon"—or, as Stephen Leacock would say, "Behind the Beyond." The play is post-Hardyan. It turns upon the paradisaic yearning that comes down to us from young Wordsworth, and that saps away the very life of drama. Much more notable as a work of art is *Lazarus Laughs* (1927). In this Whitmanian miracle-play, dramatic probability is thrown to the winds, and the author gives himself entirely to the sway of paradisaic fantasy.

The firmest mood of poetry today is not dramatic passion. It is the mood that appears preeminently in the work of Robert Frost.

It reminds us, though with certain sharp differences, of the firmest mood of Wordsworth, as in *Michael*. It seems that in looking for the way ahead in poetry, we are confronted by the potent figure of Wordsworth at every turn. He is indeed a potent figure. One may fairly say of him, as of Pope, that a century of literature grew from him and that none of his successors could equal him in the proper quality of that literature. In his best lyrics and lyrical passages, he achieved a kind of serenity, at once firm and beautiful, that has been echoed and reechoed in the best work of his successors—including Walt Whitman! This mood has undergone original and lovely developments, as in the odes of Keats, but always with a certain loss of the Wordsworthian power and elevation. It has been violently reacted from, but never really displaced: it has remained like an ever-present demigod in disguise. Well, when oppressed by one of the secondary deities, the ancients appealed to his mighty parent, Jupiter. Our poetry can get free of Wordsworth only by having recourse to his great progenitor. We must appeal from Wordsworth to Milton.

"Milton! thou shouldst be living at this hour" . . . and living much more fully *as a poet* than in the hour of Wordsworth. For him, Milton was morally alive and poetically dead—or asleep. "Milton is his great idol, and he sometimes dares to compare himself with him," says Hazlitt; the second clause being a rare instance of understatement on the part of this brilliant critic. But the incense constantly offered by Wordsworth to "his great idol," Milton the man, stifled the divinity of Milton the poet. The Miltonic mode of imagination, which we need so desperately today, was entirely clouded-over by this potent Romantic devotee. Wordsworth drew upon the ancient "dower of inward happiness" that he found in Milton, and strengthened the *spirit* of his poetry upon it; the while his Romantic imagination refused to humble itself before the Miltonic vision. Wordsworth's serenity, his "tranquil restoration," should be regarded as a fine quiet after-glow of the seventeenth-century glory, shining upon the hills and lakes that he freshly loved. His poetry of Nature is a Miltonic vacation, Milton reclining at ease in the country; and certainly the spectacle is alluring:

> Dull would he be of soul who could pass by
> A sight so touching in its majesty!

It is Milton relaxed and day-dreaming. Consider for instance the remarkable lines on the Simplon Pass:

> The immeasurable heights
> Of woods decaying, never to be decayed. . . .

A dizzy, dreamlike tone goes through the serene contemplativeness of the whole passage. The great passion and the great peace in human Personality, which Milton saw with such majestic clearness in his wakeful vision, are here reflected dreamily, confusedly, upon the giant face of Nature:

> Tumult and peace, the darkness and the light—
> Were all like workings of one mind, the features
> Of the same face, blossoms upon one tree;
> Characters of the great Apocalypse,
> The types and symbols of Eternity,
> Of first, and last, and midst, and without end.

This is Milton sleep-walking among the Alps. But Milton, on awaking, would have renewed his vows to the imaginative "Reason," reflecting that

> Oft, in her absence, mimic Fancy wakes
> To imitate her; but, misjoining shapes,
> Wild work produces oft, and most in dreams,
> Ill matching words and deeds long past or late.[30]

He would thus have dismissed the Simplon ecstasy as an harmonious chaos of Biblical, aboriginal, and vacational fancies. But Wordsworth published it.

The spiritual unity he found in Nature was the unity of mood that he had found, so quickly, in himself. The discords of his youth have been exaggerated by Wordsworthians, in sequel to the poet's autobiographic elaboration of them. After all, the explosion of the French Revolution did not lift him *very* far off his feet. His fall was easily broken by the foliage; the trees of his native country intercepted his chute and let him down easily. However, the healing of Nature, aided by sister Dorothy and friend Coleridge, could never have availed him but for a certain great power which is not duly credited in his autobiographic accounts. That power, the foundation of what is greatest in English and American literature, and deserving the full homage of our *imagination*, is called Puritanism. A great

[30] *Paradise Lost*, V, 110*ff.*

battle had been fought and won by Milton: a great shaping effort, at once moral and poetic, had engaged all his powers until the age of sixty. Wordsworth could rest upon that victory; his own little after-skirmish was over before the age of thirty. He quickly found himself in a calm unity with himself. He projected that mood into Nature and received it back from her. His "admonitory balm," as his young friend Hartley Coleridge put it, "is Nature teaching what she never knew.[31]

The life "that rolls through all things" is a poetic myth that responds always to the Wordsworthian mood, notably in the work of Emerson. But it is not suitable for poetry that is trying to represent human passions. When Wordsworth was asked why he did not write of love, he replied that he could not trust himself to do so. Properly, he could not trust his poetry to do so. It was Shelley that rushed in where the master feared to tread. He brought passionate impulses into the region of Wordsworthian calm, with the result that his poetry is never highly calm and never deeply passionate. He added sex to the single life of all things, making it quaintly hermaphroditic. In poor Browning, as I have said, confusion is worse confounded by the injection of a keen dramatic impulse. To conceive life as a single passion "rolling through all things," and to imagine this single passion as dramatic, is nothing other than grotesque. Hence, as Bagehot saw, Browning's real distinction is in the grotesque. But now we have gone a stage further. To view life as a single Desire, or conglomeration of desires, rolling through all things, and to see

[31] H. W. Garrod, a late and chastened Wordsworthian, says in his book on the master (Oxford University Press, 1927): "I doubt whether Wordsworth, in his best period, ever abandoned the doctrine that *the highest moral achievement* is that which presents itself as an inspiration, that which *is part of our natural life*, that which is bound up with childhood and its unthinking 'vision'; Duty is second-best. . . ." The italics, added by me, bring out the irony which I trust the author intended, and which is the same as that of Hartley Coleridge's epigram quoted above. Elsewhere Mr. Garrod says: "*The Prelude* is the history of a consciousness highly abnormal." But he does not bring out the most striking aspect of that abnormality, namely Wordsworth's persistent attribution to Nature of the values of Tradition. If the "highest moral achievement" may ever properly be called a "part of our natural life," this happy result is largely due to the efforts of one's forebears. They *achieved* for Wordsworth his *natural* goodness. But his poetic imagination, at its height, was too abnormal to be appealed to by that plain and profound fact.

this spectacle as dramatic, is nothing other than fantastical. Hence the poetry and drama of the present time have achieved their distinction largely in the realm of the fantastical.

To achieve a real dramatic poetry we shall first need to achieve a real dramatic vision—not the same, but essentially the same, as that which was working in our literature three hundred years ago. Alongside the sublime confusion of Wordsworth, consider the simple sublimity of a certain remark of George Fox, which unlocks for us the heart of the seventeenth century. Wordsworth had a vision of life in which all its impulses appeared to be growing together in a beautiful harmony: the "tumult and peace, the darkness and the light, were all . . . blossoms upon one tree." Fox looked at life and said: "I saw a great darkness, and above the great darkness I saw a great light." This is profoundly dramatic, born of an age which was at once poetic and Puritan. It sets the great poles of human Personality in their true position, as we find them in the work of Milton; and we sense the true current of dramatic poetry that can pass between them.

Wordsworth short-circuited the life of poetry. That is why she has such a "short uneasy motion" today. She is still caught in the round of naturalistic theory and emotion into which the magic of the greater poets of the past century conjured her; and that circuit, always limited enough, has now become (in Hobbes's phrase) "nasty, short, and brutish,"—or, at best, vivaciously galvanic. No wonder quite a few of our younger writers, especially in England, show symptoms of wanting to break away desperately from that antarctic rotation. They have impulses toward Greek humanism on the one hand, or mediaeval religion on the other. These two great traditions, however, are vitally united in Milton; and what Apollo hath joined let no poet think to put asunder. At any rate let no young poet stay caught in the nineteenth-century conceit that did so much to freeze the progress of even young Keats,—the assumption that Milton's poetic thought is obvious and outworn, and that one may get beyond it without deeply understanding it. Our poetry cannot traverse anew the great zones of the religious and moral imagination, outside of which she is now becalmed and starving, until Milton, instead of being neglected and taken piecemeal, is fully accepted as a living classic and as our chief guide. Our poetry cannot have a second real renaissance, a forward movement taking with it the social consciousness of the English race—which the eighteenth-century poets reflected shallowly and the nineteenth-century poets overrode—until Milton shall have for us as full a significance, relatively, as Homer had for the Greeks on the eve of the Periclean Age. Of course, civilization in the Renaissance had come to such a complexity that Milton (unlike Homer) had to have his Shakespeare, by way of complement, and Shakespeare had to have his Milton. Once more, whom Apollo hath joined let no devotee put asunder, on pain of a blight from the god. These two poets were complementarily designed by deity. Shakespeare without his Milton is a city wonderful, but without its citadel and crowning temple,—always liable to be overrun and spoiled by insidious emotionalists or theorists. Milton is our one great unmistakable guide to that central region of the Elizabethan dramatic imagination which was not for an age but for all time. He is the guardian spirit appointed to bring our poetry at once onward and toward home.